The Atlas of
SACRED AND
SPIRITUAL SITES

The Atlas of SACRED AND SPIRITUAL SITES

Discover places of mystical power from around the world

DAVID DOUGLAS

 A GODSFIELD BOOK

An Hachette Livre UK Company

First published in Great Britain in 2007
by Godsfield Press,
a division of
Octopus Publishing Group Ltd
2–4 Heron Quays,
London E14 4JP
www.octopusbooks.co.uk

Distributed in the United States and Canada by
Sterling Publishing Co., Inc.
387 Park Avenue South, New York, NY 10016-8810

ISBN: 978-1-84181-328-8

A CIP catalogue record for this book
is available from the British Library

Printed and bound in China

24681097531

CONTENTS

Introduction

Every atlas aspires to a comprehensive view of its subject, although its author also knows at heart that it can never achieve such completeness. This atlas takes a very broad view of what gives places their relevance and importance to humankind. All the world's major religions and philosophies are represented here and their revered sites are honoured; many of these sites are connected with key figures in each religion's history and development. Other sites are more anonymous: the people who carried out their spiritual practices are now long gone and their histories remain unrecorded, and yet the meaning of their rituals still remains open to detection by the scientist or the sensitive.

This atlas is not just a set of answers and facts. It also raises a number of questions: What makes a site sacred? How can it be that one place, which is held so dear by some, can be so unimportant, irrelevant – antagonistic even – to others? Are there places of power: locations where whole groups of people have a similar experience of spiritual meaning? Can the events of the past and the actions of remarkable humans leave impressions that, even thousands of years later, may be experienced as a distinctive, objective 'atmosphere'? Can continued religious or spiritual practice in one location strengthen and reinforce the energy felt in that place? And finally, can our questions about sacred sites and mystical places be answered by going to them and experiencing them for ourselves?

One notion that seems to unite spiritual practice at all sacred sites is the idea of gratitude. This idea, feeling or impulse is, however, expressed in very different ways in different cultures and spiritual traditions. Some will express thanks to a divine creator being – a source of all things – for its blessings, its sustenance, its forgiveness, its life-giving love. Some will praise a group of divinities: be it a trinity or a pantheon. Others will offer up prayers to saints, sages or the ancestors, to those who have gone before and who left some of their knowledge and understanding about life before they departed. With gratitude, some people say, we find our place in the scheme of things; without it there is no possibility of real joy. Can we then, through gratitude, reduce the risk of hubris and the tragedies that ensue from our ego-driven plans – the plans that make the gods laugh?

It was Atlas himself, a Titan, who challenged the gods. When his rebellion failed, he ended up with the greatest punishment of all: carrying the weight of the world on his shoulders for eternity. Perhaps this is a metaphor that earlier humans understood better than we do now: that by disrespecting the power of the gods, by 'going it alone' and following the little will of human beings, we finish up bearing all the

weight of our world and we end our days crushed in the process. Perhaps, by acknowledging a higher power, we are freed from some of that weighty burden.

WHAT THIS ATLAS OFFERS

This atlas, which does not attempt to bear the whole world's mass, tries instead to take a somewhat backward-looking view of history. It starts in the relatively modern world of 'places of worship': built environments, great cathedrals, churches and temples in which people have expressed their faith. The times of the great cathedral builders may have passed, but some unique religious buildings have survived the onslaught of natural disasters and ironic acts of God. We journey on, tracing pilgrimage routes that are both modern and ancient, seeking out the meaning of sacred journeys on different continents and in different faiths. The role of shrines is featured in the next chapter, in which locations where Mary the Madonna is honoured come together with places where other sages and saints are revered.

Places of isolation and contemplation follow: institutions and schools where sometimes-ancient spiritual practice has been concentrated and intensified to enable the greater possibility of mystical states. Arriving next at stone circles, we take a further step back in time, to discover more about the lives and rituals of early man (and woman). What drove them in their exploration of spiritual practice? With just a world of earth and stones, a sky full of stars, a

sun and a moon, and the facts of birth and death, a cosmology emerged to encode their understanding – a cosmology that left its mark in patterns of giant megaliths. And in the final chapter we discover cultures that have honoured the very earliest aspects of creation: natural features of the landscape. In a myriad ways, from a variety of mythic origins, different cultures have worshipped the very land we stand on, the objects that have formed the foreground and background of their lives.

QUESTIONING OUR SPIRITUAL CONNECTION

There are scholars and experts in spiritual traditions who would tell us that our current environmental crisis is related to our loss of a deep spiritual or religious connection with the created world. Would we really desecrate and destroy a world that was made by the same creator who made us? Wouldn't that be

Left *The mysterious and very incomplete remains at Tiwanaku in Bolivia still offer many puzzles about their true meaning and purpose. This sunken temple, with its 'stelae' and sculpted heads, is one of the few structures that remain from the pre-Incan culture that lived here.*

Right *This priest at Lalibela's Bet Medhane Alem church is part of a unique Christian tradition that has survived in a remote part of Ethiopia. Its rock-hewn churches are the largest of their kind in the world.*

'One notion that seems to unite spiritual practice at all sacred sites is the idea of gratitude. This idea, feeling or impulse is, however, expressed in very different ways in different cultures and spiritual traditions.'

like murdering a parent? Or trashing the family farm? Of course it doesn't necessarily feel like that. We just drive our cars and use our central heating and buy our food from supermarkets; our crimes seem so small on a personal level. But modern life has disconnected us from the source of our sustenance. Most of us no longer grow our food, kill our own animals, collect firewood, make our own clothes, or fetch water from the well or the river. These resources now come from shops, out of the supermarket or off the Internet. They simply appear in our lives and we have other sources to thank for their arrival. What need any longer to thank a creator, or any other source of life, for all the things that come from the Earth?

LASTLY...

And now my confession: this atlas is not complete. It is obvious, but there are of course many places not featured here that would easily qualify as sacred sites to many people, many cultures, many faiths. To all of them, I apologize. There are many thousands of places on the planet that bear witness to spiritual honouring and cultural reverence each day. Sacred sites and mystical places may not be only those that are publicly recognized as such. They could simply be places that we personally hold dear – places that bear an importance for us and that we like to visit; places that feed us on some deeper level than simply the ordinary. May all these places continue to feed those who search for greater meaning in their lives.

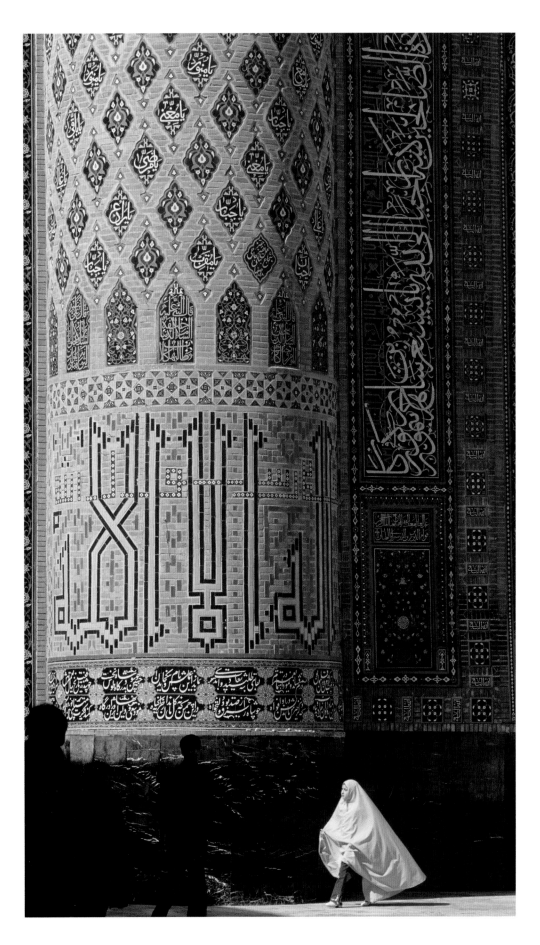

Right *The vast decorated columns of Imam Reza's shrine in Mashhad, Iran are part of a vast religious complex that encompasses mosques, shrines and libraries. Here, abstract beauty symbolizes perfection, and foreshadows a paradise that awaits the faithful.*

CHAPTER 1

PLACES OF WORSHIP

The urge to worship, to express gratitude for life and the presence of a higher power, goes back beyond the beginnings of our known religions. And yet why is there a need to locate this activity in one place? The impulse to enshrine, to contain worship, certainly demonstrates the desire of people to join together, to be part of a larger whole, to express their faith as a group and feel the power of the religious experience. It also creates a divide between the 'holy space' and the outside world, a division between perfection and the perfectible.

The creation of spaces for worship has often been in the hands of leaders of faith groups rather than their members. These buildings have been envisaged by those wishing not just to create a sacred container for worship, but to say something to the faithful without words. Buildings contain messages about the beliefs, hopes and aspirations of religious movements. Often, through their artworks, they encode the very teachings of a religion in a wordless form. They can also speak to those of the 'outside world' who are not of the same religion – conveying the message that the religion has something important that could benefit the 'unbeliever' as much as it currently sustains the believer.

In their time, these places of worship have often been perceived as miraculous, creations of the Divine through the agency of human hands. In this way they are living proof of God's existence. After all, who else could create and inspire such sacred objects?

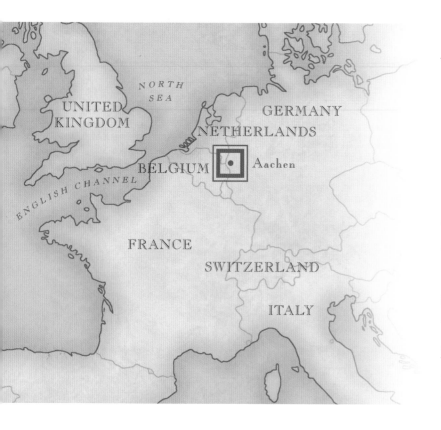

Aachen Cathedral, Germany

Aachen's importance as a city of spiritual and cultural significance in Germany and Northern Europe began in 768 CE when the Emperor Charlemagne took charge of government there. The Imperial Palace next to a site of natural hot-water sources became Charlemagne's seat of power, and the building of the new cathedral 18 years later in the same place was a symbol of his aim to bring together the powers of Church and State.

By modern standards, Aachen Cathedral is not a huge building, and many who come to worship here are surprised at its modest size. Nevertheless, the Dom (as it is sometimes known) has another claim: it is the oldest cathedral in Northern Europe, originating from 786 CE. At the time of its creation it represented the finest and most modern in church-building techniques, borrowing heavily from the Eastern Christian traditions of the Byzantines. The octagonal Palatine Chapel, the first part of the cathedral to be built, is particularly beautiful and remains today the jewel in Aachen's crown.

Left This 19th-century image of Aachen Cathedral by artist Michael Neher shows the remarkable mix of architectural styles – Byzantine, Germanic-Franconian, Classical – that has created the unique exterior. The octagonal Palatine Chapel is next to the tall, heavily glassed nave.

AACHEN AS A PLACE OF PILGRIMAGE

After Charlemagne was buried in the cathedral at Aachen following his death in 814, and with his subsequent canonization some two hundred years later, the site became increasingly attractive as a place of worship and pilgrimage. Gothic additions to the cathedral, such as the 'glass chapel', changed the building's character with their narrow, aspiring columns and impressive stained-glass panels. However, many people who come here still cite the octagonal Palatine Chapel, with its internally gilded dome, as the cathedral's spiritual centre. Charlemagne's tomb remains an important feature, and his relics, as well as artefacts that the Emperor gathered during his lifetime, are preserved in silk in the 'Charlemagne Shrine'. Every seven years (the next occasion being in 2014) the relics are brought out to be viewed by the public. The many thousands of visitors to Aachen Cathedral each year demonstrate that Charlemagne's blend of temporal power and spiritual devotion still exerts a magnetic attraction.

THE LIFE AND TIMES OF CHARLEMAGNE

For many, though, the cathedral and its creator are inseparable. Born in Aachen on 2 April 742, Charlemagne (Charles the Great, Carolus Magnus or Karl der Grosse, as he was also known) was the greatest European ruler of his time. In 768 he and his brother Carloman were crowned joint Kings of the Franks following the death of their father, Pepin III. But when his brother died in 771, Charlemagne was free to pursue his own agenda. From 772 he set out on a campaign – both military and cultural – to retrieve Europe from what he perceived as the twin evils of Barbarianism and paganism. In this way he would unite Northern Europe with a reforming zeal, the like of which had never been seen before.

Charlemagne valued education and religion above all things and achieved his ends using a contradictory mix of ruthlessness and mercy. In a time when surviving members of losing armies could expect to be executed, Charlemagne spared soldiers on a number of occasions. At the same time he was also responsible for a number of mass executions: in one case he ordered the beheading of 4,500 Saxon warriors on a single day. His conscience seemingly untroubled, he sought out religious art and high culture and attempted to live an exalted life. He brought a scholarly English monk, Alcuin, to his court, and in the palace he abandoned the entertainments of jesters at mealtimes and replaced them with readings from uplifting texts. He set up schools for the poor, revived the palace school at Aachen itself, established new money standards to support commerce and attempted to improve agricultural methods of food production. Musicians and artists were imported from other countries to inspire further appreciation. And Aachen lay at the centre of this renewal.

Through these means – a combination of military might and benign rulership – Charlemagne's empire spread and extended to include what are now France, Belgium, Switzerland and the Netherlands. It also covered half of present-day Germany and Italy, as well as some of Spain and Austria. From his palace in Aachen he ruled over most of Western Europe, re-establishing in effect a new Roman Empire – the influences of which can still be felt today. On Christmas Day 800 Charlemagne travelled to Rome, to be crowned by Pope Leo III, effectively making him Holy Roman Emperor. Although Charlemagne never adopted the title publicly, Aachen was to become the ruling centre and coronation place for a further 30 kings of the Holy Roman Empire.

Westminster Abbey, London

Westminster Abbey holds a special place in the psyche of the British people, not just because it is the place where all but two of the last 65 monarchs have been enthroned, but also because it has stood so long alongside the Royal Palace of Westminster, the political centre of the country. This important, yet sometimes uneasy, relationship between Church and State has lain at the heart of Britain's history, and the abbey stands as testament to the spiritual endurance of the country and its religion in the face of temporal change.

The first abbey on the Westminster site was established around 960 CE by St Dunstan, who was the Abbot of Glastonbury as well as Archbishop of Canterbury. Little is known about the abbey building, although it is believed to have been sited close to where the West Door of the church now stands. Less than a hundred years later Edward the Confessor, King of England, started building a larger abbey with a church dedicated to St Peter in the Norman Romanesque style, similar to the existing Durham Cathedral. It was Edward who also created a new royal palace nearby, which would, over time, become the Palace of Westminster and, eventually, the home of the Houses of Parliament.

FUNERALS, CORONATIONS AND COMMEMORATIONS

Edward died on 5 January 1066, just eight days after the new abbey was consecrated, and was buried there the following morning. By the end of the day Harold I had been elected and celebrated as the new king. (Perhaps the clearest picture of the abbey at this time is an image of the newly consecrated church and of Edward the Confessor's

Left The Lady Chapel, where Henry VII is entombed, has oak stalls either side and occupies the most easterly part of the abbey. Its ornate and delicate fan vaulting, together with carved pendants, is some of the most beautiful and complex in Christendom.

funeral march, as it appears in the Bayeux Tapestry.) Yet on Christmas Day the abbey would witness the arrival of another new king, for within months of the swift English defeat at Hastings, the crowning of William the Conqueror took place.

The next coronation, on 26 September 1087, saw William Rufus (son of William the Conqueror) take the throne. With these coronations a pattern was established: Westminster Abbey was now the venue for monarchical, hereditary, divinely inspired rule to begin its course. From that day on every monarch of England, except Edward V (one of the Princes in the Tower) and Edward VIII (who abdicated), has been crowned in Westminster Abbey, seated on the same Coronation Chair.

This tradition has placed the abbey at the centre of the country's leadership rites. In addition, the nearby presence of Parliament has added to the concentration of power in such a small area, a fact that has drawn visitors and worshippers for more than simply religious reasons. And the abbey has also become a place where the great and the good of English culture have been commemorated – through public state funeral, burial in the church or memorialization through a statue. The list of 'residents' is impressive. As well as 18 British monarchs, Westminster Abbey also contains the tombs of those who have contributed to the cultural, scientific and artistic life of Britain: Charles Dickens, Thomas Hardy, Alfred, Lord Tennyson, Sir Laurence Olivier, Sir Isaac Newton, Charles Darwin, George Frederick Handel, James Clerk Maxwell and Geoffrey Chaucer. It is also the resting place of the 'Unknown Warrior', a British serviceman killed in the First World War who represents all those who have died defending the British Empire.

CHANGING TIMES

King Edward the Confessor's building has undergone many transformations over its long history. In 1245 Henry III demolished large parts of the church and started a period of construction that was to outlive him. This initially saw the addition of the beautiful octagonal chapter house. In the 14th century

the cloisters, the abbot's house and further monastic buildings were added, and in the 16th century Henry VII completed the very tall, distinctive, French-style nave. He also oversaw the creation of the Lady Chapel with its remarkable fan vaulting. In 1540, with the reorganization of the Church under Henry VIII, Westminster briefly became a separate diocese within London, along with St Paul's. This gave the church the status of cathedral, but this was to last for only ten years. It was Elizabeth I who named the church the Collegiate Church of St Peter, and this is still the abbey's correct name today.

Sir Christopher Wren, architect of St Paul's Cathedral, and Nicholas Hawksmoor built the 'signature' west towers between

Above Westminster Abbey's west façade has welcomed some of the most powerful and important people in the history of England – in both life and death.

1722 and 1740. Since then most of the work has been decorative, with the addition of new sculptures and memorials, and restorative – attending to the needs of a building that, at its heart, is now more than 900 years old. But despite these outer changes, the role of Westminster Abbey in the life of Church and country has remained remarkably stable.

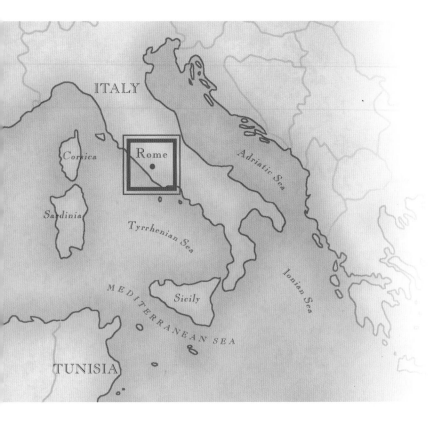

St Peter's Basilica, Rome

On 18 April 1506, Pope Julius II laid the cornerstone of the new St Peter's Basilica in the Vatican, Rome. Five hundred years later, almost to the day, the newly enshrined Pope Benedict XVI marked the anniversary with a personal invitation to the more than a billion members of the Roman Catholic Church to be 'like living stones, to build the Church'. He went on to remember with gratitude 'the Supreme Pontiffs who desired this extraordinary edifice over the tomb of the Apostle Peter'.

St Peter's Basilica (and the presence of the Pope in the Vatican) is so central to Roman Catholics around the world that it has become their main site of pilgrimage. Its importance in the Catholic mind has its roots in Scripture: Jesus said that Peter was the rock upon which his Church would be built. Jesus placed the care of the Christian Church in Peter's hands until his eventual return, and Peter's role as Bishop of Rome, Vicar of Christ and pastor is enshrined in the personage of the Pope, the Holy Father. Indeed, since Peter's death in the latter half of the 1st century CE there has been an unbroken line of 265 successions to the position of Supreme Pontiff, now occupied by Pope Benedict XVI.

EVOLUTION OF THE BASILICA AND ITS DOME

During his reign, in the 4th century CE, the Emperor Constantine built a basilica on the site of St Peter's tomb, but the basilica that now stands in St Peter's Square, begun in the 16th century, was not to be completed for another 120 years. It was designed by a succession of architects, starting with the great early Renaissance figure of Donato Bramante, who envisioned a Romano-Byzantine structure based around a Greek-cross pattern. With his death in 1514 the basilica was without a predominant guiding hand until Michelangelo took over in 1546 and developed the final design for the great dome that still stands as the building's signature today. However, he did not live to see the dome completed and it was left to Giacomo della Porta to bring the plan to fruition. Between 1585 and 1590 the dome was vaulted with the assistance of Domenico Fontana, probably the greatest structural engineer of his day. In 1591 Fontana built the 'lantern' above the dome, and the orb that supports the cross was placed in 1593.

Believed to have been partially modelled on Filippo Brunelleschi's dome for Florence's cathedral, the basilica's double-skinned dome structure replaced a single-skinned, more semi-spherical design by Bramante, which was found to be flawed. To the top of its cross, the dome is 136 m (445 ft) above the floor of the great church. Until very recently St Peter's Basilica was the largest church in the world, covering an area of 23,000 sq m (247,500 sq ft) and capable of hosting 60,000 worshippers.

THE TREASURES INSIDE ST PETER'S

It is not just the structure of St Peter's Basilica that draws worshippers: some of the most remarkable artworks and religious relics are housed there. Statues of saints and monuments to past popes line the church's walls, but perhaps the most famous and moving of all is Michelangelo's sculpture, the *Pietà*, which depicts Mary holding the crucified body of Jesus. Gian Lorenzo Bernini's altarpiece holds a fragment of the *Cathedra Petri*, the episcopal throne of St Peter when he led the Roman Church, although it is no longer used as the papal seat.

St Peter's Basilica is the resting place of 91 popes, as well as other important figures in the history of the Roman Catholic Church. James Francis Edward Stuart, of the Scottish royal family and known as the 'Old Pretender', is buried there along with his two sons. Also honoured is Christina, the 16th-century Queen of Sweden who abdicated to maintain her Catholic faith. But the most important interment is the tomb of St Peter itself, which, though it has been the subject of some controversy in the last 60 years, is believed to lie many feet beneath the altar and the huge Bernini-designed baldachin (canopy) that covers it.

There are in fact four separate basilicas in Rome and, as bishop of the city, the Pope's own church is, technically, San Giovanni in Laterano. However, recent popes have ministered mostly from the great basilica, from St Peter's Square and, in times of ill health, from the window of their apartment abutting St Peter's. It is hard to imagine the basilica without the vast expanse of St Peter's Square lying to the east of the church. With its curving colonnades, like two arms embracing the faithful and tourists alike, and the ancient Egyptian obelisk that now bears Roman carvings, the approach to St Peter's is an overwhelming prelude to the glories that await the pilgrim in the basilica's interior.

Below *St Peter's Basilica, with St Peter's Square in front of its main façade, abuts other buildings that form part of the Vatican City. These include the Sistine Chapel where Michelangelo's ceiling draws millions of admirers.*

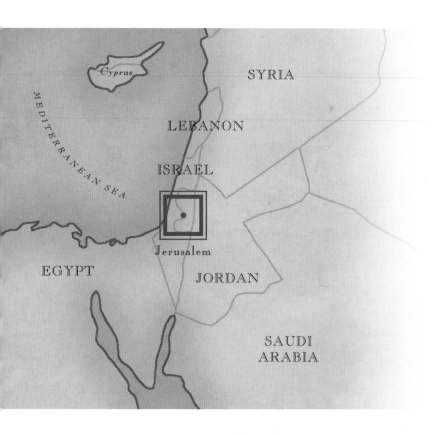

Temple Mount, Jerusalem

Jerusalem's Temple Mount – where King Solomon's Temple once stood and where the Muslim Dome of the Rock (the Qubbat As-Sakhrah) and the Al-Aqsa Mosque now dominate – has become an intense focus of Arab-Israeli conflict in the Middle East. The violence of this conflict is partly a measure of how fervently both sides hold the Temple Mount location on Mount Moriah in the history of their faiths.

The story of King Solomon's Temple is described on pages 88–89, while the Dome of the Rock is examined on pages 54–55.

MOUNT MORIAH

For both Jews and Muslims Mount Moriah, the location of the Temple Mount complex, is a holy place of great importance – the place where Abraham was prepared to sacrifice his son at God/Allah's request.

Following the destruction of King Solomon's Temple (and the subsequent building and destruction of a Roman temple to Jupiter on the same site), it was not until the Muslim conquest of Jerusalem by Caliph Umar ibn al-Khattab in 638 CE that the Temple Mount site again became a focus for religious activity. It became known as Haram-esh-Sharif, the Noble Sanctuary. Some 50 years later the first major building project – the Dome of the Rock – was initiated to enshrine the place on Mount Moriah that is not only the site of Abraham's preparedness to sacrifice his son, but also considered by many to be the point from which the Prophet Muhammad ascended into the skies during his mystic 'Night Journey' (see page 55).

AL-AQSA MOSQUE

For Muslims the true place of worship on the Haram-esh-Sharif is the Al-Aqsa ('farthest') Mosque, the construction of which was initiated by Caliph Abd al-Malik around 705 CE and was apparently completed by his son, Caliph al-Walid I.

Since its first construction, the Al-Aqsa Mosque has undergone many changes, reworkings and disasters. Even during its first century it was badly affected by major earthquakes and had to be renovated. It was significantly altered in 1033 during the Fatimid period. The Crusades saw the mosque become the *Templum Salomonis*, the Royal Palace of Solomon, when it was home to the Kings of Jerusalem and, later the Knights Templar. Further restorations and renovations took place in the 14th century and again in the 20th century. Severe earthquakes in 1927 and 1936 led to almost complete rebuilding of the mosque. Then in 1969 a member of a Christian sect, known as the Church of God, set fire to the mosque, gutting the Southeastern part of the mosque and destroying a sacred one thousand year old pulpit.

① WESTERN WALL

The Western Wall is one of the four retaining walls that surrounded the Temple Mount. It supported the platform on which the Second Temple formerly stood. When the Romans destroyed the building, they left standing most of the retaining walls.

② EL KAS FOUNTAIN

Muslims perform ritual ablutions at this fountain before entering the holy sites. Some scholars believe that the Temple's Holy of Holies was located beneath this fountain, while others believe it was located under the Dome of the Rock.

③ DOME OF THE ROCK

A shrine rather than a mosque, this is the third most important Muslim site after Mecca and Medina. The site of both the First and Second Temples is said to lie beneath or near the shrine. The bedrock of Mount Moriah is visible within the shrine.

④ AL-AQSA MOSQUE

Today worshippers at the Al-Aqsa Mosque encounter a seven-bay 'hypostyle' hall with a number of smaller halls to the east and west of the southern portion of the mosque. It's dome, covered with lead, is not as imposing as the Dome of the Rock's larger gold peak. Together,

however, they represent the current ownership of this highly charged and immensely significant site.

⑤ DOUBLE GATE

The Double Gate on the southern wall of the Temple Mount is now blocked. It once provided access to the Temple Mount through subterranean passageways.

⑥ MOUNT MORIAH

In the Jewish faith this is the site where Abraham offered his son Isaac for sacrifice to God; for Muslims, it was his elder son, Ishmael, whom Abraham was prepared to sacrifice to Allah.

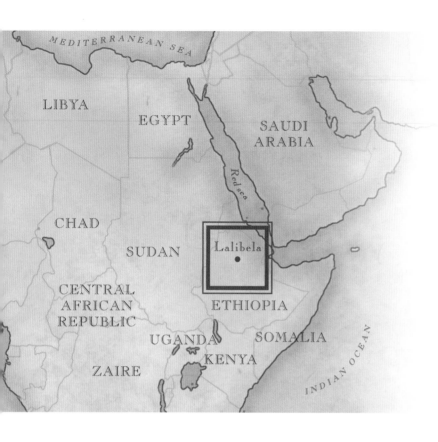

Lalibela, Ethiopia

To step into the world of Lalibela is to re-enter biblical times as here, still present, is an unalloyed faith in the miraculous life of Jesus Christ. It is as if two thousand years of history – during which debate, death, war and disfigurement have changed religious belief beyond recognition – have never happened. Indeed, Ethiopia is often referred to as the country that went to sleep for hundreds of years.

That Lalibela was allowed to stay slumbering is in part thanks to Muhammad's injunction to Muslims of the 7th century to leave Abyssinia in peace, despite its adherence to Coptic, Orthodox Christianity. It is also a function of Ethiopia's geography, which leaves its high plateaux cut off from the outside world by a dense labyrinth of narrow valleys.

THE CREATION OF LALIBELA

King Lalibela – after whom the place is named – was born in 1181, during Ethiopia's long period of seclusion. His name means 'sovereignty recognized by bees', a reference to his mother's observation that bees seemed to flock to her new baby prince. Lalibela's sovereignty was not without threat, however, and his jealous brother poisoned him in an attempt to erase his claim to the throne. The plan backfired: in fevered sufferings lasting three days Lalibela went on a spiritual journey to three heavens, during which he received the plans and inspiration to build 11 churches dedicated to his Christian God. On his recovery he set about this intensely challenging feat – the results of which have

survived remarkably intact in the dry climate of the Abyssinian uplands.

The churches of Lalibela have been described by many as representing the Eighth Wonder of the World, and there are

many reasons to recommend them. These 11 structures, which have all been hewn from the red volcanic rock that forms the ground here, divide into two groups. Seven of the churches are built above ground, in the

Left The churches of Lalibela were created by carving away the native red volcanic rock that surrounds them, revealing creations of beauty and simplicity that now contain sacred Christian relics.

Left At the festival of Timkat, or the eve of Epiphany, young 'deacons' and priests process to the River Jordan where they perform a service of communion and baptism. They carry sacred objects from all 11 of the Lalibela churches.

mouths of caves, attached on some sides, but not on others. The other four are even more remarkable. Hidden from view, they are underground buildings that were created by removing the rock from around them, as if their makers were discovering their forms in the red stone. There are stories that Lalibela's people were helped by angels in the construction of the churches, and that they were completed in 24 days or 24 years – depending on the version of the story. It is known, though, that at least one of the churches was completed by Lalibela's widow after his death.

RELIGIOUS CELEBRATIONS

Throughout the year people journey many miles, mostly on foot, to gather and join in the worship that takes place daily and, more exuberantly, around times of particular religious significance – occasions that are often accompanied by distinctive melodic music and rhythmic drumming.

Christmas is celebrated as Genna, which occurs in early January. Twelve days later, on the 18th January, is the important festival of Timkat – the eve of Epiphany – recollecting

the day when John the Baptist immersed Jesus in the waters of the River Jordan, a dove flew down from heaven to land on the Messiah's head, and God's voice was heard confirming Jesus' status as the Christ, the Son of God.

To celebrate this day the holy 'tabots' or sacred objects are taken from each of the 11 churches and carried on the turbaned heads of senior priests in a procession to the banks of Lalibela's own River Jordan. Made of stone or wood and wrapped in silk brocade, the tabots are engraved slabs representing the Mosaic tablets of the Law, which were, in Old Testament times, believed by some to have been taken to Ethiopia in the Ark of the Covenant. After a night's vigil of constant prayer, the priests conduct communion and a service of baptism. Once this ritual of renewal is complete, priests and worshippers again process, accompanied by the sounds of bells, trumpets and chanting, to return the tabots to their respective churches. In the third millennium after Christ's birth it is remarkable to find an expression of faith that seems so close to its historical roots as the worship at Lalibela.

THE BETA MEDHANE ALEM

One of the most famous of the four sunken churches, the Beta Medhane Alem (House of the Saviour of the World) is carved in the shape of a Greek cross. It is 30 m (100 ft) long, 23 m (75 ft) wide and 10.7 m (35 ft) high. The roof is level with the ground that surrounds it, and is covered to protect it from erosion. Inside is the Afro Ayigeba, a 60 cm (2 ft) long Coptic cross that has been attributed with powerful healing abilities. Despite the extraordinary buildings that contain these relics, it has been said that, without their special contents, the churches would have no meaning to the people of Lalibela.

BLACK SEA

Istanbul

Sea of Marmara

TURKEY

Hagia Sophia, Istanbul

The Hagia Sophia – the Church of Holy Wisdom, in present-day Istanbul – is widely acknowledged as one of the greatest buildings ever created by humankind. Originally built during the 6th century CE under the guidance of Emperor Justinian I, the Hagia Sophia quickly became the spiritual focus of Eastern Orthodox Christian culture.

Apart from a short period during the 13th century when it was captured by forces of the Roman Christian Church, the Hagia Sophia stayed in Orthodox hands until Constantinople was seized in 1453 by the Ottomans and the 'Great Church' was converted into a mosque. It remained a place of Islamic worship until 1935, when the Turkish ruler Atatürk secularized the building and renamed it the Ayasofya Museum.

BYZANTINE JEWEL IN THE CROWN

Byzantium, Constantinople, Istanbul: the meeting place of East and West, of Europe and Asia, the great transit port between the Black Sea and the Mediterranean has held a geographical significance dating back well before the Hagia Sophia. A temple dedicated to the Roman god Apollo occupied the same site, overlooking the Sea of Marmara, before the first Christian church was built in the 4th

Left The Emperor Justinian's 6th-century vision for the Hagia Sophia – intended to be the most beautiful building ever built – was based around a central dome that seems almost to float on a ring of glazed arches.

century CE under the Emperor Constantine (after whom Constantinople was named). This church was destroyed by fire, and a second church was itself burned to the ground by rioters in 532.

It was Justinian I who decided to create a church that would be the jewel in the crown of Byzantine architectural achievement. The Emperor appointed mathematician Anthemius of Tralles and architect Isidore of Miletus to manifest his vision of the most beautiful building that had ever existed. They had at their disposal the most accomplished builders and craftspeople of their time, who were able to bring to completion the architectural, masonic and decorative aspects required to complete this revolutionary spiritual building. With virtually every surface in the church adorned with marbles and iconic mosaics, beautiful columns supporting exquisitely carved cornices, friezes and arches, and light entering the building from 100 windows, the world had never seen such artistry or such a commitment to the Divine. At the rededication of the Hagia Sophia on 27 December 563 Justinian declared his

satisfaction with a telling phrase: 'Solomon, I have surpassed you!' It was to be another thousand years before a larger cathedral was built, at Seville in Spain.

The main architectural focus of the Hagia Sophia is the central dome, which, with a diameter of 33 m (108 ft) and rising to 62 m (203 ft), is only slightly smaller than that of the Pantheon in Rome. It is carried primarily on four pillars, and the 'footprint' of each measures more than 100 sq m (1,075 sq ft). One of the foremost achievements was to make the dome appear to float on the rest of the building, where it was supported by a continuous arcade of 40 arched windows around its rim – enabling light to flood the interior. This feature led many early worshippers to believe that the dome was kept aloft by the power of God alone.

CHANGING BELIEFS AND RESTORATION

Although remarkable mosaics are still visible in the Great Church, many of its original artistic treasures have been covered over or destroyed. During the Iconoclastic Controversy of the 8th and 9th centuries, the

Orthodox Christian Church issued decrees against displaying any images of God and Christ. When the Hagia Sophia became a mosque in 1453 there were, naturally, more radical changes. Generally the Islamic faith does not permit the making of images of Allah or the Prophet. Even so, the Ottoman sultans did not destroy all the mosaics: they were plastered over, but periodically uncovered for maintenance, then replastered. The most extensive work on the mosque was done by Mimar Sinan in the 16th century: structural buttressing was added to the exterior; the old minarets were demolished and new versions built; Islamic artwork was developed and new pulpits installed.

Perhaps the most influential and, some say, destructive restorations were carried out in the 19th century by the Swiss architect brothers Gaspar and Guissepi Fossati. Working for Sultan Abdul Mecid I, they installed a minbar (Islamic pulpit) and the four circular medallions hanging on the walls of the nave that bear the names of Muhammad and the first caliphs, although they are widely deemed to have destroyed much of the original mosaic work. For the Christian worshipper, however, it is still possible to appreciate the scale, delicacy and spiritual depth of the remaining mosaic images. Many of them depict the Christ figure with important figures in the history of the Hagia Sophia. The oldest surviving mosaic is the enthroned Virgin and Child, 'the living throne of the Pantocrator', decorating the conch of the sanctuary apse. It replaced the earlier cross of the Iconoclast period and is assigned to the second half of the 9th century.

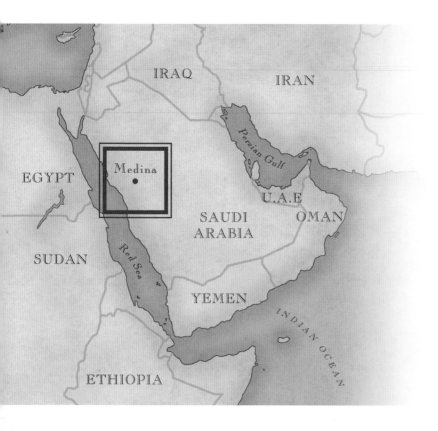

The Prophet's Mosque, Medina

The Prophet's Mosque – the Qubbat al-Nabi, the second holiest place in the Islamic tradition – is the burial place of Muhammad, the final prophet and the founder of Islam. Each year a great pilgrimage to Mecca takes place as part of the Hajj. This is a journey that every capable Muslim must make at one point in their lives, the great majority of pilgrims also make their way to Medina, the city that (along with Mecca) played such a significant part in the history of Muhammad's life.

Muhammad's family was originally from Mecca, and at the time when the Prophet was growing up, pagan religions dominated. The shrine there, known as the Kaaba, contained idols of various gods, and many pagans would make annual pilgrimages from Medina (or Yathrib, as it was then known) to the shrines at Mecca to worship the pagan god Manat. However, as Muhammad's reputation as a prophet gained strength and supporters, the pagan authorities in Mecca became increasingly uncomfortable with his teachings on strict monotheism and, in 622 CE (when Muhammad was around 52), he was forced to migrate to Medina with his followers. This event – known as the Hijra or flight – marks the beginning of the Islamic calendar and Muhammad's campaign to rid Mecca of paganism.

CONFLICT AND CONSTRUCTION

Two of the most powerful tribes who lived in the city of Medina, the Banu Aus and the Banu Khazraj, were already involved in a conflict that had escalated into war. They decided (according to Islamic texts) on the basis of Muhammad's growing reputation as a

spiritual leader, to invite him to resolve their struggle. Muhammad drew up the constitution of Medina which, while appointing him as leader, also promoted an alliance between the Muslim, pagan and Jewish communities who were living there. Medina now became the main city for the newly developing practice of Muslim worship, and the first mosque – the Masjid Quba (the Quba Mosque) – was soon constructed there.

After numerous battles with the attacking Meccans, and conflict within the tribes of Medina itself, Muhammad eventually marched his unified army on Mecca and captured the city with little opposition. The Kaaba was cleansed of all idols and, after a period in which Medina remained the capital of the Caliphate, Mecca eventually became

the main focus of worship and pilgrimage for all Muslims. The *qibla*, the direction of prayer, was changed from Jerusalem and the Dome of the Rock to the Kaaba in Mecca.

But it was only after Muhammad's death on 8 June 632, that plans for the Prophet's Mosque, the Qubbat al-Nabi (also known as the Prophet's Dome and the Green Dome), were initiated and the first structure erected next to the house where Muhammad had lived. Over time the mosque was enlarged to accommodate increasingly large numbers of worshippers. Eventually it was expanded by the Umayyad Caliph al-Waleed ibn AbdelMalek to incorporate the home of the Prophet where Muhammad had died.

After the death of the Prophet, Abu Bakr, the first Caliph and Muhammad's closest

'For many Muslims worship in Medina signifies the culmination of the Hajj experience and represents the pinnacle of their spiritual lives.'

companion, announced to mourning Muslims: 'O men, if anyone worships Muhammad, let him know that Muhammad is dead. But he who worships God, let him know that God is living and undying.'

EXPERIENCING THE MOSQUE

Today, pilgrims on the annual Hajj approach Medina from Mecca in search of the Prophet's Mosque. They find a low, brown brick enclosure with delicate, soaring minarets. They come to chant the 'unity', the chapter of the Quran that affirms the Oneness and 'uncreatedness' of God. They come also to see the tomb of Muhammad, in the knowledge that he is Allah's Final Prophet. The chamber containing the tomb is made of heavy iron filigree, painted green and decorated with burnished brass inscriptions from the Quran. A fabric drape of dark green silk completely shrouds Muhammad's last resting place, as well as those of Abu Bakr and Omar, the first two caliphs. Directly above the chamber a green dome rises towards the sky.

Though dominated by the many minarets, the rest of the building is simple in style, containing numerous pointed arches and a distinctive courtyard. For many Muslims worship in Medina signifies the culmination of the Hajj experience and represents the pinnacle of their spiritual lives.

Below *The religious complex at Medina contains both Muhammad's tomb and the very first 'Quba' mosque. The site's significance makes it an important part of the annual Hajj pilgrimage.*

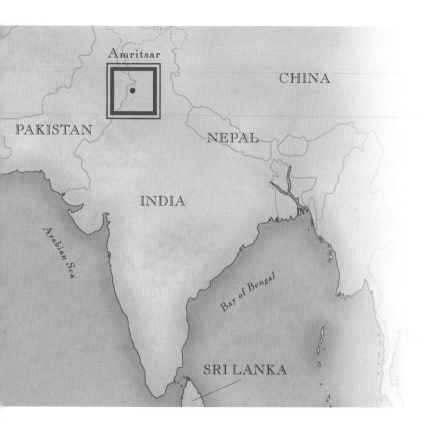

The Golden Temple, Amritsar

The Golden Temple in Amritsar is not just a peaceful and spiritually evocative place of worship for Sikhs, but also one of the most beautiful buildings in the world. The importance of the site was established long before the time of the Golden Temple: a small lake in the midst of a quiet forest was known as a place of contemplation and isolation for sages and seekers from as early as 1000 BCE.

It is known that Buddha himself meditated in this secluded spot. It was some two thousand years later, in the 16th century CE, when Guru Nanak, the first Guru of the Sikh religion, came to the shores of the lake to live and meditate, in the place then known as Kurtapur.

A MESSAGE OF EQUALITY

Guru Nanak stayed here for many years, listening and learning from the many holy men and philosophers who met and taught at the lake in the forest. When he was 30, according to Sikh tradition, he went missing one morning while bathing and was presumed to have drowned in the nearby stream known as the Kali Bein. But he reappeared three days later, perfectly healthy, and for some time would respond to every question about spiritual matters with the same answer: 'There is no Hindu, there is no Muslim.' From this moment, Guru Nanak began to spread his teachings of equality and spirituality – teachings that would eventually become Sikhism. His message was very modern for his time and countered the racism and castism that were rampant throughout the Indian subcontinent.

He made four significant spiritual journeys, which were to take him many thousands of miles. He travelled east to Bengal and Assam; south to Ceylon and Tamil Nadu; north to Kashmir, Ladakh and Tibet; and finally west to Baghdad and Mecca, before returning to Kurtapur. These journeys are reflected in the four gates of the Golden Temple, each one of which opens to a point of the compass. They symbolize the fact that Sikhism allows itself to be approached by all peoples, and turns none away. This is literally true for the whole venue of the Amritsar temple complex: those who come to worship here are welcomed, fed and sheltered without requests for payment or that they should abandon their inherited religion.

THE BUILDING OF THE TEMPLE

When he died on 22 September 1539 Guru Nanak was succeeded as the prime teacher of Sikhism by Guru Angada, the second Guru. The Guru's disciples continued to attend the site and, over the coming years, Kurtapur quickly became the most sacred Sikh shrine. The third Guru, Amardas, marked out the extent of the Holy Tank (*amritsar* or *amritsovar*), but it was the fourth Guru, Ram Dass, who enlarged the lake and gave it a more permanent containing structure. The fifth Guru, Arjan, conceived, designed and began the building of the Hari Mandir, or Temple of God, as a focus of worship for all followers of the Sikh religion. And yet the building that we see today is not exactly the one that was completed in 1601. For many years this part of the Punjab was lorded over by different Muslim factions who attempted to destroy the Golden Temple. Yet each time it was knocked down, the followers of the Guru built it up again, and each time it became more ornate and even more beautiful. From 1767 onwards the temple remained sufficiently well defended to repel Muslim attackers and the Maharaja Ranjit added marble statues, gilding to the dome and a myriad of precious stones inside the temple itself.

To approach the Golden Temple every worshipper passes through the Darshani Deori, the arch that stands at the shore end of the causeway leading across the water. The Sri Harmandir Sahib, the temple itself, is built on a 20 m (67 ft) square platform in the

centre of the Holy Tank. The bridge links to the circumambulatory path, or Pardakshna, which leads the pilgrim around the temple. After completing a number of circuits of the shrine, the pilgrim approaches the Har Ki Paure, the steps of God, which lead inside the temple. There, on the first floor of the building, recitation of the Guru Granth Sahib, the Sikh sacred texts, continues daily without cease, accompanied by peaceful, contemplative music that drifts out to worshippers all around the lake, casting its blessings as it goes.

'Those who come to worship here are welcomed, fed and sheltered without requests for payment or that they should abandon their inherited religion.'

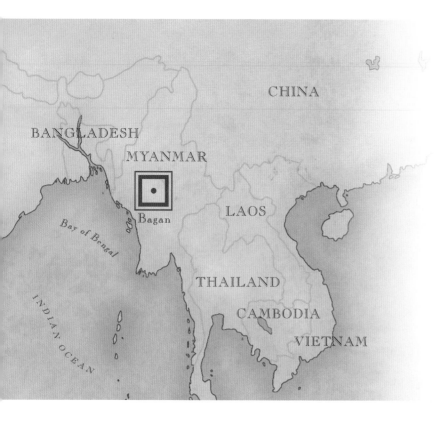

Bagan, Burma (Myanmar)

More than two thousand temples, shrines, reliquaries and stupas (sacred monuments) are spread across 41 sq km (16 sq miles) of the Bagan plain and are what remain of the spiritual outpourings of the First Burmese Empire. Their architectural styles are very varied and include buildings with Indian and Sinhalese Buddhist influence. This great ruined city stands as a testament to a culture that once valued spirituality above all else. Bagan was once the ancient capital of one of many kingdoms in Myanmar (previously known as Burma).

This remarkable place has borne many names throughout its history: Pagan; Arimaddanapura, the City of the Enemy Crusher; Tambadipa, the Land of Copper; and Tassadessa, the Parched Land.

THE RISE OF THERAVADAN BUDDHISM

It was 874 CE when King Pyinba moved the capital of Burma from Tampawadi (now Pwasaw) to Bagan and the rise of this great city began. However, according to Burmese tradition, each new ruler would choose a fresh location for his capital and, with Pyinba's death, Bagan was abandoned until King Anawratha took the throne in the 11th century and started Bagan's extraordinary development as a religious as well as a cultural centre.

Following his capture of the Mon capital of Thaton, Anawratha brought Buddhist monks and craftsmen to Bagan along with their spiritual treasures, including the Tripitaka Pali scriptures. The King later turned away from the predominant animistic religion of Nat and a form of Mahayana Buddhism known as Ari, to embrace the growing movement of Theravadan or 'southern' Buddhism, which traces its roots to Sri Lanka.

The Theravadan school of Buddhism holds the Pali Canon, also known as the Tripitaka, as the most important group of texts on the teachings of Gautama Buddha (the Buddha of our age). It also stresses a path of analysis, or reference to the adherent's own experience, as the source of spiritual progress. At the same time the wisdom of teachers is valued as an aid towards the state of Nirvana, or unbinding from the wheel of karma.

King Anawratha was eventually successful in converting the whole country to the Theravadan form of Buddhism, which has continued as Myanmar's central religion to the present day. This made Bagan the spiritual heart of the new kingdom, and the city became an even more important seat of learning and the study of Buddhist practice. The massive explosion of building was the natural manifestation of this spiritual expression. The rulers who followed Anawratha were just as prodigious in their desire to build: between 1000 and 1200 it is believed that more than thirteen thousand temples, shrines, pagodas and other religious structures were constructed.

DECLINE AND CONTINUITY

This golden age continued until 1287 when the kingdom was attacked and captured by the Mongols led by Kublai Khan. Temples were destroyed and their treasures stolen. Since that time it is believed that up to one-third of all the temples have been destroyed by the gradual washing of the River Ayeyarwady, or Irrawaddy, that runs beside the great plain of Bagan.

Perhaps the most destructive 'natural' event for the plain of Bagan was the earthquake of 1975, which destroyed and damaged many of the most treasured and revered temples and shrines, including the Gawdawpalin and Mahabodhi temples. Following the destruction wrought by the earthquake, huge restoration efforts were unleashed to bring the buildings back to their previous state, or to even more constructionally stable states. Some of these works have been carried out with care and craftsmanship, while others appear to have used inappropriate modern materials in an effort to speed up the work and reduce costs. Nevertheless, some of the reconstructions are stunning and remarkable, and the great efforts of those involved are a testament to the religious and cultural importance of the Bagan site to the people of Myanmar and the followers of Theravadan Buddhism.

Nearly 90 per cent of the population follow this form of Buddhism, one of the three main traditions along with Mahayana and Vajrayana. It is an almost universal practice for parents in Myanmar to send their children to monasteries as part of their education, and many who have had experience of monastery life decide, despite its hardships, to be ordained as monks at the age of 20. Every village in Myanmar has its own monastery, which is supported by the local people, who regard the role of the monks (Sangha) as essential to the spiritual health of their community.

While the current state political regime allows for religious freedom in Myanmar, there is a nationalistic policy of *Bama san-gyin*, which effectively equates 'Burmeseness' with Buddhism. In practice, this means that a system of preferment for those who express Buddhism as their faith operates in the fields of military and state employment.

BAGAN TODAY

Even though Bagan is now incomplete, many people regard the magical plain as one of the great religious sites in the world. The breathtaking views at dusk and dawn give Bagan a reputation as one of the planet's most sacred vistas. Perhaps the greatest threat to this remarkable site actually comes from the Myanmar authorities. A number of the stupas and temples have been insensitively restored, and there are plans to build a golf course, a paved roadway and a 60 m (200 ft) watchtower. UNESCO's attempts to protect Bagan as a World Heritage Site have so far failed. The government of Myanmar is not always renowned for its sympathy to its own people: in 1990 the government took the sudden decision to relocate all the local people who lived in the old district of Bagan city. The residents were given just seven days to move themselves and all their belongings to new homes in 'New Bagan', some 3 km (1¾ miles) to the south.

Left *The 11th-century Ananda Temple is modelled on a Himalayan cave and contains statues of the last four Buddhas, as well as a mural showing scenes from the most recent Buddha's life.*

The temples of Bagan

Of the two thousand or so temples that Bagan still offers, a small number can be singled out as exceptional examples for their religious and historical importance.

THE SHWEZIGON PAGODA

Begun by King Anawratha and completed by King Kyanzittha in 1089 CE, the Shwezigon Pagoda was built as Bagan's most important reliquary shrine, containing bones and hairs of the Gautama Buddha. During the Burmese month of Nadaw (November–December in the Julian calendar) pilgrims from all over Myanmar travel to Shwezigon for one of the country's great festivals. This attracts worshippers from the original, pre-Buddhist shamanic religion of Nat as well as Theravadan Buddhists, and this blending of religions is embodied in the architectural styles of the pagoda.

OTHER SIGNIFICANT TEMPLES

The Dhammayangyi Temple is the largest in Bagan, some 60 m (200 ft) tall. It was built by Alaungsithu around 1165, but was never fully completed. Some credit its construction to his successor, King Narathu, who reigned 1167–1170. The structure originally contained four Buddha sanctums, although three have been filled in. The fourth still contains two Buddha figures: the Gautama Buddha of the current age and the Maitreya Buddha of the coming age. The beautiful interlocking brickwork was constructed without the use of mortar, and is often considered the finest work in all of Bagan.

The Ananda Temple was completed in 1091 by King Kyanzittha and is modelled on the Nandamula cave in the Himalayas. It contains large statues of the last four Buddhas: the Kakusandha Buddha faces north; the Konagamana Buddha faces east; the Kassapa Buddha faces south; and the

Gautama Buddha, the most recent of the four, faces west. The temple also contains the story of the Buddha's life in 80 panels. The Ananda Temple was gilded in 1990 to celebrate its nine hundredth anniversary.

The Gawdawpalin Temple is a large two-storey temple that faces eastwards. This 60 m (200 ft) temple, originally built by King Narapatisithu in the 12th century, has been almost totally rebuilt following the 1975 earthquake. Around 40 per cent of the temple's stucco mouldings are still in place. Unusually for Bagan architecture, the main shrine is on the second-storey.

THE SHWESANDAW PAGODA

This pagoda is generally believed to have been built by King Anawratha in 1057. It is constructed as a series of five terraces on which there is a cylindrical stupa and a jewelled umbrella. Part of the pagoda's significance to religious seekers is the claim that it contains strands of hair belonging to the Gautama Buddha. It is also known as the Ganesh Temple, for the images of the elephant-headed Hindu god that once stood at the ends of the temple's five terraces.

① THE MAHABODHI TEMPLE

This temple is a scaled-down replica of the Bodhi temple in Bodh Gaya in north-eastern India – where the Gautama Buddha attained Samsara, the state of enlightenment, while sitting beneath the Bodhi tree. The temple in Bagan, believed to have been built by King Nantaungmya, is comprehensively decorated with niches containing more than 450 statues of seated Buddha figures. It is built in a style typical of the Gupta period and contains a large pyramidal tower. The temple was largely destroyed in the earthquake of 1975, but was subsequently rebuilt and restored to its current condition.

② NUMBER OF TEMPLES

No one knows exactly how many temples were built on the site, although it is believed that a total of more than 13,000 temples, shrines, pagodas and other religious buildings existed at Bagan. By the end of the 13th century there were officially 4,446 temples, a figure that had reduced to 2,230 according to a count in 1978.

③ OLD BAGAN

The original city is no longer inhabited – the government moved the residents to New Bagan, some miles away, in 1990. The old city is now the main archaeological site, comprising the key temples, city walls and museum.

④ RUINS IN THE JUNGLE

Like other Burmese royal cities, only the major religious buildings were built of stone. The palaces and monasteries were constructed of wood and quickly succumbed to the decaying forces of the jungle after the city was abandoned from the 14th century onwards.

⑤ THE AYEYARWADY RIVER

The Ayeyarwady, or Irrawaddy, River bisects Myanmar from north to south, running for 2,170 km (1,350 miles). The bend in the river where Old Bagan sits was originally occupied by a thriving Pyu city state. By 850 this city had grown into a complex centre of religious and administrative activity.

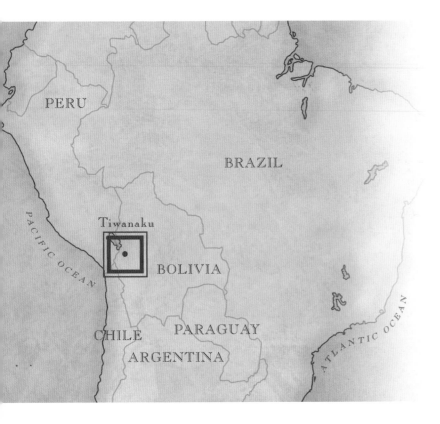

Tiwanaku, Bolivia

The ruins of the great city state of Tiwanaku lie close to the south-eastern shore of Lake Titicaca, around 70 km (44 miles) from La Paz, the capital of Bolivia. What is now an archaeological site was, for as much as five hundred years, the busy centre of the most important Andean culture preceding the Inca Empire. Time and the casual hand of humans have not been kind to the great architectural treasures of Tiwanaku, but it is still possible to appreciate the dedication, achievement and spirituality of its remarkable creators.

Opinions differ regarding the timing of the original building of the city. While some people believe that the site may date back to 15,000 years BCE, the majority of scholars believe that Tiwanaku was built between 600 and 800 CE by the Aymara people – the Native South Americans who lived in the Lake Titicaca basin in Peru and Bolivia. At the height of its power, it is possible that as many as 40,000 people lived in the city. Little is known about the pre-Incan culture that created the buildings, decorations and cultural objects, although the beauty, skill and intelligence that shine through the work have led many to speculate on their beliefs and cosmology.

Unfortunately, the architecture found at Tiwanaku is not as well preserved as it deserves to be. Over many hundreds of years it has suffered from looting of various kinds, including the worst excesses of amateur excavation work in search of valuables. Following the arrival of the Spanish conquistadors in the 16th century, this destruction continued unabated. During the 19th and 20th centuries the site has been used and abused in many different forms: it has served as a quarry for stone and even as a source of target practice for the military.

THE GATEWAY OF THE SUN

Perhaps the most famous landmark in Tiwanaku is the Gateway of the Sun, the great archway that now stands at the north-western corner of the Kalasasaya temple. There are many theories about its original location, including the idea that it formed the entrance to the temple. It carries a crack down its full height, but the gate's precisely chiselled carvings speak in a clear visual language to those who can read its symbols. Weighing more than 10 tons and carved from a single piece of granite, the Gateway of the Sun is believed to have been a form of ancient observatory dedicated to the God of the Sun himself, although its current positioning does not offer any astronomically relevant orientations. The carving is dominated by an image of the Sun God, with rays emanating from his head and tears falling from his eyes. Situated on either side of this central image is a 'calendar' frieze, which, some believe, may incorporate encoded astronomical information.

IMPRESSIVE STONEMASONRY

One feature of Tiwanaku's buildings that challenges modern cultures is the extraordinarily high level of expertise shown by the creators in working with stone. What is initially most striking is the sheer size of some of the stones used in the construction of Tiwanaku: it has been estimated that some of the stones weigh as much as 100 tons. This begs a question that has baffled many archaeologists: how did the builders move the stones? The distance from the place where the stones are believed to have been quarried to the city of Tiwanaku is several miles, and it is far from clear that the culture was even in possession of the wheel.

The second extraordinary feature of the stonemasonry is the accuracy and precision of the 'bonding'. Without using any mortar or cement, stones of many different (and often asymmetrical) shapes were brought together with absolute perfection. Not even a sheet of paper can be slid between the stones' joints. This stonemasonry demonstrates two types of achievement: the highest level of practical craft skills and a spiritual dedication to perfection.

The artistic style that typifies Tiwanaku defines, along with the related 'Huari' style, what is called the 'Middle Horizon' period of Andean prehistory. It is thought that both these styles grew out of an even older style developed by the 'Pukara' culture who lived in the northern part of the Titicaca basin.

A PUZZLING BEGINNING AND END

Perhaps the most important feature of the site is the Kalasasaya Temple. Although it has been subject to many restorations over the centuries – much of the work being inferior to the original constructions – this large area continues to engage the interest of scientists wishing to understand the cosmology of the people who lived here. The temple's boundary is defined by a series of 3 m (10 ft) high stone stelae, or slabs, of simplified

human figures, each with a carved face, which appear to stand guard over the temple. From the solar alignments that seem implicit in the organization of the structure, and from a knowledge of the changes in the Earth's orbit over long periods of time, some experts have dated the Kalasasaya to around 15,000 BCE – making Tiwanaku one of the oldest cities in the world.

If its beginnings were uncertain, then so was Tiwanaku's end. The city is thought to have been abandoned around 1000 CE, although it is far from clear what caused the residents to leave. The exodus may have been linked to a fall in Lake Titicaca's water level. Whereas the city may once have been a port on the lake's edge, it now lies some 16 km (10 miles) from the shore. Other experts have speculated that different factors may

Above The entrance to the Kalasasaya mound can be seen here from the Sunken Courtyard. The stairway is a single block of carved sandstone, worn by the footsteps of centuries.

have played a part: whether it was other environmental factors, a loss of faith in the religion or an invasion by another culture from the south. It is unlikely, though, that a definitive answer will emerge. What the people of Tiwanaku left, however, has continued to enthral those who came after them – and will do so for many years yet.

The collapse of Tiwanaku

Since farming was central to the economy of Tiwanaku, its people developed a distinctive agricultural technique suitable for high altitudes. Reliance on this technique, however, made the city particularly vulnerable to environmental changes such as drought. This may be the explanation for the collapse of the city around the 11th century CE.

HIGH-ALTITUDE FARMING

The key to growing enough food to sustain a growing population in a valley more than 3,220 m (10,500 ft) high is controlling the temperature. Surrounded on three sides by mountain ranges and on the fourth by Lake Titicaca, Tiwanaku's growing season was short and its crops were at risk from frost at any time of the year. Only crops that grew below ground, such as potatoes and hardy grains, could survive at this altitude.

To protect their crops from frosts, Tiwanaku's farmers developed a sophisticated technique known as 'raised-field' agriculture. Artificially raised planting mounds were separated by canals filled with water. The water flow to the canals was controlled by a system of aqueducts, causeways and dykes. The canals irrigated the crops but, more importantly, the water in the canals collected warmth from the sun. During the day the water temperature could be as much as seven degrees centigrade above the air temperature. This heat transferred both to the air and to the soil in the beds, keeping the plants from freezing. Modern-day experiments with this method have produced yields two to three times greater than conventional farming. Experts estimate that the extent of the raised fields in Tiwanaku could have fed a population of as many as 500,000 people.

DECLINE AND REDISCOVERY

Many experts believe that a significant long-term drought led to the collapse of Tiwanaku. Without sufficient water, raised-field agriculture could not produce enough food to feed the population. By 1000 CE the city fell into decay and was largely abandoned. About the middle of the 15th century, after the city had been empty for more than five hundred years, the Inca people came to Tiwanaku. Impressed by the monoliths, the carvings and stonework, they absorbed Tiwanaku into their own mythology, saying that their creator deity, Viracocha, had created the first Andes people at Tiwanaku, including the Inca themselves, whom he sent to Cuzco to found an empire.

① DESERT SETTING

Situated high on the windswept altiplano, Tiwanaku lies close to the south-eastern shore of Lake Titicaca on its Bolivian side, roughly 70 km (44 miles) west of La Paz. Its setting, coupled with a weather system of alternating droughts and torrential downpours, meant that creative farming and irrigation methods had to be established. Large canals were dug 10 m (33 ft) apart, with banks of crops planted between, allowing for irrigation and ensuring that, despite the bitter winters, frost did not kill the crops. Fish were also kept in the canals both as a foodstuff and as an automatic fertilizer.

② GATEWAY OF THE SUN

Many scholars have likened the Sun God figure on the Gateway of the Sun to Viracocha, the creator god of the Inca people. This deity has a long history in the Andes and is also found at Nazca (see pages 154–157). However, since no written record exists, this can never be verified beyond doubt, and there has also been dispute over the carved figures on the gateway. Some people claim that a carving of an elephant proves that a highly sophisticated, well-travelled people occupied the site; others contest that it is in fact an image of a condor.

③ STONE SCULPTURES/ MONOLITHS

Although much of the detail has rubbed off the stones, there are several monoliths on the site that probably represent deity figures, such as the Ponce monolith found in the Kalasasaya complex.

④ AKAPANA TEMPLE

Akapana is the largest pyramid on the site and was once thought to be a modified hill. Its base was later found to be constructed of perfectly cut and joined facing stone blocks, a trademark of its creators' architecture. There were also six T-shaped terraces with vertical stone pillars, another distinct design. The floors were made of packed dirt, probably from the dug-out moats surrounding each structure, and the top of Akapana held a sunken courtyard, which filled with water.

⑤ WORSHIPPERS

Despite the citadel-type appearance of the central buildings and the inclusion of a moat around Kalasasaya, the buildings were probably used purely for ceremonial purposes, not for defence. Tiwanaku's population of around 40,000 at its peak, most of whom lived in settlements on the outskirts of the city, probably made regular journeys to the main temple buildings to worship what is presumed to have been a sun deity.

⑥ KALASASAYA TEMPLE

The main temple of Tiwanaku, Kalasasaya is believed to have been the focal point of major ceremonies. The Gateway of the Sun is now in its north-western corner, after being moved from its original location.

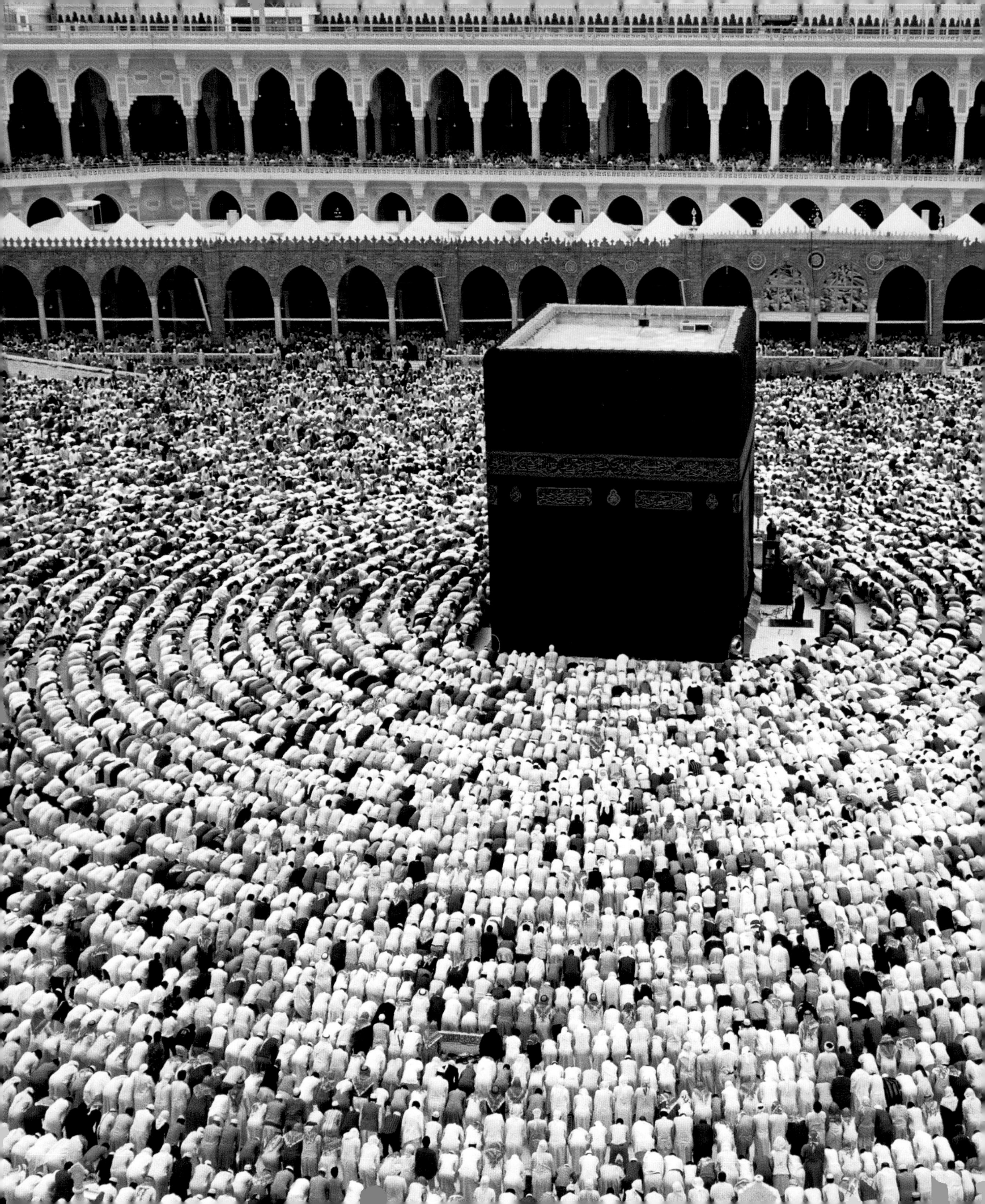

CHAPTER 2

SITES OF PILGRIMAGE

Pilgrimage is one of the most ancient human impulses, so embedded in our culture and our psyches that we have lost sight of its ever-presence. Every time we go on a journey we hope to improve our lives in some way, whether materially, spiritually or both. This is a pale shadow of the pilgrimage, the craving to improve our spiritual condition by undergoing a journey that demands our sacrifice. The pilgrim embarking on a journey knows that he or she is in a state of 'lack', that there is something the psyche calls out for. The sacred destination offers the hope of salvation or enlightenment, and the journey is the means to that end. What many stories of pilgrimage reveal is that the journey – far from being simply a way to arrive at the destination – contains much of the meaning and purpose of the pilgrimage experience.

Nothing, though, can prepare the pilgrim for arrival at the sacred place. Through the preparation and the hardships of the journey, the devotee is opened up to new ways of experiencing. It is precisely this process that transforms individuals and, when they finally arrive at their chosen place, they are in a condition to receive the spiritual benefits of the sacred site and its incumbent rituals. Without the preparation of the journey, the pilgrim is simply a tourist.

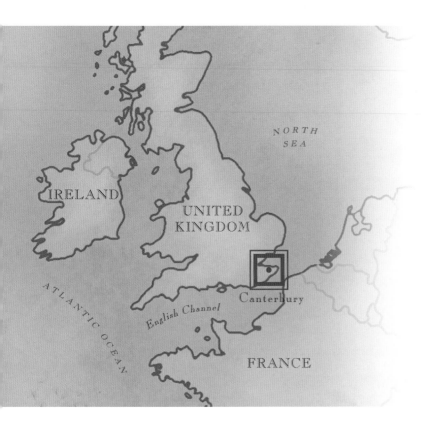

Canterbury Cathedral, Kent

Canterbury Cathedral, the headquarters of the Church of England, seems to have had its earliest origins in Rome. In 597 CE Pope Gregory sent Bishop Augustine to convert the 'Angles' (the English) to Christianity. Augustine formed an alliance with local King Ethelbert, whose French queen, Bertha, was already a Christian, and was given a church at Canterbury. He established his seat within the Roman walls of the city and built the first cathedral there.

As the first Archbishop of Canterbury, Augustine started a line of succession that now sees the stewardship of the Church of England in the hands of its 104th archbishop: the Most Revd and Right Honourable Dr Rowan Williams.

MARTYRDOM AND MIRACLES
One of the most chilling and important chapters in the history of the cathedral occurred during the 12th-century reign of Henry II. Henry had appointed Thomas Becket to be Archbishop of Canterbury and had believed that he could rely on Becket's personal loyalty. However, Becket soon demonstrated that his first allegiance was not to the King, but to God and the Pope. Henry grew tired of Becket's non-compliance and, at his Christmas court in France in 1170, issued the challenging words: 'Who will rid me of this meddlesome priest?' Whether Henry intended his words to be taken literally remains unknown, but within hours a group of four knights were on their way to Canterbury, eager and proud to do the King's bidding. Richard Brito, Hugh de Moreville, Reginald FitzUrse and William de Tracy

arrived in the abbey on the evening of 29 December to find Becket at prayer during Vespers. They challenged him to comply with the King, but Becket made his loyalties clear. 'For the name of Jesus and the protection of the Church, I am ready to embrace death' were his last words. The knights set about their grim execution, decapitating Becket on the stone floor of the abbey.

Following his death a number of miracles were reported, and three years later Becket was canonized by Pope Alexander III. Another year on, Henry, walking barefoot and wearing sackcloth along with other pilgrims, made his way to Becket's shrine. His wish to pay public penance was clear, though

whether Henry's inner torment was as real as his outer show has been debated ever since. Nevertheless Thomas Becket's martyrdom brought a new vigour to Canterbury. Pilgrims came from all over the British Isles and Europe and, in the 1380s, the pilgrimage became the setting for the first great work of English literature, *The Canterbury Tales* by Geoffrey Chaucer.

The Canterbury Tales represent a cross-section of English social life at this time and, according to some scholars, were inspired by the form of *The Decameron* by the Italian writer Giovanni Boccaccio. They are a series of stories told by a disparate group of pilgrims as they make their way towards Canterbury and

'Each year some two thousand services are performed within the cathedral – testament to Augustine's vision and the enduring faith of the English Church.'

Left The nave of Canterbury Cathedral is one of the finest examples of the Perpendicular Gothic style. Here, the cloisters surround a peaceful, grassed quadrangle, overlooked by Bell Harry Tower.

the tomb of Thomas Becket. *The Canterbury Tales'* lasting appeal seems to lie in their combination of humour, bawdiness as well as their extraordinarily perceptive observation of character.

TESTAMENT TO A LASTING FAITH

Throughout its long history there have been many developments to the structure of Canterbury Cathedral, and the building that now stands would be only partly recognizable

to the pilgrims of Chaucer's time. Its tall 14th-century Perpendicular Gothic nave with elegant vaulting and gilded roof bosses is one of the most exceptional examples of its kind. The quire, chapter house, trinity chapel and corona chapel are all unique features of this grand building, which has survived destruction and change of many kinds. Such events have included the dissolution of the monastic community and the destruction of Becket's shrine in 1538 by Henry VIII, the

smashing of the cathedral's stained glass by Oliver Cromwell's men during the English Civil War of the 1640s and the incendiary bombs of Hitler's Luftwaffe during the Second World War. Nevertheless, Canterbury Cathedral has managed to flourish as an active religious community for 1,400 years. Each year some two thousand services are performed within the cathedral – testament to Augustine's vision and the enduring faith of the English Church.

Lough Derg, Ireland

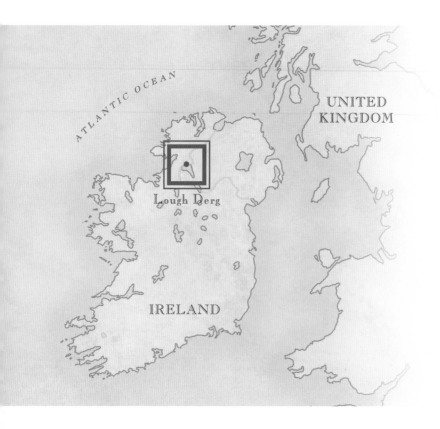

Lough Derg – literally St Patrick's Purgatory – is one of the oldest Christian pilgrimage centres in Western Europe. Situated 6.5 km (4 miles) north of the village of Pettigo in County Donegal, Station Island (as it is also known) has been attracting Christian seekers since St Patrick, Ireland's patron saint and the man who brought Christianity to its people, first came here in 445 CE.

Legend reports that Patrick was struggling to convince the people of Ireland of the importance of his message of Christianity and that he retreated to a cave on Station Island, where he prayed to God for assistance. In response he was shown a disturbing image: a vision of purgatory – the terrifying condition that sinners could expect to experience after death if they were to continue in their ungodly ways. In some reports Patrick's image of purgatory was a pit: not just a picture in his imagination, but a real depression in the very soil of Station Island. Alongside the image that he was sent, Patrick was told that by communicating the grim nature of purgatory, he would also help people to understand the attraction of reaching heaven by renouncing sin and living a blameless Christian life.

A SITE OF PILGRIMAGE

The event became an important milestone in Patrick's personal mission to convert the Irish to Christianity and marked a turning point in the country's religious history. From this time on, St Patrick's Purgatory became more widely known and people started to

make the journey to Station Island in an attempt to replicate Patrick's mystical experience or gain forgiveness for their sins. In the latter part of the 5th century a local abbot, later to become St Dabheog, took on the stewardship of the Lough Derg site as its importance grew. The beehive 'cells' on Station Island – the remains of which still form part of religious life today – date from this time and were used during the preparation period of fasting and meditation before the pilgrim entered the pit of purgatory, where he or she might experience all the potentials (both good and bad) of the afterlife.

By the 12th century Augustinian friars had taken over the stewardship of Lough Derg. They built a monastery on the nearby Saints' Island, where the increasing numbers of pilgrims were readied for their journey to purgatory. The pilgrims would even receive the final sacraments before being taken by boat to Station Island. Such was the international renown of the place that travelling Christians were coming from all over Europe in their desire to experience a taste of the afterlife.

The importance of the pilgrimage in medieval times is evidenced by the fact that Lough Derg was often the only Irish location labelled on international maps. Records demonstrate that pilgrims from European countries have been coming here from the 14th century onwards.

PRESENT-DAY LOUGH DERG

Today Lough Derg no longer has the same hold over the psyche of Irish Christians as it did in earlier times, but thousands of people still make the journey every year to experience this sacred place. Many come to take part in the traditional three-day pilgrimage, which, although it may not be as demanding of the contemporary seeker as it would have been for his or her medieval counterpart, it is still very challenging.

Over the three-day period (and starting before they arrive) participants follow a fast and are permitted only one meal of dry toast, water and black tea or coffee each day. They perform repeated 'stations', in which they walk barefoot and repeat the Lord's Prayer, the Hail Mary and the Creed. Parts of these stations are carried out while walking circuits through the 'beds', the remains of the 6th-century cells from the time of St Dabheog. Other stations are performed in the basilica. In the middle of the three days, pilgrims are required to perform a 'vigil', in which they go without sleep for a 24-hour period as they continue their 'stations'. This undertaking mimics – in a way more acceptable to 21st-century sensibilities – the challenges of St Patrick's original purgatory. Many participants report that the experience brings them closer to their fellow pilgrims, with whom they form unusually supportive groups; as well as bringing them closer to God, on whose grace and beneficence the deprived are forced to throw themselves.

Below *The pilgrim's journey to Lough Derg, also known as Station Island, was originally taken by St Patrick, in 445 CE. His visionary experiences have inspired thousands to follow him.*

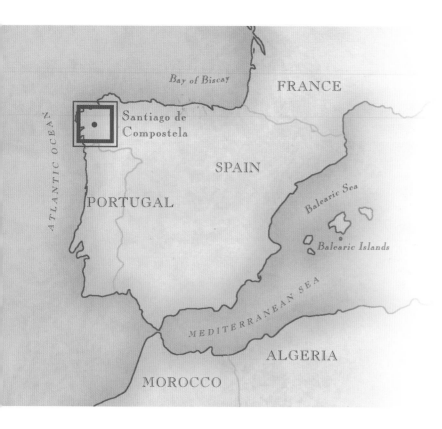

Santiago de Compostela, Spain

'St James of the Starry Field' is the literal translation for the name of the small, yet beautiful medieval city of Santiago de Compostela, set in the rolling hills of Spain's north-western province of Galicia. 'The Starry Field' is the metaphorical Spanish name for the Milky Way, the cloudy constellation of stars that looks down on the many hundreds of pilgrims as they journey towards the Cathedral of St James in the heart of the city.

There are a number of traditional, well-defined pilgrim routes – or *caminos* – to Santiago, many of which start in Spain, France, Germany and other European countries. Every year around ten thousand pilgrims make this journey of meditation, contemplation and hardship through the beautiful, rugged landscape of northern Spain, stopping on the way at rudimentary pilgrims' hostels known as *refugios*. Each pilgrim's progress is very personal and, as testimony to this, the *camino* is walked by Christians, Jews, Hindus, Buddhists and, indeed, members of all the world's religions, as well as by those who profess no faith at all.

THE JOURNEYS OF ST JAMES THE APOSTLE

But why do all of these different people come to Santiago de Compostela? The literal answer is that the city's cathedral claims to play host to the remains of St James the Apostle. James, one of the first disciples to be called by Jesus, was the son of Zebedee and Salome and, if some readings of the Bible are correct, also the first cousin of Jesus. After the crucifixion and resurrection of Jesus in 33 CE, James proselytized the good news of Jesus' teachings until he was executed by Herod Agrippa in Jerusalem in 41 CE. Some traditions believe that James visited Spain as a missionary during this period, before he returned to Jerusalem and his martyr's death.

How James' corpse made the journey to north-western Spain is the subject of an extraordinary legend: it is said that his body (contained in a stone sarcophagus) was cast adrift in an open boat, which floated west across the Mediterranean, out through the Straits of Gibraltar and up the coast of the Iberian peninsula before landing on the rocky beaches close to Cape Finisterre ('The End of the World' – the most westerly point of the then-known world). Some versions even say that the voyage took just seven days. From there it is said that the saint's body was carried on a cart pulled by oxen to its final resting place, where it was buried along with two of James' disciples, Athanasius and Theodore.

Strangely, nothing more was heard of James the Apostle until 813, when a hermit named Pelayo received a vision, or 'shining', that led to the uncovering of the tomb in a

field. The location was soon given the name *Campus Stellae* (Latin for 'field of stars'), later Hispanicized to *Compostela*. Following the discovery of the relics, King Alfonso II came to pay his respects, built a chapel on the site and established James as the saint most likely to rid Christian Spain of its current problem: occupation by the Moors.

MIRACLES AND DISPENSATIONS

St James was soon credited with a number of miracles – particularly in aiding the Christian forces to repel the Islamic invaders. After one battle, King Ramiro I claimed that James had fought beside him and had personally dispatched sixty thousand of the Moorish army. James' image as the saviour of Christian Spain meant that Santiago de Compostela soon became an important goal for pilgrims wishing to express their gratitude.

As the popularity of the pilgrimage grew, so did the need for a grander setting for the saint's relics. The building of a cathedral dedicated to St James was completed in 1188 under the supervision of architect Master Mateo. The current ornate façade, built in the 18th century, is credited to the Santiago-born architect Fernando Casas y Novoa. Over time, too, the significance of the journey developed. For the faithful, completion of the pilgrimage meant a dispensation from the Pope – if not total forgiveness of sins, then at least a reduction of the time required to be spent in purgatory.

Each year the Apostle's saint's day is celebrated on 25 July, and when this date falls on a Sunday the year is considered especially auspicious. One of the features of the celebration is the swinging of the giant incense burner, the *botafumeiro*, over the heads of the congregation. This is considered a great blessing on all those present – another example of the power of place and ritual working together.

Left The Tree of Jesse is the central support for the Portico de Gloria. Fingerprints have been worn into the marble by the millions of pilgrims who arrive here. Some also place their hands in the holes at the base of the column, which are the carved mouths of fishes.

Below The 18th-century Obradoiro Façade dominates the western end of the cathedral. Many pilgrims arrive in this vast square, before ascending the steps to the cathedral entrance.

The pilgrimage, ancient and modern

Although the most popular starting point for the pilgrimage to Santiago is Saint-Jean-Pied-de-Port, just a few miles over the Spanish Pyrenean border into France, pilgrims set off on their journeys from all over the world and take many different routes. The favoured route across the north of Spain takes in some of the most beautiful and rugged scenery that the country has to offer.

APPROACHING THE CATHEDRAL

Passing through large cities such as Pamplona, Burgos, Leon and Ponferrada, and a collection of small villages and pueblos, pilgrims stop at *refugios* for the night, before resuming their journey the following day. Although there are pilgrims who make the journey by horse, donkey, bicycle, motorcycle and even car, the route by foot is considered the only real way to travel.

With the journey taking some people a month or two to complete, the pilgrim's day of arrival in Santiago brings much joy after the hardships of the road. There are particular ways to approach the cathedral, and at certain times the Porta Santa, or sacred door, at the east end is opened for pilgrims. Most, though, will make their way to the vast square, the Praza do Obradoiro, facing the cathedral's west façade. With its multiple images of the behatted James and ornate bell-towers, this 18th-century confection is one of the most exuberant pieces of baroque architecture in the world.

Mounting the ornate steps, the pilgrims enter the cathedral's outer doors and meet the Portico de Gloria, one of the most beautiful pieces of medieval stone carving in the Christian West. With its dominant figure of Jesus and, beneath him, St James, the portico displays a combination of ethereal lightness and worldly seriousness in both the modelling of the faces and the design of the reliefs. For the pilgrim, there is one sacred duty to perform at the portico: on the central pillar – a marble effigy of the Tree of Jesse – are the marks made by many millions of human hands. This gradual wearing away has left imprints of fingers and palm, which invite the visitor to place his or her hand along with that of every other traveller who has passed this way and made this sacrifice.

VIEWING THE RELICS

The pilgrim is then drawn towards the east end of the cathedral, to the altarpiece and its ornate baldachin framing the gilded statue of St James himself. To climb the steps and embrace the figure of the saint in his bejewelled cape is, for some, the climax of their pilgrimage. For others, that moment comes when their eyes first fall on the silver casket containing the relics of St James. These are reached by a set of descending steps beneath the altar and well protected behind layers of glass. It is the significance of the bones within the box that keeps many pilgrims on their magnetic journey to the third heart of Christendom.

The location of Santiago close to the most westerly point of the European mainland is not without significance. This coast, from where Christopher Columbus' ships first left for the New World, was once the end of the known world. And for some pilgrims their journey is not complete until they have travelled on a further 100 km (60 miles) to the ragged, granite coastline of Cape Finisterre, touched the water and returned to Santiago.

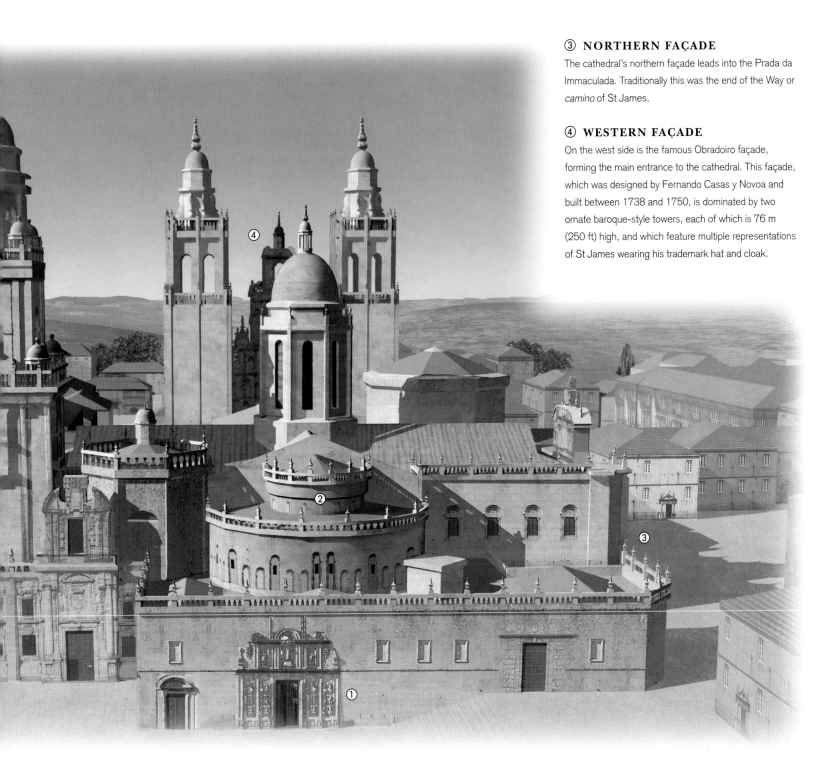

③ **NORTHERN FAÇADE**

The cathedral's northern façade leads into the Prada da Immaculada. Traditionally this was the end of the Way or *camino* of St James.

④ **WESTERN FAÇADE**

On the west side is the famous Obradoiro façade, forming the main entrance to the cathedral. This façade, which was designed by Fernando Casas y Novoa and built between 1738 and 1750, is dominated by two ornate baroque-style towers, each of which is 76 m (250 ft) high, and which feature multiple representations of St James wearing his trademark hat and cloak.

① **PORTA SANTA**

This special eastern entrance to the cathedral (known as the Sacred Door) is opened only in those years when the saint day of St James falls on a Sunday. Its baroque façade was built in the year 1611 by Fernandez Lechuga who incorporated earlier statues of the prophets and patriarchs sculpted by Master Mateo.

② **APSE**

The apse survives from the original Romanesque cathedral begun in 1075, and is situated behind the altar. The baroque eastern façade now hides the five chapels radiating from the apse, which are designed to offer pilgrims places to pause and reflect during their time in the cathedral.

⑤ **THE CLOCK TOWER AND SOUTHERN FAÇADE**

The ornamental baroque clock tower with its distinctive pyramidal spire dates from the 17th century. It rises beside the southern façade of the cathedral, which is situated by the Praza das Praterias or the silversmiths' square.

Sainte-Anne-de-Beaupré, Canada

St Anne, the mother of Mary and the grandmother of Jesus, is one of the most important saints in the Roman Catholic canon. Catholics have prayed to her, particularly for healing, over the past two millennia and many miracles have been attributed to the power of her blessings. Following the arrival of Catholic pioneers in eastern Canada, the first shrine to St Anne was erected on the shores of the St Lawrence River in 1620.

The fertile valley of the St Anne River soon formed the home for a small community of farmer-settlers, with the first houses appearing there in 1650.

THE GENESIS OF THE SHRINE

One member of the small village, Etienne Lessard, wished to donate some land for the building of a chapel dedicated to St Anne, and he invited a missionary priest named Father Vignal to decide on the precise location for their worship. On 13 March 1658 Vignal came and blessed the site, inviting villagers to join in placing the new foundation stones. A man named Louis Guimond, who suffered from severe rheumatism, stepped forward to place his three stones and, at the very moment of their placing, found himself suddenly relieved of all pain. The healing was quickly attributed to St Anne and his affliction never returned.

A larger church was built of stone and timber in 1676 and lasted for two hundred years, before being replaced by an even more impressive building in 1876 – the same year that St Anne was pronounced patroness of the Province of Quebec. In 1887 the church

was raised to the status of a minor basilica by Pope Leo XIII. In 1922 this building was destroyed by fire and replaced with the beautiful stone structure that stands today – a testament to the support of the Canadian Catholics who contributed to its funding, and a symbol of the place's spiritual importance.

HEALING MIRACLES AND SACRED RELICS

Over the three hundred or so years since Louis Guimond's first miracle, many other healing miracles have occurred at the same site, which have brought Sainte-Anne-de-Beaupré a significance in the Catholic Church similar to that of Lourdes in France. Indeed, one of the sights that greets pilgrims as they enter the basilica is a huge pile of crutches, walking sticks, leg-irons, bandages and other medical equipment, which the faithful have cast off following the granting of their healing prayers. Many Catholics now attribute the particular power of Beaupré to the presence of the relics in the basilica. There are believed to be five separate fragments of bones from St Anne herself, the presence of one piece dating back as far as

1670. Probably the most important, the 'Great Relic' of Beaupré, is a 10 cm (4 in)-long wrist bone, which was brought from Rome and presented to the church by the Canadian Cardinal Taschedreau in 1892.

The basilica itself is arranged on two floors. As well as chapels of the Immaculate Conception and the Blessed Sacrament, the lower floor contains a number of artworks, including the only known life-size copy of Michelangelo's *Pietà*. This is also the site of the tomb of Venerable Father Alfred

'From some twelve thousand people per year in 1875, there are now more than a million and a half pilgrims each year.'

Pampalon, a Redemptorist priest who played an important role as an apostle of St Anne's shrine, as well as being remembered for his work with people suffering from alcohol and drug dependencies. He died in 1896 and was honoured with the title 'Venerable' by Pope John Paul II in 1991.

The upper floor of the basilica is a shrine decorated with mosaics and stained glass, and is where many pilgrims come for quiet reflection and the opportunity to meet the Divine in a place of beauty and silence.

On the hillside close to the basilica is a Memorial Chapel, which commemorates the third church that welcomed pilgrims between 1676 and 1876. On the second floor of the Memorial Chapel is the 'Scala Santa', a set of steps that are an image of the Holy Stairs that Jesus ascended to meet Pontius Pilate just prior to his crucifixion.

Pilgrimage to Sainte-Anne-de-Beaupré has continued to flourish over the centuries. From some twelve thousand people per year in 1875, there are now more than a million and a half pilgrims each year, and the influence of St Anne as the most important saint to Canadian Catholics shows no sign of diminishing.

Imam Reza's Shrine, Iran

Imam Reza, the eighth Shi'ite imam, was born in Medina, the burial place of the Prophet Muhammad, in 765 CE. As a Shi'ite, he followed the line of Islamic succession that passes from Ali, Muhammad's son-in-law, the husband of Fatima. Imam Reza was considered by the Shi'ites to be of great religious and intellectual development, and his shrine in Mashhad has become an important place of pilgrimage.

The regard in which Reza was held was not limited to his own people, for when he was 51, the Sunni Abbasid Caliph Mamun summoned Imam Reza to Sannabad to announce publicly that the Imam would be his successor. At the same time Mamun gave Imam Reza his daughter in marriage. For many Sunnis, however, this act of reconciliation between the two main branches of Islam was seen as a capitulation to the minority Shi'ites and was followed by violent demonstrations.

BUILDING THE 'NOBLE MAUSOLEUM'
In 817 Caliph Mamun and Imam Reza set off on a journey to recapture Baghdad from political enemies, but on the journey Reza was suddenly taken ill and died. His Shi'ite supporters suspected the Imam had been poisoned by Mamun or his close allies, in order to placate the Sunni people. The Caliph, however, showed great sadness at Reza's death and decided to build a mausoleum over the Imam's place of burial, immediately next to his own father's tomb.

The site soon became a place of pilgrimage for Shi'ite Muslims – particularly after Imam Reza's father was reported as saying that a pilgrimage to Reza's tomb would grant the spiritual rewards of seventy thousand pilgrimages to Mecca. To the Shi'ites, the site also became known as Mashhad ar-Rizawi: the place of the martyrdom of Reza. Today this important pilgrimage site is known as Mashhad.

Since its establishment the shrine has undergone great changes – either by those who embellished the tomb or by those who wished to destroy it. In 993 Sabuktagin, the Ghaznevid sultan, demolished much of the tomb, only for his son Mahmud of Ghazni to rebuild and enlarge it around the year 1009. The shrine was decorated with tiling, some of which still survives in the dome chamber. It came under threat again in 1120 when the Mongols invaded the city. Then, almost a hundred years

***Right** Shi'ite worshippers spend time in the Dar-el-Salaam, or Chamber of Salutation, just one of the important spaces within Imam Reza's shrine complex.*

Right *Behind the highly decorated walls of the Tala-ye Fath Ali Shah Iwan, the Golden Dome is the dominant feature of Imam Reza's shrine site.*

later, the Mongol leader of Persia, Sultan Muhammad Khudabandeh, converted to Shi'ism and began a grand programme of improvements for Reza's shrine. When the well-known Muslim traveller Ibn Battuta came to Mashhad in 1333, he told of a 'large town with abundant fruit trees, streams and mills. A great dome of elegant construction surmounts the noble mausoleum, the walls being decorated with coloured tiles.'

SAFAVID EMBELLISHMENT

Around Imam Reza's shrine are many further buildings and courtyards, which have been erected in the hundreds of years since Ibn Battuta's visit. Much of this was achieved during the reign of Shahrukh Mirza, the son of Tamburlaine the Great, and during the time of the Safavid kings who ruled Persia from 1501 to 1786. It was they who gilded the domes, erected minarets and laid out the airy courtyards that make the complex so atmospheric. They were also responsible for encouraging Shi'ite pilgrimage. Although more recent times have seen attacks on the site – in 1912 the Russian army shelled the complex – any destruction has always been a trigger for even further expansion.

Today the golden dome of great height – reaching over 31 m (100 ft) – and beautiful construction still marks the location of Imam Reza's tomb directly below. Inside, the shrine room has been decorated with craftsmanship of the rarest quality. The lower parts of the walls are covered with fine marble, above which are Sultan Sanjari tiles bearing verses from the Quran and from the Hadiths, which contain guidance on the teachings of Muhammad. Even higher up the wall, making its way around the entire building, is a calligraphic inscription by Ali Ridha Abbasi (the well-known calligraphist from the time of the Safavid kings) of the Jumah Sura, the 62nd chapter of the Holy Quran itself.

THE 'OTHER' DOME

Pilgrims coming to the site are often overcome by Mashhad's skyline, which is dominated by two domes as well as the impressive minarets. The 'other' dome (adjacent to the golden dome of Imam Reza's tomb) is the glistening blue dome of the Gowharshad Mosque. Perhaps the largest place of prayer at the shrine complex and, many say, the most important mosque in Iran, its library is home to more than thirty thousand religious books – confirmation that the whole shrine complex is not simply a place of worship and pilgrimage, but it is also an important centre for religious scholarship and learning.

Each year as many as twenty million Muslim pilgrims visit Imam Reza's tomb, and remember the man who played such an important role in the development of the Shi'ite faith.

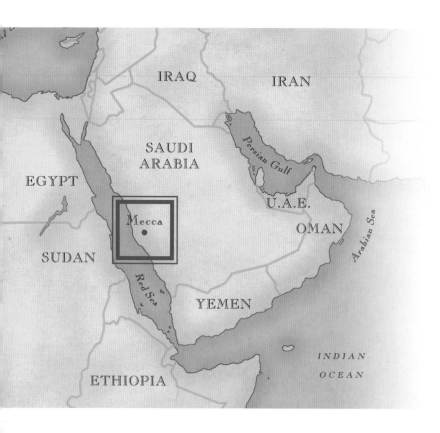

Mecca, Saudi Arabia

It is hard to overestimate the importance of the city of Mecca to the Muslim faith. Not only does it play a large part in the history of Muhammad and the development of Islam, but Mecca is also the ultimate destination for the Islamic pilgrim. Muslims regard the al-Masjid al-Haram (the 'Sacred Mosque') in Mecca as the holiest place on Earth, and to make a pilgrimage there – the Hajj – is one of the five Pillars of the faith for every able-bodied Muslim who can afford the journey.

Every year between two and three million Muslims go on the Hajj during the month of Dhu al-Hijjah, although more minor pilgrimages – Umrah – are taken to shrines and mosques in and around Mecca at other times during the year.

SHIFTING ALLEGIANCES

After the time of Abraham and Ishmael, Mecca become a centre of pagan worship and, at the time of the Prophet Muhammad's birth in 570 CE, the Kaaba contained as many as 360 religious idols of various kinds. So when Muhammad recaptured Mecca in 630 (see pages 24–25), one of his first acts was to cleanse the Kaaba of all idols as part of his establishment of strict monotheism among the people of the city. The only object that remained was the Black Stone, the Hajar al Aswad. Muhammad declared Mecca to be a place of pilgrimage for the new Islamic faith, even though it was never the capital of the new Islamic Empire. The first capital of the caliphate was Medina, although it was soon moved to Damascus and later to Baghdad.

For many centuries Mecca was governed by the Hashemite Sharifs, who were descendants of Muhammad by his grandson Hassan ibn Ali. The Sharifs ruled Mecca on behalf of the Muslim Caliph, who was declared Guardian of the Two Shrines (Mecca and Medina). However, in the 10th and 18th centuries Mecca was temporarily captured by other Muslim groups. The rule of the Sharifs did not finally end, though, until 1926, when Mecca was captured by the Saudis and incorporated into Saudi Arabia.

THE KAABA

With the rise of Islam over the centuries and its spreading empire, pilgrims came from further away and the city became a focus for scholars and devout Muslims who wished to be close to the Kaaba. Compared with today, though, the city was very small. Even 18th- and 19th-century maps show a little walled city of mud-brick houses close to the al-Masjid al-Haram mosque. Naturally the mosque itself has grown and expanded over the centuries and is now a vast arena in which hundreds of thousands of worshippers can congregate at one time.

The Kaaba, or Cube, that stands in the centre of the mosque is one of the great spiritual mysteries of the Islamic faith. It is also known as the Baitullah, the house of Allah, because it is regarded as an image of Allah's house in heaven, the place where the Divine and the mundane meet. The original Kaaba that stood in this place is believed to have been built by Adam, the first man, at the request of God himself. Its importance to Muslims also lies in the fact that Abraham and his son Ishmael, from whom all Arab people are descended, rebuilt the Kaaba. It is said that the Angel Gabriel gave Ishmael the enigmatic Black Stone that still forms its cornerstone.

THE BLACK STONE

The actual composition of the Black Stone is unknown, but one observer believed it to be 'a block of volcanic basalt, whose circumference is sprinkled with little crystals, pointed and straw-like, with rhombs of tile-red feldspath on a dark background, like velvet or charcoal, except one of its protuberances, which is reddish'. Some people believe that the Black Stone is actually a meteorite, possibly made of tektite, and originally found in a meteorite crater some

Above When the five-day ritual of the Hajj reaches its height there can be as many as one and a half million Muslim pilgrims in Mecca at one time.

'Every year between two and three million Muslims go on the Hajj.'

160 km (100 miles) from Mecca. The size of the Black Stone is surprisingly small – it is only about 30 cm (12 in) in diameter, and has a silver strap around it to hold it together, following damage in the 10th century when it was temporarily stolen.

Many pilgrims attempt to touch and kiss the stone, just as Muhammad did in his day, and the Black Stone is now accessed through a silver orifice. The significance of this act is questioned by some parts of Islam, as it appears to be a form of worship for the stone itself: 'No doubt, I know that you are a stone and can neither harm anyone nor benefit anyone,' said the second Caliph, Umar Ibn al-Khattab, when he came to kiss the stone. 'Had I not seen Allah's Messenger [Muhammad] kissing you, I would not have kissed you.' Others say that the stone is simply to be thought of as a marker – a device to help pilgrims keep count of their circumambulations or *tawaf*. Still others believe that the stone can erase the sins of the sincere believer: that the Black Stone was

once a shining white, but has turned black with all the sins it has absorbed. Still more say that, on the Day of Judgement, the stone will testify in favour of those who have kissed it. Whatever the truth, there is no denying its importance to the faithful.

THE HAJJ

The Hajj is a journey that only Muslims can make – there are even roadblocks along the routes leading into Mecca, ensuring that non-Muslims are not attempting to enter the city. This has not deterred all non-Muslims: one of the most detailed accounts of the Hajj by a non-Muslim was made by Sir Richard Francis Burton in the 19th century. His *Personal Narrative of a Pilgrimage to Mecca and Al-Madina* tells the story of his travels as a Qadiri Sufi and of his strict observance of the prayers, rituals and religious practices that give the Hajj its vital significance in Islamic life.

The pilgrim's tasks are well defined and marked by specific prayers at particular

places on the pilgrimage route within the mosque: on entering, he or she asserts the intention to circumambulate the Kaaba seven times in the ritual known as the Tawaf. Then, with each cycle around the Kaaba, he or she recites further prayers. There are also specific prayers that can be performed at certain points of the circling – for instance, at the place where Abraham and Ishmael mixed the mortar for the construction of the Kaaba, and at the place where Abraham is said to be buried. In fact, as well as the Kaaba itself, there are some 13 other sites of honour where prayers may be given. On completion of the seven cycles of the Kaaba, pilgrims normally proceed to the well of Zamzam, where they receive and drink the holy water that flows there. Many Muslim pilgrims also fill a container with water to take back to their homes and use in holy rituals.

An important part of the Hajj is the journey to the village of Mina, where the ritual stoning of Iblis (the Devil) – symbolized by stone columns – takes place.

Right *The silver orifice gives access to the black stone within the Kaaba. Muslim scholars disagree about the symbolic importance of touching the stone: some say it can result in the remission of sin, others are wary of appearing to worship an object.*

Right *The black cloth covering the Kaaba is called the Kiswah and is embroidered in gold with verses from the Quran.*

THE KISWAH

The structure of the Kaaba, measuring 18 m (60 ft) on each side, is covered by the kiswah, the gold-embroidered piece of black fabric that envelops it. With the passing of so many pilgrims each year, the kiswah becomes worn and dirty. In the past, small pieces of the cloth were also taken by pilgrims. In the month following the Hajj, the mosque is closed while it is washed and cleansed and the kiswah replaced.

The Kaaba is the focal point of worship for the Islamic world. Every time that Muslims throughout the world pray, they direct their prayers towards this place, and this focus is expressed in the concept of *qibla*, the direction of prayer towards Mecca to which Muslims adhere. And in the life of each Muslim there is the wish that the direction of their prayer becomes the direction of their pilgrimage.

Many pilgrims also make the 400 km (250 mile) journey to the city of Medina, the first capital of the Islamic Empire and home to the tomb of the Prophet Muhammad (see pages 24–25).

MECCA TODAY

The city of Mecca has grown considerably over the last decades – particularly due to the increased affordability of airline travel.

Around five to six million people a year now travel to Mecca, which has led to an increase in the number of Saudi Arabians staffing the hotels, shops and other facilities that serve the pilgrim. There have also been many large building projects: shopping malls, hotels, motorways and new skyscrapers, such as the Abraj Al Bait Towers. More recently there have been concerns that many of the oldest and architecturally significant parts of the

Great Mosque are being systematically taken down and replaced with modern additions. Some experts believe that 90 per cent of the original features of the mosque have been lost in the last 25 years. However, this in no way deters the faithful, whose sacred duty is to make the journey of their lifetime in demonstration of their love for Allah as the one god of all, and of their utter respect for the Prophet Muhammad.

The Dome of the Rock, Jerusalem

Jerusalem's Temple Mount, or the Haram esh-Sharif as it is known to Muslims, is identified by both Jewish and Islamic traditions as the place on Mount Moriah where Abraham offered up his son in sacrifice (Genesis 22:1–18; the Quran, Sura Al-Saffat 37:102–10). The religions disagree, however, as to which of his two sons Abraham chose. Jews say it was Isaac, one of the founding fathers of the Jewish people; Muslims say it was Ishmael, antecedent of the Islamic faith.

To understand the significance of the Dome of the Rock, and its location on the Haram esh-Sharif, it is important to trace some of the history of this sacred place in the times after Abraham's experience on Mount Moriah had already given it special significance to the Jewish people.

THE BUILDING OF THE DOME

The presence of King Solomon's Temple (see pages 88–89), and the later Second Temple that was finally destroyed in 70 CE by the Romans, had reinforced the importance of the place for the Jews. The site now entered a period of Romanization, with a temple dedicated to the god Jupiter. Later, in the 4th century when it was Christianized under the Emperor Constantine, Jupiter's temple was itself destroyed and the Temple Mount left in ruins.

Islamic interest in Mount Moriah began in 638, just six years after the death of the Prophet Muhammad, when Jerusalem was captured for the new Muslim religion by the Caliph Umar. Soon the whole area of the Temple Mount – the Haram esh-Sharif or 'Noble Sanctuary' – was cleansed of all other influences and a small mosque erected. It was 687 when the ninth Caliph, Abd al-Malik, initiated the building of the Dome of the Rock, the Qubbat As-Sakhrah, the structure that would enshrine the very piece of Mount Moriah's bedrock on which – Muslims believe – Abraham prepared to sacrifice Ishmael.

When the new captors arrived in Jerusalem, the most dominant building was the Church of the Holy Sepulchre. Fearful that the Muslim faithful might be tempted back to Christianity, they built the Dome of the Rock to rival the Christian church in beauty and sophistication. Inside, in classical

Right *The rock beneath the Dome is believed to be the very location on Mount Moriah where Abraham was willing to sacrifice his son to please his God.*

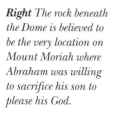

Arabic, one of the ornate inscriptions affirms that God is One and not three; and that Jesus was an apostle of God and His Word, and not His only son. This was a message to the faithful concerning the new Islamic religion's superiority. It was also an invitation to the rest of the Islamic world to regard Jerusalem – rather than Mecca – as the *qibla*, the geographical focus of worship.

A GLORIOUS ACHIEVEMENT

Designed by Byzantine architects employed by the ninth Caliph, the Dome of the Rock borrows styles from Christian-Byzantine traditions, and the 16 internal arches that surround the sacred rock were taken from Christian buildings destroyed by the Persians. The final effect was remarkable: the Qubbat As-Sakhrah was the greatest monumental building of early Islamic times. Even so, it is not vast: the top of the dome is 35 m (115 ft) above ground level and around 10 m (33 ft)

in diameter. Its main covering was of lead and was originally covered in pure gold; more recently this has been replaced by anodized aluminium. The interior glass mosaics in the drum and dome contain representations of Byzantine imperial jewellery.

The Dome of the Rock is not, as many imagine, a mosque for public worship, but rather a *mashhad*, a shrine for pilgrims. Even though some consider it the third most important Islamic site (after Mecca and Medina), the main focus for actual Muslim worship on the Haram esh-Sharif is the Al-Aqsa Mosque (sees pages 18–19) at the southern end of the complex.

THE 'NIGHT JOURNEY'

The whole site gains much of its importance from a particular passage in the Quran. 'The Night Journey' describes Muhammad's meeting with the Archangel Gabriel and his flight on a horse-like creature called El Burak

Above *Designed by Byzantine architects, the decoration is typically Islamic with elements borrowed from other traditions.*

from 'the sacred temple to the temple that is remote'. It is believed this meant a journey from Mecca to Jerusalem's Noble Sanctuary site, where Muhammad met Abraham, Moses, Jesus and other prophets before – as some believe – proceeding to the 'As-Sakhrah', the pinnacle of the rock, where a ladder of golden light appeared and Muhammad ascended through seven heavens to meet Allah himself. Other sources locate Muhammad's point of departure at different places on the Noble Sanctuary; some even say it was not from Jerusalem at all. Whatever the truth, the Dome of the Rock continues to draw new pilgrims.

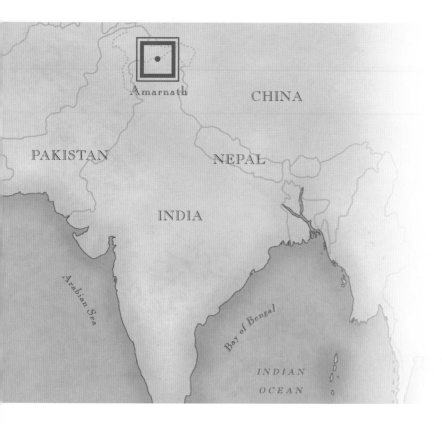

Amarnath Cave, Kashmir

In July and August each year, throughout the 45-day Hindu festival known as Sharvani Mela, 400,000 pilgrims make a sacred journey to a cave high in the Himalayas to worship and give thanks to their god Shiva and to ask for his blessings. This journey through the Kashmiri Himalayas reaches a height of 3,888 m (12,750 ft) and has many dangers. Every year some pilgrims will not return home, victims of exertion or, more recently, of extremist Kashmiri terrorists intent on killing the Hindu faithful.

The importance of Amarnath Cave has been enshrined in legends dating back as far as 3000 BCE. Hindu texts, including the Rig Veda, tell the story of Lord Shiva, one of the three 'gods' of the Hindu Trinity. While Brahma is the creator of life and Vishnu the sustainer of life, Lord Shiva is both the perpetuator of good and the destroyer of evil. Shiva is seen by Hindus as an eternal being who also took earthly form; with his consort Parvathi, he had a son named Ganesha. Through his dialogues with Parvathi recorded in the Rig Veda, Shiva revealed his wisdom – and it was when they were in the Amarnath Cave that Shiva told Parvathi about the nature of life and eternity, explaining his birthless, deathless existence.

THE ABODE OF SHIVA

The story of how Shiva's dwelling place in the cave at Amarnath came to be discovered is enshrined in an ancient legend. A Kashmiri shepherd named Buta Malik was given a sack containing coal by a stranger in the mountains. When Buta Malik reached home, however, and emptied out the sack, he discovered that it was filled with gold coins. At this point he

Right The ice 'lingam' is a physical representation of the Hindu god Shiva. The stalagmite varies in size throughout the year, but is believed to have existed – and been worshipped – in its present form for many hundreds of years.

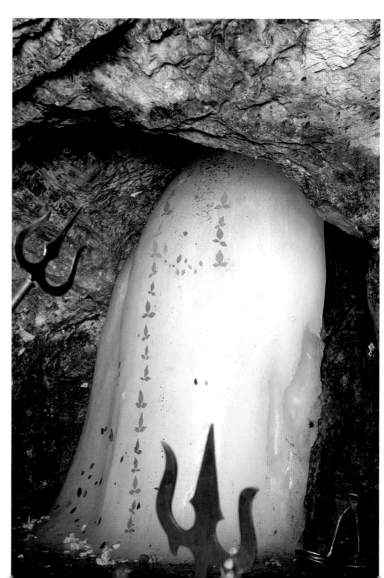

realized that the man who had given him the gift was a saint and decided to go back and thank him. Yet when he arrived at the original place he could not find the saint. Instead he discovered a cave, which to his knowledge had not been there before, and in the cave he found a 'lingam', an abstract phallic shape made of ice, which he knew to be an expression of the Living God Shiva. Exploring further, he found two more lingams: one representing Shiva's consort Parvathi and the other playing the part of Ganesha, their son. Soon Buta Malik's discovery convinced his entire village that Shiva's abode had been revealed, and Amarnath Cave quickly became a place of Hindu pilgrimage.

This is not the only version of the story telling the origins of the cave. There is a further legend that attributes its uncovering to the draining of the Kashmir Valley by a Hindu *rishi*, or wise man, named Kashyap. Whichever story is correct, the significance of the place is clear. The ongoing presence of the ice lingams is, for many Hindus, evidence of the holy presence of Lord Shiva, his consort and their son. These extraordinary phenomena – which are in fact ice stalagmites – vary in size with the seasons, becoming larger between May and August and waning through the rest of the year. They nevertheless maintain their basic lingam form from year to year, and are not known to have required any intervention for hundreds (if not thousands) of years. To witness these expressions of Shiva in this remarkable location is, for many Hindu devotees, the experience of a lifetime and a source of great spiritual upliftment – especially as the journey to the site is so harsh and demanding.

THE PILGRIMAGE ROUTE

There are two main ways to make the pilgrimage, or *yatra*, to the Amarnath Cave. The shorter, more popular route is around 45 km (28 miles) long, and it takes pilgrims four

Above *At least two legends describe how the Amarnath Cave and its sacred contents were revealed. Belief in the presence of the Living God Shiva within the cave draws pilgrims to make the harsh and dangerous journey.*

to five days to complete the return journey from Pahalgam to Amarnath. The longer, more difficult route begins 141 km (88 miles) away in Srinagar, and some pilgrims (particularly if they are older) may undertake this journey on horseback. The steepness of the climb, the effects of altitude and weather, and now the dangers of attack from Islamic terrorists all threaten to stop the pilgrims on their path. That they continue to climb, chanting holy names as they go, is a testament to their faith in the power of Shiva, the power to conquer evil and bring peace to the world.

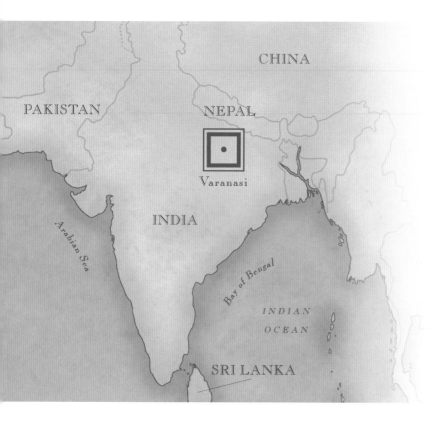

Varanasi, India

The name Varanasi is the ancient, abiding name for the city that lies between two rivers: the Varuna and the Assi. It is here that both rivers also join the Ganges (or Ganga), the most holy river for Hindus, the source of so much life and the very reason for Varanasi's flourishing. The city has also been known as Baranasi (in Pali), Benaras and, in the time of the British Empire, as Benares; the name Banaras is still popular with many.

Left *The Kashi Vishwanath Temple (also known as the Golden Temple), built by the Birlas, was planned by Pandit Madan Mohan Malaviya, who also founded the Hindu University in whose grounds the temple stands.*

In literary works the city is often known as Kashi, meaning 'luminous', or 'place of enlightenment', referring to its high status as a centre for culture and learning. It is also called the city of temples, the holiest city and the religious capital of India. For most of its million or so inhabitants, though, this remarkable city will always be called Varanasi.

AN ANCIENT, SACRED CITY

Varanasi is believed by some experts to be the oldest continually occupied city in the world, rivalled only by Aleppo, Byblos and Damascus. References to the city in ancient texts put its age at more than five thousand years old. Mark Twain, the famous American author, wrote that 'Benares is older than history, older than tradition, older even than legend, and looks twice as old as all of them put together!'

According to legend, the city was founded by the Hindu god Shiva, and this link to the Hindu pantheon has made Varanasi one of Hinduism's eight sacred cities. Indeed, for many Hindus of all denominations it remains the holiest city of all. More than one million adherents attest to its importance each year

with a holy pilgrimage. It is the site of the holy
shrine of Lord Kashi Vishwanath, one of only
12 specially revered *jyotirlinga* shrines of the
Lord Shiva on the Indian mainland.

The River Ganges, or Ganga, is the focus
for many of the people who travel here,
because they believe that by bathing in the
river's sacred waters they can receive
remission for their sins in this and previous
lives. It is thought by many that by actually
dying in the holy city, they will avoid the need
for rebirth and escape further turns on the
wheel of karma.

A MULTI-FAITH SITE

Varanasi is not just important to Hindus. In
Samath (now a residential area in the city)
there was once a deer park where Gautama
Buddha gave his first sermon about the
principles of Buddhism. The place is marked
by the Dhamek Stupa shrine. The Buddha is
also believed to have met his first disciples
here, and this event is commemorated by the
Chaukhandi Stupa monument and, more
recently, by a further octagonal tower. Later
the Buddha designated four pilgrimage sites
for Buddhists to visit: Kushinagar, Bodh Gaya,
Lumbini and Samath.

Members of the Jain faith also identify
Varanasi as an important site of worship and
pilgrimage, as it is recognized as the
birthplace of Parshvanatha, the 23rd
Tirthankar, or fully enlightened teacher.

There are also Islamic sites of significance,
dating back to the occupation of the city by
Muslim peoples. The first of these invasions
was led by Mahmud of Ghazni in 1033 CE and
resulted in the demolition of all the Hindu
temples. The materials were then used for
the building of mosques. After some recovery
under the Mughal emperor Akbar in the 16th
century, the city's temples were again
destroyed at the end of the century by
another Mughal emperor, Aurangzeb. It fell
to the Hindu Maratha clans to rescue
Varanasi from Aurangzeb for the Hindu
peoples. It was not until the 18th century that
Varanasi gained its independence as an
Indian kingdom and a period of relative
stability ensued. Even with the arrival of the
British in India, and the creation of the state
of Varanasi, the city was still allowed its own
independence.

With this historical mix of religions, each
of which expresses its own ideas and forms of
worship, there has often been tension. At
certain times in the modern age this has led
to acts of terrorism. On 7 March 2006 around
20 people were killed and many more were
injured when a series of explosions was
unleashed on Varanasi. The most significant
of these was at a Hindu place of worship, the
Sankat Mochan Temple, which is dedicated
to the Hindu god Lord Hanuman.

THE GHATS OF VARANASI

Significant to both the holy traveller and the
inhabitants of Varanasi are the riverside holy
sites known as ghats: stretches of the river
where pilgrims can descend via steps into the
waters of the Ganges to bathe and perform
other rituals. For thousands of years people
have been coming to the ghats to offer their
prayers to the morning sun as they look out
over the peaceful waters. Of the more than 80
ghats at Varanasi, some of the best known are
the Manikarnika Ghat, the Kabir Ghat, the
Assi Ghat and the Dasaswamedh Ghat. It was
at the Dasaswamedh Ghat that it is believed
the old kings of Varanasi would perform the
ritual *ashvamedha* sacrifice of a horse, while
Jalasi Ghat (at Manikarnika) is Varanasi's pre-
eminent cremation ground and is always
crowded with funeral parties.

Varanasi: temples and ghats

Because of the many conflicts over Varanasi throughout history, there are actually few genuinely old temples left in the city. For the pilgrim, however, this does not seem to diminish the importance of the many temples that now bear witness to the power of religions to withstand change and setback.

SIGNIFICANT TEMPLES

Also called the Golden Temple, the Kashi Vishwanath Temple represents the most holy man-made site for Hindus in Varanasi. Since it is one of only 12 *jyotirlinga* shrines of Lord Shiva on the Indian mainland, simply being there is said to bring the pilgrim great religious merit. The Birla Temple, or New Vishwanath Temple, is a replica of the original Vishwanath Temple, which was destroyed at the end of the 16th century by the Mughal emperor Aurangzeb.

The Durga Temple was built during the 18th century by a maharani from Bengal and is often called the Monkey Temple because of the presence of so many monkeys at the site. Next to the temple is a rectangular tank called the Durga Kund, which was once connected to the River Ganges, although it is now refilled by rainwater. Each year, on the festival day known as Nag panchami, the Kund plays host to a depiction of Lord Vishnu and his consort Lakshmi.

The Annapurna Temple is dedicated to the goddess Annapurna who provides all with plentiful food. She is considered to be the mother of all three worlds in the Hindu universe (heaven, earth and hell). The Bharat Mata Temple is dedicated to 'Mother India'. It was inaugurated by Mahatma Gandhi and contains a remarkable relief map of India carved from marble.

① THE GANGES

Hindus regard the River Ganges as a goddess and as *amrita*, the elixir of life, which brings purity to the living and salvation to the dead. Pandit Nehru, the first Prime Minister of India, expressed the importance of the River Ganges to the Indian people when he described it as: 'beloved of her people, round which are intertwined her memories, her hopes and fears, her songs of triumph, her victories and her defeats. She has been a symbol of India's age-long culture and civilization, ever changing, ever flowing, and yet ever the same Ganga.' Everyday life and activities – from bathing to cremating the dead – revolve around this holy river, and its ghats are a focus for both locals and visitors.

② MANIKARNIKA GHAT

This ghat (a riverside holy place) is one of the oldest and most sacred in Varanasi. Beside its stone steps lies the Manikarnika Kund, a sacred well, which is said to have been dug by Vishnu at the time of creation. Its origins rest on the legend that the god Vishnu dug a pit with the power of one of his chakras (energy centres) and the sweat generated by the task filled the pit. The god Shiva then shook his head in disbelief at the feat and one of his jewelled earrings fell into the newly formed lake.

The idea that those who die in Varanasi are freed from the cycle of death and rebirth is particularly strong at this ghat, where many ritual cremations take place on the waters each year.

③ SHIVA TEMPLE

The Shiva Temple lies partially submerged in the river, having partly collapsed and tilted under the sheer weight of the Scindia Ghat's construction around 150 years ago.

④ SCINDIA GHAT

Just north of the Manikarnika Ghat lies the beautiful Scindia Ghat, which was constructed around 150 years ago. Just above the ghat several important shrines are hidden within a maze of alleyways called Siddha Kshetra, 'the field of fulfilment'. Here, Vireshvara, the Lord of all Heroes, receives invocations from parents wishing for a son. Agni, the Lord of Fire, is also thought to have been born here.

'For thousands of years people have been coming to the ghats to offer their prayers to the morning sun.'

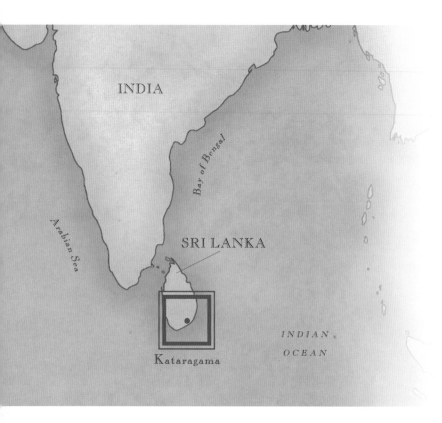

INDIA

Bay of Bengal

Arabian Sea

SRI LANKA

Kataragama

INDIAN OCEAN

Kataragama, Sri Lanka

The Kataragama Pada Yatra is probably the oldest and best known of all Sri Lanka's living traditions. The pada yatra, *or foot pilgrimage, starts in the island's far north on the Jaffna peninsula, follows the eastern coast of Sri Lanka and ends a couple of hundred miles south – and around 60 days later – at the Kataragama shrine in the remote jungle.*

Pilgrimage is not limited to travel by foot, and many pilgrims travel from India and other parts of Asia with the wish to show their devotion to Kataragama. The worship of this deity can be traced back to a time before the arrival of Sri Lanka's major contemporary religions and is known to be a tradition that came from the island's indigenous forest-dwelling peoples, the Wanniya-laeto or Veddas, who worshipped the deity that lived on top of the mountain just outside Kataragama, called Wædahiti Kanda.

FAMOUS PILGRIMS

Because of the gruelling distance and the two months or so that it takes to complete, the Kataragama Pada Yatra has, since ancient times, tended to be the preserve of *swamis* (Hindu religious teachers) and others following a religious vocation. Most are unknown, but some great saints and wise men and women have trodden the *yatra* path. Perhaps the most famous was one of the first, the man-god Skandha-Murukan, also known as Lord Murukan. Like his spiritual father Shiva, Skandha-Murukan was intimately connected with mountains and hilltops, and

his Wanniya-laeto devotees refer to him as 'Kande Yaka', the hunter spirit of the mountain. In the 15th century the Tamil psalmist Arunagirinathar also walked the Pada Yatra route and composed a number of famous hymns on his journey.

Despite differences of caste and religious belief, most present-day Sri Lankans still revere Kataragama and regularly offer prayers to God asking for assistance in every area of their lives. In times of distress and calamity – such as the aftermath of the recent disastrous tsunami – many Sri Lankans turn their prayers towards Kataragama, in the belief that his power can heal and help them.

HINDU AND BUDDHIST BELIEFS

It might seem strange that such worship is compatible with Sri Lanka's other religions of Hinduism, Buddhism and Islam, but this is a city that contains temples for all faiths, including an Islamic mosque.

For followers of Hinduism, Kataragama is known as Katirkamam and his mountain home as Vedahitikanda, 'the Peak where he was'. The main Hindu temple is dedicated to Lord Katirkamam, although it is also

identified with Lord Murukan or Skandha. The same deity is also recognized by a number of other names in Hindu texts: Kandasamy, Katiradeva, Katiravel, Kartikeya and Tarakajith. He is portrayed in two ways: with six heads and 12 hands, or with one head and four hands, and is often seen riding on a peacock. Typical of Hindu ritual, the local river has a vital importance: Manik Ganga, the river of gems, is a place where devotees can wash away their sins and be healed of physical ailments. It is believed that the river has a high gemstone and mineral content, as well as containing medicinal compounds released from the roots of bankside trees.

Buddhists believe that Kataragama is one of the 16 sites of pilgrimage to be visited in Sri Lanka. The Kiri Vehera Dagoba temple, which lies close to the Hindu Katirkamam Temple, was built by King Mahasena. Buddhist legend, which tells of Gautama Buddha's three visits to Sri Lanka, reports that the Buddha met King Mahasena somewhere in the Kataragama area in 580 BCE. After listening to the Buddha's discourse, King Mahasena was moved to build the Dagoba Temple where it stands today. After the Buddha's death, around the year 300 BCE, a sapling from the Bodhi tree under which he had become enlightened was brought to Anuradhapura in Sri Lanka. Present at the planting of the sacred tree were warriors from Kataragama, eager to pay their respects to this symbol of Buddhahood and enlightenment.

There is also a strangely synchronicitous relationship between Kataragama and Mount Kailash in Tibet, where the god is believed to have originated. Mount Kailash is sacred to both Hindus and Buddhists and is also one of the great pilgrimage destinations for both religions. What is almost unbelievable is that Mount Kailash and Kataragama lie on virtually the same line of longitude (81° 10´ and 81° 20´ respectively) – a fact that it has only been possible to determine with modern measurement techniques.

Below The Water Cutting ceremony in the river Manik Ganga – river of gems – marks the end of the annual festival. The river contains large amounts of gemstones and minerals, which are thought to possess healing properties.

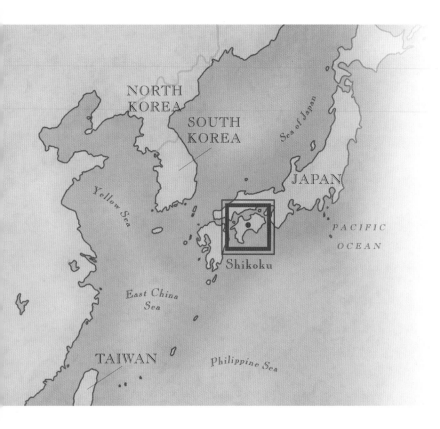

Mount Koya, Shikoku, Japan

Shikoku Island is Japan's fourth largest island, lying south of Honshu's south-western tip. Since the 9th century the island has been intimately associated with Kobo Daishi (also known as Kukai), one of Japan's great masters of Buddhism. Kobo Daishi is credited with introducing the Shingon teachings of esoteric Buddhism to Japan.

Shingon, which originated in China, focuses on the potential for individuals to attain Buddhahood in their present lifetime through specific practices and rituals related to the body, speech and mind, or 'mudra, mantra and meditation'.

THE KOBO DAISHI STORY

Kobo Daishi founded the Shingon School of Buddhism in Japan, and in honour of his contribution many pilgrims still trace the 1,400 km (870 mile) circular route around the 88 temples on the periphery of Shikoku Island. Each temple represents one of the 88 'evil passions' requiring mastery and release on the path to enlightenment.

Kobo Daishi was born into a wealthy family in 774 CE in Sanuki province on Shikoku Island. At this time Japan was still struggling to find its own religious and cultural identity; Buddhism had recently arrived in Japan via Korea, and there was conflict between this new teaching and the older philosophies of Taoism and Confucianism, which had been imported from China.

As a young student, Kobo Daishi joined a university in Japan's capital of Kyoto, but his strong spiritual search led him to drop out of conventional education and pursue the Mikkyo form of esoteric Buddhism. In 804 he travelled to China to study Shingon Mikkyo Buddhism. Within months he was told by his teacher Hui Kuo that he would be the person to carry on this teaching, and – following Hui Kuo's death in 805 – he returned to Japan. With permission from the Emperor Saga, Kobo Daishi was free to spread Shingon teachings throughout the country. Although he lived and taught in temples close to Kyoto, he eventually founded the Koyasan (Mount Koya) school of Shingon Buddhism close to Osaka in 817.

THE FATHER OF JAPANESE CULTURE

Although his spiritual home was always in Shikoku, Kobo Daishi continued to travel as part of his mission to bring new cultural ideas to the people of Japan. He founded the first private school in Japan devoted to the education of children from ordinary backgrounds. He is also credited with writing the first Japanese dictionary and inventing the Japanese 'syllabary', the unique form of writing for the Japanese phonetic language. In the practical realm he offered new knowledge on the construction of roads, dams and bridges. He also instructed people in the use of coal, discovered hot springs and was an expert in many artistic fields. Through these multiple expressions of cultural renewal he became known as the father of Japanese culture.

It is not clear when the pilgrimage around Shikoku Island started, but the idea that it was inspired by Kobo Daishi's own spiritual journeying between temples is very strong. It is known that although all 88 temples on the island have an association with Daishi, at least 50 of them were already in existence before his

'Each temple represents one of the 88 "evil passions" requiring mastery.'

birth. One legend, however, attributes the very beginnings of the pilgrimage to a man named Uemon Saburo. In the history of the Ishide-ji Temple it is recorded that he visited the 88 temples 21 times, as a penance for his refusal to help Kobo Daishi and the subsequent deaths of his eight sons. In 831, on his 22nd circumambulation, Saburo died, and his grave can be seen close to the Shosan-ji Temple.

Today pilgrims on the route will find a shrine or building dedicated to Kobo Daishi at all 88 temple sites. Many of the pilgrims wear white costumes, often decorated with the Japanese characters that mean 'Together with Kobo Daishi'. As the pilgrimage has developed, it has become increasingly ritualized, with particular routes and practices being required of the

pilgrim at each temple. Much of the ritual is focused on honouring and acknowledging the presence of Kobo Daishi and his helpful influence in the pilgrim's life. Some locations have also become associated with honouring the landscape and its sacred features.

One aspect of the pilgrimage that expresses the Buddhist idea of loving kindness has been the development of *settai*, which originally saw the residents of Shikoku Island taking care of pilgrims by providing them with food, drink and shelter as they made their way around the temple circuit. This has now expanded to a movement of its own, called *settai-ko*, in which Buddhist people from all over Japan spend the entire pilgrimage season offering help to pilgrims.

Above A Buddhist pilgrim passes stone Buddhas at the Hongo Fuku Temple near Tosa Shimizu on Shikoku Island. All 88 temples on the pilgrimage route are dedicated to Kobo Daishi, the man who brought Shingon Buddhism to Japan.

In Shingon Buddhism the notion of 'making merit' is very strong and on Shikoku Island, it seems, the spirit of Kobo Daishi's teachings is still very much alive today.

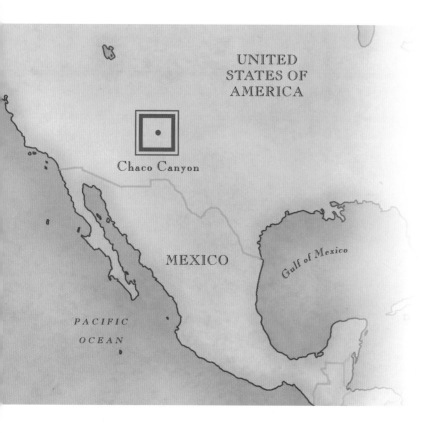

UNITED
STATES OF
AMERICA

Chaco Canyon

MEXICO

Gulf of Mexico

PACIFIC
OCEAN

Chaco Canyon, New Mexico

Chaco Canyon is one of the most important and impressive cultural centres built by ancient Native Americans (also known as Anasazi or Puebloans). Located in north-western New Mexico, Chaco Canyon comprises around 30 buildings, each containing hundreds of rooms. One of the best known of the 'great houses' is Pueblo Bonito, originally four storeys high and with more than 650 rooms. It contains at least 33 kivas or large rooms, and three even larger 'Great Kivas', whose purpose may have been ceremonial.

The buildings at Chaco Canyon appear to have been well planned, and many of the walls are composed of 'core-and-veneer' masonry, a technique that gave structural integrity to the larger buildings. Some are 1.2 m (4 ft) thick at their base and taper as they ascend. Roofing structures would have been made of timber, often brought from many miles away.

ASTRONOMICAL OBSERVATORIES

Thought to have been occupied between around 900 and 1150 CE, the buildings of Chaco Canyon are believed by some to have functioned as astronomical observatories and calendrical sites, as well as simply being dwelling and meeting places. More recently these aspects have brought modern seekers to the site, wishing to understand more about the spirituality behind the Puebloan or Anasazi culture.

The Anasazi were very interested in the movements of heavenly bodies, and a number of features of their buildings and surrounding rock structures demonstrate this very clearly. On Fajade Butte, a rock feature in the centre of Chaco Canyon

bearing a petrograph (rock carving) known as the 'Sun Dagger', the summer solstice is marked when a shaft of sunlight passing between two stone slabs hits the centre of a spiral marked on rock. At Casa Rinconanda's

Great Kiva, a square of sunlight is projected onto a notch in the wall on the summer solstice. Some people believe this Great Kiva holds other evidence of its earlier use as a stellar observatory.

ENIGMA OF THE PETROGRAPHS

Throughout Chaco Canyon and the San Juan Basin in north-western New Mexico there are many similar phenomena, of which perhaps the most impressive is the petrograph given the number-name 1054 to indicate the year of its significance. Around 4 July 1054 the remains of a supernova appeared in the night sky, an exploding star that would subsequently become the Crab Nebula. Glowing some six times brighter than Venus, it remained visible for around 23 days and was so bright that it could even be seen during the day.

Just outside Peñasco Blanco, one of the great houses at West Mesa, Chaco Canyon, there is a panel showing three important symbols: a crescent moon, a hand and a large star. It has been suggested that the visual relationship between the elements of the petrograph record the positions of the moon and the extraordinary supernova at the time of its appearance nearly a thousand years ago. Many other petrographs seem to hold further mysteries.

OUTLIERS AND ABANDONMENT

The first discoveries at Chaco Canyon were not made until 1822 and archaeological activity there has continued ever since. Initially the buildings were believed to represent an isolated community. Yet what has emerged over time gives a quite different picture. Many roads, around 10 m (33 ft) wide and dead straight, fan out from Chaco Canyon, some travelling as far as 80 km (50 miles) across the desert plains. Many of these roads lead to other villages, or *pueblos*, forming a web of 'outliers' from the main centre. At least 80 outliers have been discovered so far, some composed of fewer than ten rooms, others with more than a hundred. The roads are another sign of the main site's importance to ancient peoples –

though whether people came as pilgrims, traders, farmers or simply as part of a wider community of people wishing to meet with their own kind is unclear.

Indeed, without any written records to reveal the purpose of Chaco Canyon, archaeologists have struggled to understand the function of this and similar sites in the deserts of New Mexico, Colorado, Utah and Arizona. Farming would certainly have been difficult in the dry and windy desert, and some experts believe that the people of Chaco Canyon would not have been self-sufficient in foodstuffs. It is thought that the abandonment of the site may have coincided with severe droughts in around 1150–80, when the people who lived here may have left in search of more sustainable lands.

The site is now part of a National Park and is well protected from 'collectors' and from the ordinary ravages of an overenthusiastic public. Perhaps, with this protection, it will survive long enough to give up all its enigmatic mysteries.

Below The buildings at Chaco Canyon comprise a great variety of structures, some of which were four storeys high. The circular Kivas are believed to have been used for ceremonial purposes.

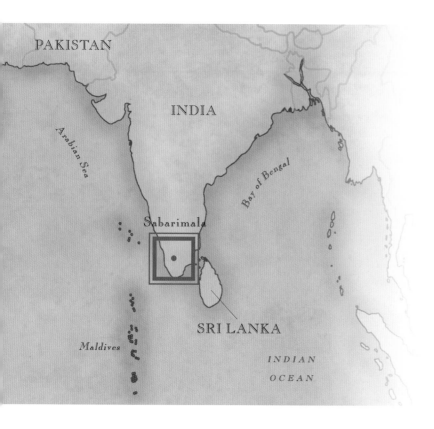

Sabarimala, Kerala

The Lord Ayyappa is an important deity within the Hindu pantheon. Also known also as Dharmasastha, Hariharasuthan, Manikant, Manikanta, Manikantan, Manikandha, Ayyanar and Bhoothnath, he is worshipped in a number of shrines across India. At Kulathupuzha he is worshipped as a child and at Sabarimala in Kerala he is revered as an important deity and celibate ascetic, who prays and meditates for the benefit of all humankind.

The Sabarimala pilgrimage is one of the most important events in Indian Hindu cultural life and takes place between late November and mid-January each year, culminating in Makarasankranti Day. This is when, according to both legend and pilgrims' reports, a series of specific miracles happens each year.

THE 'HUMAN SOJOURN' OF LORD AYYAPPA

The central legend concerning Lord Ayyappa and the creation of the Sabarimala Temple relates to his 'human sojourn', or lifetime in human form. The story tells of a time when Raja Rajasekhara was the ruler of the kingdom of Pandalam. During a hunting expedition the Raja heard the cries of a child coming from the banks of the River Pampa. Among the reeds he found a beautiful baby with a bead, or *mani*, around his neck, and the child was named Manikantan. The Raja, a pious, devoted and just ruler, had wished to have a child with his wife, but she had been unable to conceive. He felt that the arrival of the little baby was an answer to his prayers for an heir to his throne, and he took Manikantan into his home.

The Raja began to bring up the child as his own, educating him in the ways of Hindu learning and martial arts and preparing him for kingship. In the meantime, his wife gave birth to a son. Despite the arrival of a natural heir, the Raja decided that Manikantan should still be the one to succeed him and that he would crown him as the Yuvaraja, or king-in-waiting. Unfortunately, the Raja had a corrupt minister who decided to stir up trouble by persuading the innocent queen that tragedy would befall her if Manikantan were to ascend the throne. She was persuaded to join the minister in a plan to get rid of Manikantan so she pretended to have an illness that could be cured only by the milk of a leopard. The Raja believed that only he could face the dangerous mission to capture the leopard's milk, but the youthful Manikantan volunteered to go in his place and, despite the ruler's protests, the young man headed for the woods where the leopards were known to live.

An agonizing few days later Manikantan reappeared from the forest, riding a leopard and pursued by her cubs. At this miraculous sight the conspirators confessed their guilt, and the overjoyed Raja realized that Manikantan was a being of Divine origins.

Manikantan himself declared that he must now leave them and, in response to the Raja's prayers, promised blessings on his family and initiated the Raja on the path to the attainment of *moksha* (salvation). Their spiritual conversation is recorded in a text

> *"The possibility of* moksha, *and the potential for miraculous happenings, makes Sabarimala a heady draw for the serious Hindu devotee."*

known as the *Bhuthanathageetha*, in which Manikantan's identity as the Lord Ayyappa is clearly established. In the final dialogue between the two Lord Ayyappa asked the Raja to build a temple at Sabarimala, north of the holy river of Pampa where he had been discovered in the reeds as a baby, and promised that his blessings would always be available to those who came here and expressed their *bhakthi* or devotion to God.

PILGRIMAGE AND AUSTERITIES

At the same time Lord Ayyappa required that those who came in search of *moksha* underwent *vratham* (austerities) – strictures that many of the fifty million present-day pilgrims who come each year still undergo. These may include 41 days of refraining from intoxicants and various pleasures of the flesh, the regular chanting of prayers and mantras, and an attitude of service and devotion to the

other spiritual seekers on the Sabarimala pilgrimage. Tuition and wisdom in the practice of the austerities are offered by a guru, the Guruswammy, who is appointed from among the elder pilgrims who have completed the Sabarimala pilgrimage at least seven times.

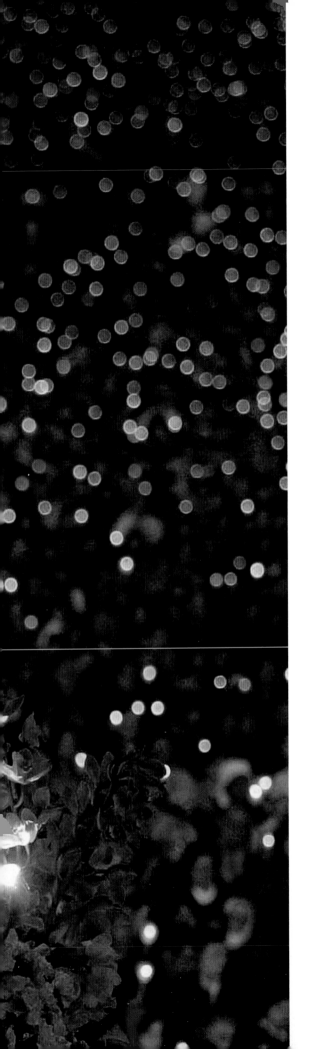

CHAPTER 3

KINGS, SAINTS AND SAGES

Many sacred sites gain their importance through their association with inspirational people and their mystical experiences. Shrines, churches and temples have often grown up around the very places where those blessed by contact with the Divine have achieved their special states. In this idea there is the promise that we all have the potential to have transcendent experiences ourselves; that, given the right conditions, devotion, spiritual practice and intentions – we can all receive what the mystics have talked about for centuries. And if we cannot aspire to such spiritual heights ourselves, then at least we can come and express our appreciation for a higher being who is willing to bless the faithful.

Most major religions seem to accept the idea that the acts of its most devoted followers are an inspiration to the rest of us. Even in the most organized of religions there is room for new spiritual pioneers. Perhaps the reason for this is that spirituality requires constant renewal. If we are not inspired by the spiritual courage of the ascetic, the campaigner or the wise, then a link in the chain is lost and the potential for spiritual evolution disappears. The places where sages and saints have received enlightenment often act as a catalyst for the chain to be remade.

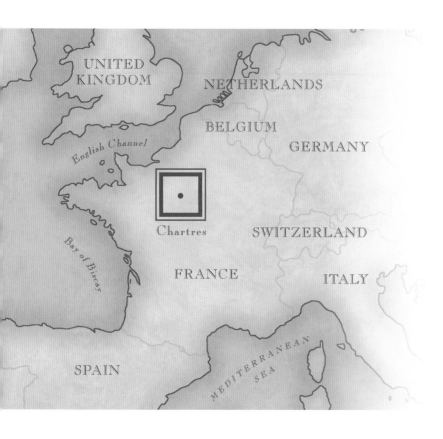

Chartres Cathedral, France

On a clear day in summer, Chartres Cathedral, France's most perfect Gothic cathedral appears to float above the buildings of its surrounding town. Situated some 80 km (50 miles) south of Paris, the cathedral's two asymmetric spires pierce the sky in an unforgettable silhouette.

The first churches stood on the cathedral site from around the 4th century CE, in the time of Constantine, and a cathedral is known to have existed until its demise by fire in 1020. During this time the cathedral's link with the cult of Mary the Virgin was established. Some believe that in 876 Charlemagne, head of the Holy Roman Empire, gave to the cathedral of Chartres the *Sancta Camisia*, the blouse or shirt worn by Mary, the mother of Jesus, when she gave birth to him. It was once thought that Charlemagne had captured the *Camisia* while on crusade in Jerusalem, but it is now believed that the *Camisia*, rather than being Charlemagne's gift, was given to the cathedral by Charles the Bald some time later, and that the relic is actually made from Syrian cotton woven in the 1st century CE. Whatever the truth, this garment was to play an important role in the cathedral's story.

After the first cathedral fell foul of fire, it was replaced by a grand Romanesque basilica, which survived until its own partial destruction by fire in 1134. Then in June 1194 much of the basilica, and most of the timber-framed town buildings that surrounded it, were engulfed by another conflagration, in which it was thought that the sacred *Camisia* had been consumed by the flames. In fact, three days after the fires subsided, rescue workers discovered three priests who had locked themselves into the cathedral's treasury room with the relic. Alive and relatively unharmed, the three emerged with the *Camisia* intact.

The survival of the sacred object seems to have been one of the key inspirations for those who rebuilt the cathedral. With a fresh constructional zeal, they began work immediately on the new Cathedral of Our Lady of Chartres (Notre-Dame de Chartres) and it was completed in the form we now see in around 1220 – a remarkably swift achievement. From its enshrining in 1260, the cathedral became a humming centre of life for local people and an increasingly important site of pilgrimage for those in search of religious enlightenment and the blessing of Mary and her son, Jesus.

Today, visitors to Chartres still have much to marvel at, for it is regarded as the apotheosis of all French Gothic cathedrals. Every part of this cathedral, it seems, aspires

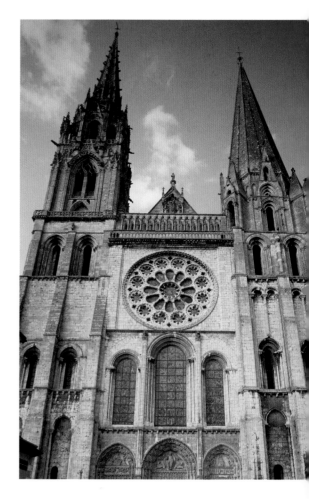

Left The Western
Facade, with its
circular rose window,
is dominated by two
strangely mismatched
spires: one is a 105 m
(349 ft) tall pyramid,
dating from the 1140s.
The other is a 113 m
(377 ft) tall ornate
16th-century spire on
top of an older tower.

to God. Externally it is dominated by its two strangely (but perfectly) mismatched spires, together with the elevating buttressing. Inside, one's senses are overawed by the tall, vaulted interior with its remarkable stained glass. In true Gothic spirit, every aspect of the cathedral seems to guide the worshipper towards the power of what is 'above'.

THE STAINED GLASS PANELS

It is the cathedral's external flying buttresses that permit such height in the building's walls. In turn these expansive walls provide a 'canvas' onto which the painters of glass placed their work. Whenever the sun shines, Chartres' stained-glass windows are illuminated, shedding brilliantly coloured light onto the walls and floor of the cathedral.

Altogether around 152 separate windows now occupy the walls, although there were 186 panels until the 18th century, when a

number of overzealous clergymen attempted to modernize the overall glazing pattern. During the Second World War all the stained glass was removed and hidden while German bombing raids and subsequent occupation continued, and was replaced at the end of hostilities. Current plans for further renovation and restoration depend on an enormous fundraising venture.

Perhaps the most impressive of all the panels are the enormous 'rose windows' that occupy key stations within the structure, notably the west façade and the north and south transepts. In his book *The Doors of Perception*, Aldous Huxley likened the intensity of colour contained in the stained-glass windows to a vision of heavenly reality. Perhaps, in the drabness of medieval life, the beauty of the coloured light visible within the cathedral was indeed the closest many people would come to heaven on Earth.

Above The Cathedral's
Lancet Window depicts
events from the life
of Christ. On the left
Mary receives the
visitation from the
Angel Gabriel; the
right-hand image
shows the Nativity.

Chartres: the labyrinth

Among the many architectural glories of Chartres Cathedral, one of the most celebrated is the intriguing labyrinth laid out on the floor of the nave, which has been an important focus for pilgrims over the centuries.

WALKING THE LABYRINTH AS AN ACT OF FAITH

The famous labyrinth embedded in the nave floor at Chartres has raised as many questions as it has answered. For many, the labyrinth is not a Christian symbol and its roots lie in spiritual cultures as diverse as Celtic, pagan and ancient Greek. There is now a resurgent interest in the power of labyrinths as tools for meditation and spiritual transformation; copies of the Chartres labyrinth currently exist all over the world for these very purposes. For the medieval seeker, labyrinths were often said to offer a symbolic (and definitely shorter) alternative to a pilgrimage to Jerusalem. For today's pilgrim, labyrinths are seen by some religious thinkers as a way to the very heart of God. In a journey that mirrors the real pilgrimages of older times, the person who enters the labyrinth surrenders control to the directions of the journey's twists and turns. From ground level it is impossible to see the route taken by the path – only from God's own view can this be seen and known. The journey through the labyrinth is an act of faith.

In this state of unknowing, the pilgrim releases his or her everyday concerns and becomes gradually more involved with the process of obedient following. To some, this part of the journey is a form of purgation, a necessary cleansing of the spirit on the way to the ultimate destination: peace in the heart of God. But arrival in the still centre, and time spent in contemplation there, is not the end of the journey: for pilgrimage is as much to do with what is brought back as with what is found. The return to the 'ordinary world' – the world outside the labyrinth – has to be negotiated at least as carefully as the leaving of it. Integration of the gifts of grace, and the personal broadcasting of these gifts in the life of the pilgrim, represent the new challenge. 'If I am changed for the better, what now do I have to offer?' What pilgrims thought was just for them often turns out to be of benefit to others, too.

Perhaps one journey in the labyrinth is not enough. Knowledge of the power at the heart of things invites a return to discover more, to learn more and to be further transformed by the process. But can all these possibilities and potential experiences really be offered by a simple pattern on the ground – a design that some visitors will simply trample on and ignore? It is undoubtedly up to each individual to explore this question and come to his or her own conclusion.

① LABYRINTH

Created around 1200 CE, the design for the labyrinth at Chartres would have been quite common in other churches and cathedrals around Europe. Most labyrinths have been removed or changed – often because they were viewed as an expression of pagan values. Perhaps uniquely, the labyrinth has come to be highly valued as one of Chartres' remarkable features. It is now carefully preserved and often roped off from use by the general public. The sight of repentant pilgrims, prostrating themselves through the 11-circuit route, is now the remnant of a more religiously fervent time.

② STAINED GLASS

Constituting one of the most complete collections of medieval stained glass in the world, Chartres' 13th- to 16th-century windows are renowned for their clarity of colour, especially the vivid blues found in the representations of the Madonna and child, and of Noah.

③ NAVE

Standing 36 m (120 ft) in height, the soaring nave, with its almost unimaginable weight of masonry, is supported by a complex series of flying buttresses that press against the cathedral's exterior. The effect of this is striking: a tall, unbroken view from the western end of the cathedral right through to the magnificent dome of the apse in the east.

④ GROTTO OF THE VIRGIN MARY

Beneath the altar lie what are believed to be the remains of the original Christian chapel on the site. Others claim that it is in fact a dolmenic chamber – a site of original druidic worship, located at the crossing of important earth energy lines.

⑤ ALTAR

As with many cathedrals and churches, the altar here represents the timeless focus of worship. At least five churches and chapels stood on the same site before the current cathedral was built 1194–1220. All the previous places of worship were burned down, and yet each subsequent version shared the same altar position.

Rocamadour, France

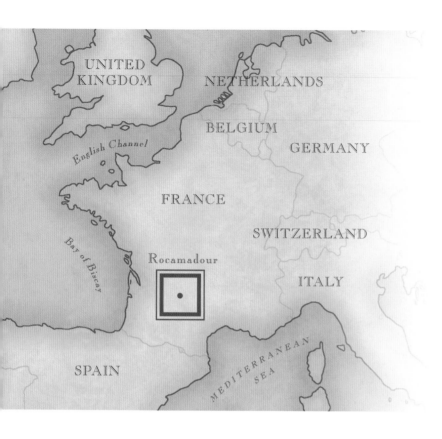

Rocamadour – the rock of St Amadour – is an ancient town containing a shrine to the Virgin Mary. Uniquely, the buildings of the town, together with its shrines and chapels, are built against a vertical sandstone cliff overlooking the Alzou Canyon in south-western France. The eponymous St Amadour (a name meaning 'lover') was originally identified as a man called Zacchaeus who appears in St Luke's Gospel.

Zacchaeus was the owner of the field that protected the Holy Family during their flight from Egypt, by miraculously growing tall maize plants among which Jesus, Mary and Joseph were able to hide from Herod's pursuing army.

THE BLACK VIRGIN

Zacchaeus, a tax collector, later married a woman called Veronica, who was herself made a saint in due course for her act of kindness to Jesus when she mopped his brow as he carried the cross to Calvary. Following Jesus' death and the persecution of Christians that ensued, Zacchaeus and Veronica fled from Palestine and took a small boat across the Mediterranean, eventually landing on the French coast. From there they travelled to Rome where they witnessed the executions of both St Peter and St Paul, before returning to France.

On Veronica's death, Zacchaeus retreated to the remote area of Quercy, where he established a shrine dedicated to Mary, installing the image of the 'Black Virgin', which various legends say was carved either by him or by St Luke, the author of the Gospel.

The Black Virgin, which is still enshrined in the cliffside town's Chapel of Our Lady, and which has been a hugely significant focus of Christian pilgrimage, apparently portrays the Virgin Mary with the baby Jesus on her left knee. Both mother and child wear crowns to indicate the special status that grants them access to God's grace. The Black Virgin of Rocamadour is one of many such carvings that are enshrined throughout the Christian world and are often associated with miraculous occurrences and Marian worship. Much speculation and scholarship have gone into the origins of these Black Virgins, and, although many dismiss their importance as

special objects, there are experts who see them as expressing pre-Christian, pagan ideas of worship. More specifically, the figures are often viewed as the Egyptian partnership of Isis and Horus – which is in itself an expression of the Mother principle in union with the God principle.

THE PILGRIM'S ASCENT

Along with the rise of Marian worship, it was the discovery of St Amadour's (Zacchaeus') body in 1166 CE – and a number of attendant miracles in the months that followed – that really brought Rocamadour to the attention of the religious faithful in medieval times

'At its height, Rocamadour was considered the fourth most important pilgrimage site in Christendom, behind Jerusalem, Rome and Santiago de Compostela.'

and led to the development of the town as a centre of pilgrimage. At its height, Rocamadour was considered the fourth most important pilgrimage site in Christendom, behind Jerusalem, Rome and Santiago de Compostela. The shrine of the Black Virgin – together with the relics of St Amadour in the crypt beneath – became the focal point of the pilgrimage. In its fortress-like location, pilgrims would ascend from the secular part of the town, prostrating themselves as they climbed the 216 steps of the Great Staircase until they reached what became known as the 'holy city' – a small central area surrounded

by seven churches and chapels where the pilgrims would await their entrance to the sanctuary. This *parvis*, or courtyard, was once decorated with paintings showing scenes from the life of Christ. So great were the number of people travelling to Rocamadour that it was necessary to build 11 gates to restrain and contain the faithful as they progressed through the stations of their journey. Only seven of these gates still remain today.

On the top of the cliff is a castle, built in medieval times to defend the sanctuaries. Although the castle still stands, it was not

enough to defend Rocamadour from the many religious wars that inflicted damage on the town's shrines. Many of the town's treasures were plundered as conflicts raged. Nevertheless, the important elements appear to have survived and many still believe the Black Virgin of Rocamadour to be original and authentic. In the 19th century significant restorations were carried out on the town's buildings, and the 20th century saw a rise in the numbers coming to worship here. It seems that the power of the Virgin Mary today to induce religious reverence is far from diminished.

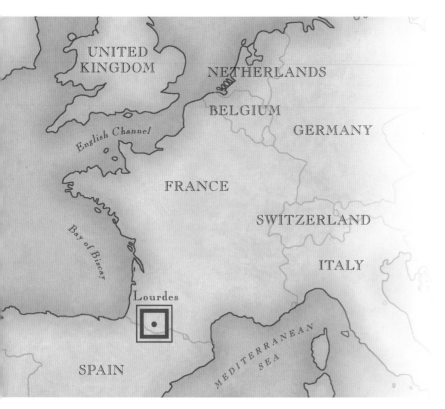

Lourdes, France

Lourdes, a small town in the foothills of the Pyrenees in south-western France, plays host to five million pilgrims each year. The year 2008 is the 150th anniversary of the time when a poor, pious peasant girl named Bernadette Soubirous experienced a series of appearances of the Virgin Mary. Her experiences resulted in the building of a chapel on the site of the apparitions. Lourdes is now the most important Marian shrine in the Catholic world.

Bernadette was just 14 years old on 11 February 1858 when she, her sister and a school friend went for a walk to the River Gave de Pau to collect firewood. Separated from the others who had crossed to the other side of the river, Bernadette sat down to take off her stockings, close to a grotto once dedicated to the Greek goddess Persephone, Queen of the Underworld.

THE APPARITIONS

At first Bernadette was startled to see a light – the silhouette of a figure, which resolved itself into a young lady wearing a white dress with a blue girdle, and a yellow rose on each of her feet. She also held a rosary of white

beads with a chain of the same yellow. Frightened by the apparition, Bernadette started to pray with her own rosary, an act repeated by the figure. Unsure whether the silent figure was to be feared or adored, Bernadette at first refused the Lady's beckoning signs to approach her. The figure

then disappeared, leaving Bernadette unsure as to what she had experienced.

When the young girl returned to the same spot three days later she initiated a series of 18 apparitions that took place over the next few weeks and months. Each time Bernadette would return to the same Grotto of

Right *The Grotto of Massabielle, where Bernadette Soubirous experienced her visions of the Virgin Mary in 1858, is still the focus for intense worship by Catholic pilgrims.*

Left The Lourdes 'Rosary' Basilica, and particularly its Upper Basilica of the Immaculate Conception with its central spire, welcomes pilgrims in search of healing.

Massabielle with increasing numbers of friends and followers, none of whom would share her visions, although many would be impressed – even overwhelmed – by the state of religious ecstasy engendered in the young girl by what she was experiencing.

THE SPRING EMERGES

It was during the third apparition on 18 February 1858 that the Lady spoke to Bernadette, asking her to continue to come for a fortnight, but also revealing that she would not promise to make her happy in this world, but rather in the next.

On 25 February, the ninth apparition, the Lady encouraged Bernadette to drink from a fountain. Scrabbling in the grass and finding only a muddy puddle, she drank the murky water. The next day a spring started to flow from the spot. During the 12th apparition a young woman bathed her paralysed arm in the water, and immediately full movement of the limb was restored. This was to be the first of the many claimed healing miracles of Lourdes.

At the 13th apparition the Lady asked Bernadette to request the local priests to attend her and to start building a chapel on the site of the apparitions. It was not until the 16th apparition on 25 March that the Lady finally answered Bernadette's oft-repeated question as to her identity, with the phrase *Que soy era Immaculada Conceptiou* – 'I am the Immaculate Conception'. This was a particularly significant choice of words, because although the phrase 'immaculate conception' is now familiar to us, it had come into religious usage only four years earlier and would not have been part of public vocabulary at this time. It was, as Bernadette said, unknown to her.

By the time of the 18th and final apparition, Bernadette had both supporters and detractors. Some eight thousand people accompanied her final attendance at the grotto – final because the place was fenced off by the police with support from certain religious authorities. There were also those who believed Bernadette to be mad, deluded or simply a charlatan. Nevertheless, within a year Lourdes had become a significant place of worship and pilgrimage for Christians wishing to affirm their faith and remains so to this day.

THE POWER OF FAITH

There are now numerous recorded cases of people who believe they have been healed by the waters of Lourdes. Although Bernadette stressed the power of faith above that of the water itself, the Roman Catholic authority in charge of reviewing such cases has publicly verified 68 of the thousands of apocryphal stories of healing from the last 50 years or so.

Although the Lady of Lourdes did not speak a great deal during the 18 apparitions, she stressed the need for penance, poverty and prayers for sinners. Bernadette also reported that the Lady gave her the words of a prayer that she repeated every day for the rest of her life. Bernadette Soubirous died in 1879, hidden from the world in a remote convent.

Fatima, Portugal

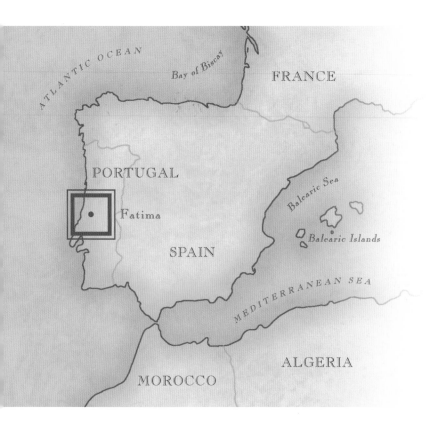

It was 13 May 1917 – at the height of the First World War – when ten-year-old Lúcia Santos, together with her cousins Jacinta and Francisco Marto, first saw the woman they referred to as 'Our Lady of the Rosary' in a field outside Aljustrel, close to the Portuguese town of Fatima. Five more apparitions, one of which took place before a crowd of seventy thousand has resulted in Fatima becoming a major site of pilgrimage for Catholics.

Lúcia described the figure as 'more brilliant than the sun, shedding rays of light clearer and stronger than a crystal glass filled with the most sparkling water and pierced by the burning rays of the sun'. With just one exception, for the next five months on the 13th day at almost exactly the same time, the Virgin Mary appeared to the children again and spoke to Lúcia on many topics, including the need for people to say the rosary each day in order to bring peace to the world. She also revealed three secrets – the three secrets of Fatima – that quickly became the focus of interest for those who took the apparitions seriously.

ARREST AND APPARITIONS

On 13 August 1917 the provincial administrator Artur Santos effectively arrested the children as they were on their way to rendezvous with the Lady of the Rosary for the fourth time, and imprisoned them in the local jail. As part of his investigation Santos even pretended to have a pot of boiling oil in another room and withdrew the children from the interrogation one at a time, saying to the two that remained that the

Left Jacinta Marto (left), Francisco Marto (centre) and Lúcia Santos (right) in 1917. While Lúcia lived on to carry the secrets of 'Our Lady of the Rosary' until 2005, Jacinta and Francisco were to die as a result of the great influenza epidemic of 1919.

others had been boiled alive. Nevertheless, Jacinta, Francisco and Lúcia were unwilling to divulge any information about the secrets.

That month the children met Mary at the nearby hamlet of Valinhos on 19 August. At the fifth apparition on 13 September the children were told that proof would be provided for the mass of people, 'so that all may believe' Mary's messages. And so, on 13 October 1917, a crowd of some seventy thousand people gathered in the same field, the Cova da Iria, where all but the August visions had occurred. What the people experienced that day would change the lives of many of them for ever.

THE 'MIRACLE OF THE SUN'

It had been raining heavily since the morning, with heavy cloud cover, and yet there was a sudden opening in the clouds that revealed the sun as a spinning disc, throwing off light of many colours. Then, even more miraculously (and apparently confirmed by the great majority of those present), the sun appeared to detach itself from its place in the sky and move around in a rapid, zigzagging motion before returning to its original place. It is recorded that many of the crowd were screaming, praying, staring in wonderment and shock as the 'Miracle of the Sun' unfolded. Over the days that followed, many reports appeared in newspapers all over the world of the extraordinary events that had apparently been seen by so many.

The young children, who had become important religious figures in their own right, continued in their devout practices, saying the rosary for long periods, prostrating themselves and performing strict forms of painful self-mortification. They also practised forms of self-denial, including fasting and even avoiding drinking water. Jacinta and Francisco both died in the great influenza epidemic that followed the end of the First World War. That left Sister Lúcia to protect the meaning of the messages and to work with the hierarchy of the Roman Catholic Church over the future of the secrets, and it was not until 1941 that the contents of the first two secrets was made public. The first

Left The neo-classical basilica of 'Our Lady of the Rosary' at Fatima, with its sweeping steps and colonnades is linked to convent and hospital buildings. The tombs of all three child seers are now in the basilica.

concerned a vision of hell, while the second secret described how another world war and the 'errors' of Russia and Communism could be prevented by devout individuals rededicating themselves to Mary's Immaculate Heart.

THE THIRD SECRET

While Lúcia had said that the mysterious third secret could be revealed at any time after 1940, and apparently no later than 1960, the Church decided to withhold the facts. This level of secrecy within the Church led different people to draw a variety of conclusions about what the third secret had to say: a prediction about the end of the Catholic Church, a message about the future of Russia and Communism and their role as an enemy of religion, or information about an apocalyptic end of the world. It was not until June 2000 that the Church finally relented and released a mild and quite non-specific text of the third secret. This has led some sceptics to believe that the revealed text is either altered or not the full version. With the death of Sister Lúcia on 13 February 2005 at the age of 97, the hope of further elucidation seemed to fade.

UNITED
STATES OF
AMERICA

MEXICO

Gulf of Mexico

Guadalupe

PACIFIC OCEAN

Caribbean Sea

HONDURAS

GUATEMALA

NICARAGUA

Guadalupe, Mexico

On 9 December 1531, just 13 years after the arrival of Hernando Cortés and his Spanish conquistadors, a Mexican peasant named Juan Diego Cuauhtlatoatzin had a vision of the Virgin Mary on a hill named Tepeyac just outside Mexico City. Most Mexicans now see themselves as 'Guadalupans', under the spiritual protection of the Lady. As the Mexican novelist Carlos Fuentes once put it: 'One may no longer consider himself a Christian, but you cannot truly be considered a Mexican unless you believe in the Virgin of Guadalupe.'

In his own report of the event, Juan Diego said that during a walk from his village towards the city, the figure of the Virgin was suddenly in front of him and – speaking in the native language of Nahuatl – asked him to build an abbey on the spot where she appeared. Juan Diego immediately went to the Spanish bishop, Juan de Zumárraga, and told him of the Virgin's wish. A sceptical Zumárraga asked Juan Diego to return when he had a miraculous sign to prove his story.

THE MIRACLE OF THE FLOWERS

Three days later the devout Mexican had a further visitation from the Virgin Mary, this time telling him to go to the peak of Tepeyac hill and gather flowers there, even though it was winter and no plants normally bloomed at this time. When he reached the top of the hill he discovered roses, which he picked and placed on his *tilma* or cloak. The Virgin told him that he should keep the flowers wrapped in the cloak until he gave them to the Bishop. When the *tilma* was opened, an extraordinary colourful image of the Virgin Mary was revealed, apparently imprinted onto the material of the cloak. The Bishop's request

for a miracle seemed to have been granted and a chapel was soon built on the hill where Juan Diego had first seen 'Our Lady of Guadalupe', as she came to be known.

There is some question about the source of the apparition's name of 'Guadalupe'. It may be a literal translation of the Nahuatl word *Coatlaxopeuh*, meaning 'one who crushes the serpent', although some sceptics have speculated whether the name is simply an adoption of another Marian visitation that occurred in Extremadura in Spain during the 14th century CE. However, the Mexican story asserts that Juan Diego's uncle – who is also said to have seen Mary – was told directly of the Virgin's identity as 'Our Lady of Guadalupe'. Whatever the truth, the worship of Our Lady of Guadalupe soon strengthened the growing Catholic Church in Mexico and when Juan de Zumárraga was installed as Archbishop of Mexico City, he oversaw an increase in Christian faith and worship. Nevertheless, in a teaching published close to the end of his life, the Bishop stated that 'The Redeemer of the world doesn't want any more miracles, because they are no longer necessary.'

CONTROVERSY AND SPECULATION

Some have questioned the whole series of events and this first appearance of Mary as 'Empress of the Americas', and have speculated whether the Catholic Church may have been using 'Our Lady of Guadalupe' to adopt more ancient female deities from the native culture of Mexico. When the first shrine to Guadalupe was erected, many of the worshippers were found to be honouring the indigenous Mexican goddess Tonantzin and the Aztec mother goddess Coatlicue. Was this, as some have suggested, an example of 'syncretism', a deliberate confusion of the object of worship? Questions have naturally been asked concerning the *tilma* and its origins; more recently it has undergone a number of scientific tests. While not conclusive, they reveal some controversial aspects – there appear to be three layers of images, and one is very similar to that of the Black Madonna in Guadalupe, Spain. Nevertheless the pigments used in the image are paints contemporaneous with the apparition, although the material of the *tilma* is not cactus fibre, as originally thought, but hemp or linen.

Left A large crowd gathers outside the Old Basilica of Guadalupe in Mexico City during the annual pilgrimage to the shrine of the country's patron saint, the Virgin of Guadalupe.

The importance to the Catholic Church of the visitation of the Virgin Mary in Mexico has been well demonstrated by the succession of popes who have spoken positively about the appearance and the miraculous icon. It was 1754 when Pope Benedict XIV declared Our Lady of Guadalupe the patron of Central and North America – or New Spain, as it was then known – and approved specific forms of worship in her honour. Pope Leo XIII oversaw the coronation of the *tilma* image in 1895. In 1992 Pope John Paul II dedicated a chapel in St Peter's Basilica in the Vatican to 'Our Lady of Guadalupe'. And on 31 July 2002 another significant step was taken when the 16th-century peasant Juan Diego Cuauhtlatoatzin was finally made a saint.

'It was 1754 when Pope Benedict XIV declared Our Lady of Guadalupe the patron of Central and North America – or New Spain, as it was then known.'

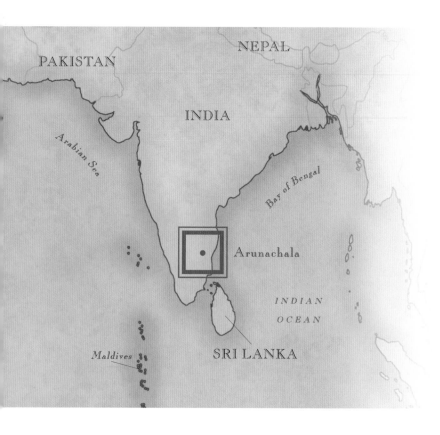

Arunachala, India

Arunachala, also known as Tiruvanomalai, in Tamil Nadu, southern India, has been associated with gods and sages for thousands of years, but its position in the Hindu world as a sacred place can be traced back to a particular legend about the great god Shiva and his lingam, or phallus. The Arunachaleswar Shiva Temple, dedicated to Shiva, is one of the oldest and largest temples in Southern India.

When Shiva was mourning the death of his wife Sati, he wandered naked through the forests of Daruvana, arousing some of the wives of the sages who lived there. Their husbands became jealous and issued a curse that Shiva's lingam, or phallus, would fall off. However, when it landed on the ground, it grew up into the sky like a great shining tower. The gods Vishnu and Brahma decided to find its root and peak, but could not do so. Vishnu confessed his failure to find the source of the phallus, but Brahma claimed to have reached its summit. When Shiva arrived, he turned on Brahma and accused him of lying; but, out of respect for Vishnu's honesty, Shiva decided to honour his request to leave part of his lingam, in its 'fire form', on Arunachala Hill, and the place has been regarded as sacred ever since.

Right Arunachala mountain, standing 980 m (3,234 ft) high, is India's holiest Hindu peak. Here legends bring together the Hindu gods: Shiva, Brahma and Vishnu.

THE ARUNACHALESWAR SHIVA TEMPLE

This legend, like so many involving the god Shiva, has been enshrined with a temple: the Arunachaleswar Shiva Temple in Tiruvanamalai, the Tamil name for Arunachala. This temple complex, with its beautifully constructed and strangely modern towers, is one of the oldest and largest temples in southern India. The exact time of its establishment is unknown, but it is thought to have grown up over at least two thousand years and now covers an area of 10 ha (25 acres). Its large and distinctive towers, or *gopurams*, were built between the 10th and 16th centuries. Of the nine *gopurams* – all

ornately carved, layered pyramid structures – the largest is 60 m (197 ft) high and contains 13 storeys.

The central, inner temple contains the shrine to Shiva in his Tamil manifestation as Lord Annamalai. Every year Shiva's presence here is celebrated during the Hindu month of Kartikai (around November and December in the Julian calendar) with the great Deepam festival. Lasting ten days and bringing Tiruvanamalai alive with music and processions, Deepam is an extrovert celebration of the great fire lingam left by Shiva on Arunachala Hill and culminates on the eve of the full moon, when a large beacon fire is lit on the peak of Arunachala Hill to symbolize the god's presence there.

RAMANA MAHARSHI

Arunachala Hill and its surroundings have been home to many great Indian sages over the centuries, including Arunagirinathar, the author of the *Tiruppugal*, and Sri Ramana Maharshi, known in his early life by the birth name Venkataraman. Born in 1879, Venkataraman lived a relatively normal life among a devout Hindu family until the age of 16, when the name of the place Arunachala was first mentioned to him. He immediately knew that he must go there, although not knowing how this might happen. Following a spiritual, near-death experience the following year, Venkataraman decided to leave school and make his way to Arunachala, carrying just a few rupees in his pockets. Members of his family tried to persuade him to return, but he had already established a reputation as the 'little swami' and knew that his vocation lay in this place.

Although his life in Arunachala started in the Arunachaleswar Shiva Temple, Venkataraman was forced to move to different locations to avoid too much attention from those who would not permit him the peace he required. In 1916 his mother, who had once begged him to return home, finally came to join him in Arunachala and follow a path of spiritual asceticism.

Now known as Ramana Maharshi, he moved to a hermit's cave known as Virupaksa on Arunachala Hill, and later to

Skandasramam, another cave further up the hill. Following his mother's death in 1922, Ramana and his devotees formed an *ashram* (a sanctuary or retreat), where increasing numbers of spiritual seekers came to be in his presence and ask questions of the 'young swami', as he was also known. Many people – including seekers from the West – were very moved by their meetings with Ramana and wrote fondly of their time with the sage in articles and books.

Ramana's teachings on non-attachment to the body were tested during his final illness with cancer. Nevertheless his positive outlook, and his insistence that identity should not be invested in the physical body,

Above *At the Arunachaleswar Shiva temple, a mahout guides his temple elephant past two of the nine* gopurams *(gate towers), that dominate the site.*

was maintained until his death in 1950. In the modern age, Ramana Maharshi and Arunachala will forever be linked, not just in the psyche of southern Indians, but in the minds of those from further afield who experienced the deep peace of an important spiritual presence.

Czestochowa, Poland

Czestochowa in southern Poland is home to the most important religious shrine in the country: the Jasna Góra Monastery. This spiritual community is the site of an icon painting of the Black Madonna, which has a special place in the psyche of Roman Catholic Poles. The origins of the painting itself are obscure, but many believe the image was originally created by St Luke, author of the Gospel, and painted on wood from a tabletop formerly in the Holy Family's home in Nazareth.

According to some documents in the Jasna Góra Monastery, the image arrived in Czestochowa in August 1382 in the hands of Prince Ladislaus Opolczyk, but some of the details of its journey to Czestochowa are harder to pin down.

THE ICON'S HISTORY

There are stories that the painting was taken to Constantinople in the 4th century CE by St Helena, the mother of Constantine the Great. There the painting was held in high esteem and was credited with bringing both spiritual comfort and healing from epidemic illnesses to the Eastern Christian faithful. It is believed to have been taken from Constantinople sometime in the 9th century and to have been carried to Northern Europe, where it was held in Belz Castle, north-east of Lwów, in Red Ruthenia. When Tartar tribes were besieging the castle in the 14th century, it is believed that a rogue arrow pierced the image at Mary's neck. Concerned for its safety and acting on behalf of King Louis of Hungary, Prince Ladislaus Opolczyk smuggled the icon out of Belz Castle, intending to take it to Silesia. But on the way

Left The Jasna Góra Monastery is the most famous catholic sanctuary and pilgrimage destination in Poland – an importance it maintains as container and protector of the Black Madonna icon.

he stopped at Czestochowa and, sensing that this was the icon's natural spiritual home, decided to create a temporary shrine there, appointing a group of white-robed Pauline fathers from Hungary to protect the holy image in a newly commissioned monastery to be called Jasna Góra, or 'bright mountain'.

In 1430 the Jasna Góra shrine was robbed by a group of unscrupulous thieves and many valuable sacred objects were stolen from the monastery, including the icon. The picture was eventually found close to a nearby river, but it had been badly damaged: the wooden base was broken, ornaments had been removed from its surface and the canvas had been cut with a sword, leaving two marks on Mary's cheek. The Pauline monks took the painting to King Ladislaus Jagiello and his wife Hedwig in Kraków, where the difficult job of restoration was carried out.

THE PORTRAYAL OF THE BLACK MADONNA

Many people have commented that the style of the Czestochowa painting is more in keeping with icons of the Eastern Orthodox tradition than with other approaches to the depiction of Mary and the Christ child. The design shows Mary dressed in a robe with a distinctive fleur-de-lis pattern. She is portrayed as the *Hodegetria* or the 'One Who Shows the Way', gesturing with her right hand towards the Christ child, who holds a book (presumably the Gospels) indicating his role in the transmission of God's word.

The image is an example of the Black Madonna tradition, in which the faces of Jesus and Mary are dark or dark-skinned. There are scholars who link this portrayal with older, pre-Christian figures, such as Isis and Horus of the ancient Egyptian world. In the case of the Black Madonna of Czestochowa, there is also a legend that the Jasna Góra Monastery was miraculously saved from destruction by fire, owing to the presence of the icon – but not until Mary's and Jesus' painted skin tones had been darkened by the smoke of the fire.

Left Some people believe that this image of the Black Madonna with the Christ child was painted on wood that was once a table in the Holy Family's house in Nazareth. Many spiritual and healing powers have been attributed to the icon.

OUR LADY AS SPIRITUAL MONARCH

The idea of the icon as a protective force for the Polish people has grown since the 17th century when Poland was invaded by the Swedes. Her presence is said to have inspired King Jan Kazimierz in his struggle to resist the invading enemy, and when the battle was over he announced in Lwów Cathedral on 1 April 1656 that Our Lady of Czestochowa would henceforth be Queen of Poland, Protector of her people for ever. Since that time, prayer to Mary, Our Lady of Czestochowa and Queen of Poland has been a major feature of the Polish people's worship during the succession of wars and other disasters that have befallen them over the centuries.

In more recent times, authorized copies of the image have been created and taken to other parts of the country to enable worshippers to experience the blessings of the image and, by association, the Marian presence. The remarkable attraction of these events, supported by successive popes, demonstrates that – despite the general rise of secularism – for many Poles Our Lady of Czestochowa remains their spiritual monarch.

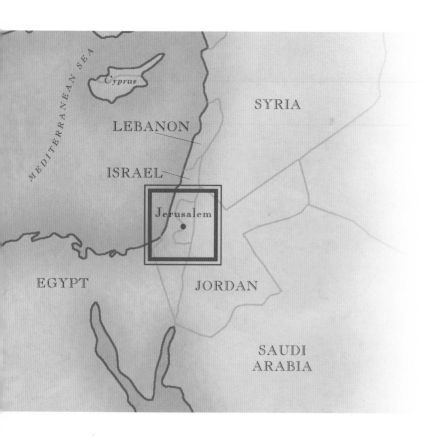

King Solomon's Temple, Jerusalem

It is hard to overestimate the significance of King Solomon's Temple in the religious psyche of the Jewish people. Even though little trace of the temple appears to have survived its destruction nearly 2,600 years ago, such are the power and importance of this iconic structure that Jews all over the world pray daily for its restoration to the manifest world.

Once the Jews eventually took hold of Jerusalem after their long period of wandering, King David wanted to build a temple as their first, fixed place of worship, but was told by God that his son Solomon would have this privilege.

THE FIRST TEMPLE

King Solomon's Temple – the First Temple, as it became known – was built around 1000 BCE and its design is described in great detail in the Tanach, the Hebrew Bible: 'The length by cubits after the ancient measure was threescore cubits and the breadth twenty cubits. And the porch that was before the house, the length of it according to the breadth of the house, was twenty cubits, and the height a hundred and twenty; and he overlaid it with pure gold.'

Right This 15th-century woodcut from the Nuremburg Chronicle by Hartmann Schedel shows King Solomon's Temple in the city of Jerusalem, or 'Hierosolima'.

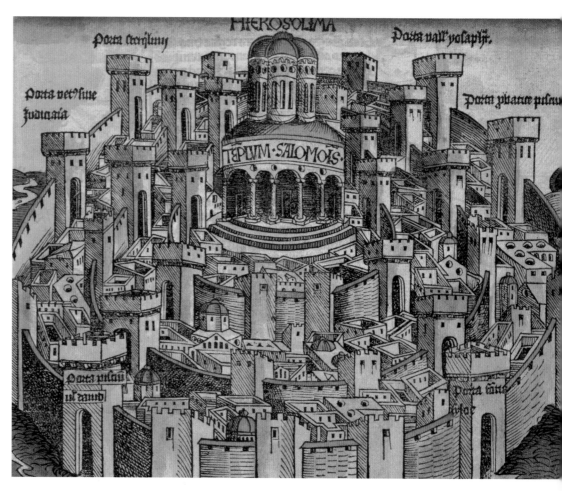

The Tanach goes on to describe not only the design and the method of building, but also the great inventory of exquisitely crafted sacred objects – such as vessels and ornaments – that were to adorn the interior of the temple. The most important room was called the Holy of Holies and was created to house the Ark of the Covenant. The Ark, which had become a focus of worship and an object of great power and protection for the Jewish people, is believed to have contained not only the Tablets of the Ten Commandments, but also the Pentateuch: the first five books of the Bible, supposedly dictated by Moses.

The Tanach also records how Solomon enlisted the help of King Hiram of Tyre, the Phoenician ruler, in the building of the temple. He first requested great quantities of cedarwood and vast blocks of the finest quarried stone, which the King willingly provided. Solomon then also received the help of Hiram's great craftsmen, including the famous Huram, who was responsible for many of the temple's important ritual artefacts, including the winged beasts that reputedly guarded the Ark of the Covenant.

To ensure the swift completion of the project, Solomon imposed a regime of forced labour on his people. So grand and overreaching was his plan for the temple that he incurred huge debts – debts that eventually led to the handing over to King Hiram of 20 towns in the region of Galilee. On the occasion of the First Temple's initiation, Solomon invited all his people, and even those of other religions, to join him in prayers of thanksgiving to God. The temple containing the Ark of the Covenant was now at the centre of the Jews' worship, and on the holiest of all days, Yom Kippur, the most sacred rituals were performed in the Holy of Holies, where only the most elevated of the priests were permitted to perform specific prayers to invoke blessings on the entire Jewish people.

THE SECOND TEMPLE

King Solomon's Temple maintained its key role at the heart of Jewish religious life for four hundred years until the Babylonians completely destroyed it in 587 BCE, stealing its treasures in the process. No remains of the First Temple have ever been found, and the fate of the Ark of the Covenant is one of the many mysteries surrounding the temple's destruction. Seventy years later, however, the Jews rebuilt the temple when King Darius gave permission for some Jews to return to Judaea. The Second Temple was in turn substantially altered under the new King Herod in around 20 BCE.

According to ancient sources, Herod acquired a thousand wagons with oxen to transport the stones from the quarry to the building site, hired ten thousand skilled workmen and trained one thousand priests as masons and carpenters, for only priests could build the temple proper. According to the ancient historian Josephus, during the time the Second Temple was under construction, no rain fell during the day, but only at night, so as not to hinder progress.

The Second Temple was to last until the destruction of Jerusalem by the Romans in 70 CE, when all but a section of its Western Wall (Wailing Wall) was completely destroyed. It is said the Romans left a section of wall standing in order to show the scale of the edifice they had razed to the ground. In its place the Romans erected a temple to Jupiter in around 135 CE, which was in turn destroyed by the Emperor Constantine after his conversion to Christianity in 312.

According to Orthodox and Conservative Judaism, a Third Temple will be built prior to the coming of the Messiah.

CHAPTER 4

PLACES OF ISOLATION AND MEDITATION

The way of the monk and the way of the nun – of spiritual devotion to the exclusion of the temporal world – have always aroused mixed reactions from the outside world. Something about the rejection of life's normal pleasures, in favour of a life lost in the possibility of the Divine, challenges the ordinary person's sense of what life is for. Others simply see the retreat into solitude or a religious community as a selfish rejection of a world that needs people of good heart to solve its problems. These hermits provoke endless questions: Is it really necessary to cut oneself off from the world in order to live any kind of spiritually valuable life? Is such a sacrifice the only way we have of gaining spiritual uplift? In other words, does the existence of monks and hermits negate the very value of my life, my efforts?

Is their purpose really quite different, though? Are such people simply a reminder of another way of life? Some mystics claim that the prayerful activities of hermits and monks through the ages have sustained the planet – that without their outpourings of intercessional requests, the Divine might have given up on the rest of us. Others would simply say that to maintain a dialogue with the Divine requires concentration and focus. A place without distractions is simply a mandatory requirement for such a difficult task, and a community of people with the same aim helps to reinforce and maintain such a commitment. Here are places where such a life has been lived.

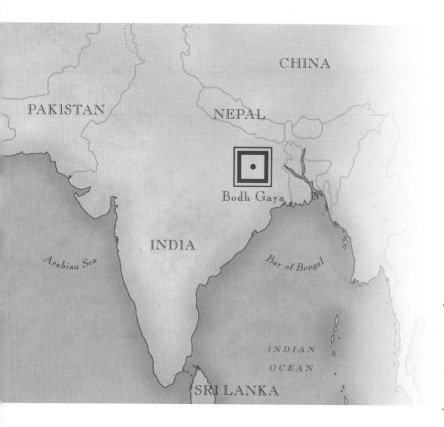

Bodh Gaya, India

Bodh Gaya is, perhaps the most important location in the story of Buddhism. According to Buddhist tradition, it was around 500 BCE that Prince Gautama Siddhartha arrived at the Falgu River, close to the town of Gaya, some 96 km (60 miles) from present-day Patna. He found shelter under a peepal tree, and started to meditate. For three days and three nights Siddhartha continued his contemplation until he achieved the state of Nirvana, or enlightenment. At this time he became fully realized as the Gautama Buddha.

The Buddha spent a further seven weeks in the nearby area, continuing his meditations and integrating what he had experienced under the peepal tree (a type of fig now known as *Ficus religiosa*). He then travelled to Sarnath and started to teach what he had learned: the four noble truths, the noble eightfold path, the five precepts, the three jewels, the concept of Nirvana and the many other ideas that formed the core of his philosophy.

DECLINE AND REBIRTH OF THE MAHABODHI TEMPLE

As the popularity of Buddhism grew, the Buddha's followers started to travel to the place where he had been enlightened – particularly at full moon during the Hindu month of Vaisakh (April or May of the Julian calendar). In time the place became known as Bodh Gaya, and the tree that had sheltered the Buddha gained the name of the 'Bodhi tree'.

In around 250 BCE the Emperor Ashoka came to Bodh Gaya to worship as a pilgrim. Some experts believe that Ashoka initiated the building of the Mahabodhi Temple, although others put its origins in the 1st century CE during the Kushan period. Originally this famous temple consisted of a tall spire topped with a miniature stupa. Two flights of steps led to a platform and an upper sanctum; multiple images of the Buddha adorned the niches on the spire. Pilgrims came from all over the world, many of them writing accounts of their experiences. Some of the best known are those of the Chinese pilgrims Faxian in the 5th century CE and Xuanzang in the 7th century. Pilgrimage and worship all but ended, however, when Turkish armies conquered the area in the 13th century and the temple complex gradually fell into disuse. Over time the temple was forgotten, and sand gradually covered it from view.

It was not rediscovered again until the 19th century when Sir Alexander Cunningham of the British Archaeological Society led a thorough excavation of the site. A great deal of renovation was required to bring the temple back from obscurity. The last hundred years, however, have seen the Mahabodhi gradually return to its full glory and once again become an important focus for Buddhist pilgrims.

UNITY IN DIVERSITY

Many monasteries and temples have been built in the area around the Mahabodhi Temple by Buddhist practitioners from Bhutan, China, Japan, Myanmar, Nepal, Sikkim, Sri Lanka, Thailand, Tibet and Vietnam, and all the buildings demonstrate the architectural styles of their creators. The Buddha from the Chinese Temple dates back more than 200 years and was brought to Bodh Gaya from China. The Nippon Temple erected by Japanese Buddhists is in the shape

'As the popularity of Buddhism grew, the Buddha's followers started to travel to the place where he had been enlightened.'

of a pagoda. The temple of the Myanmar (Burmese) people is also in pagoda form and contains elements of the famous temples of Bagan. The Thai Temple has a curved roof covered with golden tiles, typical of Thailand's architectural style; it contains an impressive statue of the Buddha, cast in bronze. The collection of buildings is intended to convey both the unity and diversity of Buddhism's expression throughout the world. At the same time it demonstrates the remarkable and widespread effect that the Gautama Buddha's realizations – his experiences in this very place – have had throughout the Asian world. The Bodhi tree that currently stands at the site of the Buddha's enlightenment is actually a sapling of the Sri Maha Bodhi tree in Anuradhapura, Sri Lanka, which was itself taken from the original Bodhi tree in Bodh Gaya. At around 2,200 years old, the Bodhi tree in Sri Lanka is believed to be the oldest tree planted by human hand, a delicate symbol of Buddhism's own longevity.

Below Tibetan Buddhist monks prostrate themselves at the stupa close to the Bodhi tree where the Gautama Buddha achieved a state of enlightenment.

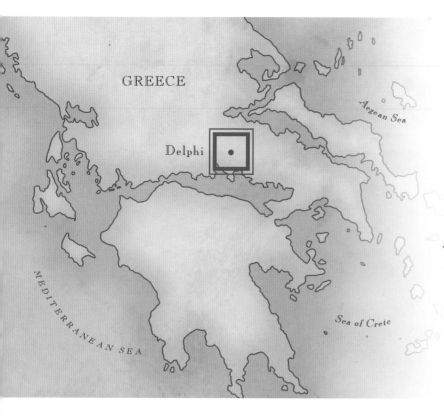

Delphi, Greece

Delphi was one of the most important locations in ancient Greek culture. Sited on a plateau cut into the lower slopes of Mount Parnassus, it was the home of the Delphic Oracle – the source of knowledge dedicated to the god Apollo, where the 'eternal flame' (the original 'Greek fire') burned inside the inner temple. Delphi was also the site of the omphalos, *an egg-shaped stone that marked the centre, or navel, of the known universe. Mount Parnassus had its own role in the ancient Greeks' world as the home of Apollo, the Nine Muses and many other important members of the Greek pantheon. It also played host to Pegasus, the famous winged horse of Bellerophon.*

Situated some 14 km (9 miles) north-east of the coastal town of Kirrha on the Corinthian Gulf, Delphi's origins as the home of the Oracle are obscure.

ORIGINS OF THE ORACLE

Remains of pottery and offerings show worship activity from as early as the 8th or 9th century BCE, but many believe that the Oracle (or a form of spiritual guidance) functioned at the site from much earlier, when the place was dedicated to Poseidon and, even longer ago, to Gaia, the earth goddess. As with much of Greek history, legend and truth are often intertwined, but what is clearly known is that the Oracle at Delphi functioned as a source of wisdom for Greece's leaders.

In legend, the priestess of the Oracle was known as the Pythia. In images shown on pottery she is depicted sitting on a tripod, or a three-legged stool, holding the leaves of the bay tree. It is often said that she chewed the bark of the bay tree and drank the water of the sacred Castalian spring before entering the altered state in which she provided information gleaned from supernatural or spiritual sources.

Though some have imagined that she was a type of fortune-teller, predicting the future, most of the Pythia's information was guidance on the conduct or ritual behaviour that supplicants should pursue, if they were to cleanse their spirits and avoid disaster befalling either themselves or the nation. She was consulted before major battles, campaigns and other events that affected the wider populace. Her influence was not limited to the Greeks, and there is evidence that the peoples of Lydia, Caria and Egypt also came to meet her. Many of her utterings were challenging to the recipient, but the fact that the Oracle survived for so long in one form or another demonstrates that her words of wisdom held value. The temple of the Apollonian Oracle, as it is also known, is famous for the wordings that adorn the site: 'Know Thyself', 'Nothing in Excess' and an enigmatic letter E or *epsilon*.

THE ORACLE'S PROPHECIES

Of the Oracle's prophecies there are about 500 that have survived and originate from as early as the 9th century BCE until 393 CE, when the Oracle declared itself effectively destroyed by the tide of anti-pagan Christian thought. In 560 BCE King Croesus of Lydia tested many oracles, before deciding on Delphi to provide him with an answer to his burning question concerning the future longevity of his reign. Herodotus reported that the Oracle gave its response as: 'Nay, when a mule becometh king of Medes, flee, soft-soled Lydian ... and stay not, nor feel shame to be a coward.' Believing it impossible that a mule could ever become King of the Medes, Croesus then asked for advice about attacking the Persians. The Oracle responded: 'After crossing the Halys, Croesus will destroy a great empire.' Croesus liked this reply and made war on the Persians. Unfortunately he had forgotten that Cyrus, the leader of the Medes, was indeed a mule of sorts – his mother was Mede, his father Persian. Croesus destroyed a great empire: his own.

In the 4th century BCE King Philip II of Macedon was told that whomsoever could ride a particularly wild colt in his possession would conquer the world. When neither he nor his best generals proved up to the task, Philip was astonished to see his son

THE *OMPHALOS*, PARNASSUS AND THE NINE MUSES

The origin of the *omphalos* stone, which is said to give Delphi its centrality in the Greek universe, lies in the story of how the god of gods, Zeus, released two eagles from opposite sides of the Earth, and the place where they met was then marked as the centre of the world. The presence of the egg-like stone at the heart of the Apollonian Temple is further evidence of the site's association with the earth goddess and the symbol of her womb as both the seed of all things and the container of vital knowledge.

The relationship between Delphi and its location on the side of Mount Parnassus adds much to the power of the place. There are further associations with Pan, the god of nature, and with the Corycian nymphs who were said to have dwelt in a cave on the mountainside. Mount Parnassus' name derives from Parnassos, the son of a nymph named Kelodora and a mortal called Kleopompous. Parnassos was the leader of a city until it was flooded by terrible rains. Together with his surviving citizens, he escaped the flood waters by climbing up the nearby mountain. There they built a new city called Lykoreia, but from then on the mountain would forever be associated with the name of Parnassos.

The Nine Muses account for many of the links between Mount Parnassus and art, poetry, music and other forms of learning and creative activity. Even now – despite the place's role as a bauxite mining resource and a skiing centre – many people still come to Delphi in search of inspiration from the Muses and the self-knowledge and wisdom offered by the Delphic Oracle.

Alexander tame the wild beast. Alexander would become Alexander the Great and the horse, named Bucephalus, would be his companion for the majority of his conquering campaign in Asia. Later Alexander consulted the Oracle himself; when the Oracle refused to respond to his questions about his future, he forcefully dragged the Pythia priestess by the hair from the adyton within the temple until she spoke: 'Let go of me: you are unassailable!' Having his answer, he released her.

Delphi: the sanctuary

The water of the Castalian (Kassotis) spring played an important part in the cult of the Oracle: according to Pausanias, the Greek traveller and geographer, it 'brought the women in the adyton of the god into a condition in which they could prophesy'. The adyton is a small room in a temple reserved for the most sacred of activities and for the use of priests and priestesses.

Delphi is one of the most significant ancient sites in Greece, and its magnificent art and architecture are a reflection of its political importance. Most of the sanctuary ruins that survive today date to the 6th century BCE, when Delphi was at the very height of its power.

THE PYTHIAN GAMES

Over the centuries Delphi became a major centre for Greek cultural events and festivals. The Pythian Games were initiated in the 6th century BCE in honour of Apollo's slaying of the great Python, although there are those who say that it was the god himself who started the Pythian Games as a competition amongst mortals who aspired to honour the gods in poetry and music. Later the Pythian Games included athletic events, and when the Olympic Games started sometime later, the same physical activities were adopted. The two Games then alternated – each taking place two years after the other. A four-horse chariot race also formed part of the programme for the Pythian Games, and took place on a plain close to the sea. Athletics events were run in Delphi's impressive stadium, while the music and theatrical events were housed in the Theatre. The winners of the various events would receive laurel wreaths and would return to their home cities as heroes.

① TEMPLE OF APOLLO

The Temple of Apollo was first built around the 7th century BCE by the two legendary architects Trophonios and Agamedes. It was rebuilt following a fire in the 6th century BCE and was then named the Temple of Alcmeonidae, in tribute to the noble Athenian family who oversaw its construction with funds from all over Greece and from foreign emperors. This temple was destroyed in 373 BCE by an earthquake and was rebuilt again in 330 BCE. Above the door were carved snippets of wisdom such as 'Know Thyself' and 'Nothing in Excess'. Answers to written questions were channelled through the priestess known as the Pythia. She sat on a sacred tripod close to a cleft in the rocks that emanated vapours. Under the combined influences of these gases and the ingestion of bay leaves, the Pythia was able to access altered states of mind in which she received her prophetic, often encoded answers.

② ATHENIAN TREASURY

This Doric building was constructed around 490 BCE. Most of the metopes (decorated panels) show the adventures of Herakles and Theseus. Other metopes and the acroteria (roof sculptures) show the Amazons, who fought battles against both of these heroes. Some fragments of sculpture from the pediments also survive: chariots and a frontal Athena from one pediment, and a fight from the other pediment. The walls of the Athenian Treasury also served as a giant message board, where visitors could inscribe honours and dedications onto the smooth stones.

③ SIPHNIAN TREASURY

The Siphnian Treasury, which was Ionic in style, was built in 525 BCE from Parian marble and was paid for from the gold and silver profits from the mines of Siphnos. Instead of columns, the treasury was decorated with two caryatids (pillars in the form of female figures).

⑤ MOUNT PARNASSUS

According to Greek legend Apollo, the son of Zeus, travelled from his home on top of Mount Olympus to Mount Parnassus in order to slay the great serpent known as Python. Feeling remorse for his actions, Apollo then erected a temple on the site. Today Mount Parnassus is a popular place for skiers. It is also mined for its wealth of bauxite.

⑥ THE SACRED WAY

We are told that on first passing through the main entrance gate into the sacred Delphic Precinct, the pilgrim was immediately set upon a path that would lead him through the most extraordinary architecture, statuary (most of which have now gone) and votive offerings. This path was known as the Sacred Way and took the seeker on a serpentine road heading first west past the first of

the Treasuries, before heading back east and further up the hillside, until finally he reached the Temple of Apollo. The religious ambiance in the precinct would have been powerful, perhaps even more intense than the sense of history and political power at Delphi. The opulence of the place was due in large part to the grand gifts of the various Greek city-states, donated in order to both thank and appease the gods.

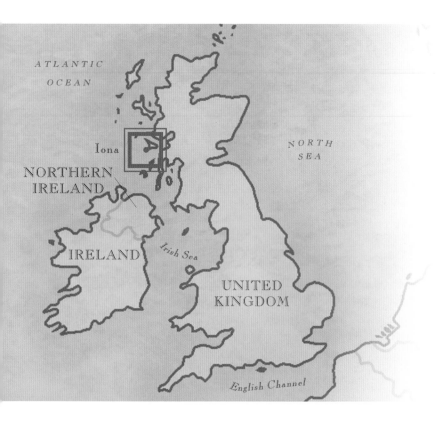

ATLANTIC
OCEAN

Iona

NORTHERN
IRELAND

IRELAND

Irish Sea

NORTH
SEA

UNITED
KINGDOM

English Channel

Iona, Scotland

It was 563 CE when a priest named Columba set sail from Ireland with 12 monastic brothers on a mission to Scotland. Columba had become involved in a conflict over the ownership of a psalter manuscript that had led to a battle in which many people died. Out of guilt and wishing to do penance, he decided to exile himself from his homeland and travel to the land of the Picts, where he intended to convert as many souls to Christianity as had died in the battle that he felt he had caused.

The 13 monks in Scotland first arrived at Southend, on the southern tip of the Kintyre peninsula. Moving northwards, Columba made contact with the Picts and was granted land on the island of Iona, a tiny speck just 1.6 km (1 mile) wide and 5.6 km (3½ miles) long, lying just off the western tip of the island of Mull. Columba established a monastic community on Iona, initiating the building of an abbey, and this religious centre, dedicated to the training of missionary priests, soon became the base for his evangelical work.

THE CREATION OF THE BOOK OF KELLS

Columba travelled to many parts of Scotland, working to reconcile the disparate warring tribes of the 6th century. He gained a reputation as both a capable politician and a fervent evangelical priest, securing the trust of many of the Pictish leaders who ruled Scotland. He also established a number of churches in the Hebrides, and his proselytizing work was to be carried on by monks who travelled throughout Europe, establishing Christian communities as far away as Switzerland.

Columba was a cultured man and much of the monks' work at Iona focused on the

Right Iona Abbey, with the Island of Mull in the background, is still a functioning Christian community and retreat centre. The peaceful and remote situation of the abbey is highly conducive to prayer and meditation.

IONA AS A SPIRITUAL HOME

Iona Abbey became a focus of worship for the Scottish people, and particularly for Scottish royalty. Over the years kings and tribal leaders of Scotland, as well as kings of Ireland, Norway and France, have been buried in the grounds of Iona Abbey. They include King Kenneth I, Donald II and III, Malcolm I and Duncan I, who was killed – as told in Shakespeare's play – by Macbeth (also believed to have been buried here).

Present-day pilgrims approach the island by ferry from Mull and pass the Celtic cross of St Martin and a copy of the cross of St John on their approach to the remarkable stone-built abbey (the original Celtic cross of St John, now restored, stands in the abbey museum). Significantly renovated over the past 70 years, the abbey now boasts beautiful cloisters with freshly carved columns. Many worshippers attend the regular services that take place there throughout the day and bear witness to the faith and achievements of the man who sailed here more than 1,400 years ago to clear his conscience. St Columba is buried in the abbey that he founded.

translation and transcribing of the Gospels and other religious texts. It is thought that Columba personally transcribed around 300 books in his lifetime, as well as being the author of a number of hymns.

Iona – and in particular Columba – has become inextricably bound up with the monks' achievement in creating the Book of Kells. This remarkable document (sometimes also known as the Book of Columba) is an ornately illuminated and beautifully scripted Latin version of the four Gospels, together with other relevant writings. Comprising some 340 vellum pages

or folios, the book is believed by some to have been initiated or at least inspired by Columba, although other experts see the Book of Kells as one of a number of illuminated sacred Gospels. Although it was never fully completed, there are a number of theories about how much of the work had been carried out when it left Iona in around 800, in order to protect it from the growing threat of Viking invaders. As proof of the reality of this threat, in the year 806 a Viking raiding party killed every monk they could find at the abbey and was to return a number of times in the years that followed.

The text ended up in a Columban monastery in Kells, in present-day County Meath in Ireland, from where it gained its name. During the 17th century the Book of Kells became the property of Trinity College Library in Dublin, where it has remained – except for occasional exhibitions – to this day. The preservation of the book has now become a continuous task although, with improvements in scanning technologies, it has now become possible to create digital versions of the book for those who wish to appreciate the workmanship and artistry of the early fathers.

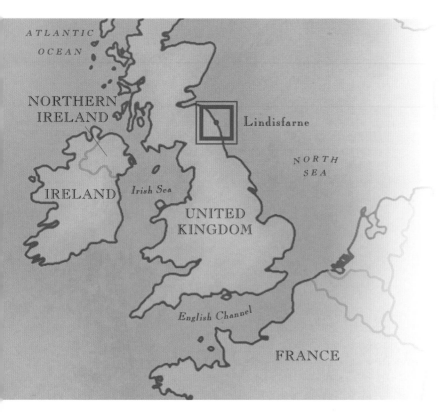

Lindisfarne, Northumberland

When King Oswald needed an evangelical leader to reconvert the pagans of Northumberland, he called on Aidan, an Irish-born monk who was then living at Iona Abbey. Oswald had spent time on Iona island as king-in-exile and, following his baptism in 634, decided to draw on the Celtic form of Christianity, rather than the more Roman culture of the English monasteries. It was 635 when Aidan arrived in England with a small band of monks and chose the island now known as Lindisfarne to be his diocese and the home of his new monastery.

Supported by King Oswald, who often acted as translator for the Irish-speaking monks, Aidan and his gentle form of Christianity quickly garnered many new adherents. An inspirational and patient man, he would travel around the villages of Northumberland simply talking about Christianity with the ordinary people he met.

AIDAN'S MANTLE PASSES TO CUTHBERT

Soon stories of Aidan's compassionate acts spread. One legend told of Aidan being given a horse by Oswald and his deciding to pass it on to a beggar, as he preferred to travel on foot. When Oswald died in 642 he was succeeded by Oswine of Deira, who continued the close friendship with Aidan until the new king was murdered in 651. Aidan was to die of illness just 12 days later, leaning against the wall of a local church. He had been Bishop at Lindisfarne for 17 years.

At the time Aidan died, a young man named Cuthbert, who was then living in Northumberland, had a vision of Lindisfarne's bishop 'flying to heaven'. However, Cuthbert did not act on this experience for a number of years, opting instead for the life of a soldier. Nevertheless he eventually became a great missionary, travelling the country and converting many to Christianity. In around 676 Cuthbert ended up living as a religious hermit on one of the Farne Islands, close to Lindisfarne. There he welcomed those who came in search of inspiration and blessing, and even washed their feet, as the Samaritan had done for Jesus Christ. The poor, penitent monk had a love of nature, and particularly of the sea birds that he saw each day from his cell. In 684 he was asked to become abbot of the monastery on Lindisfarne and reluctantly left his solitude. He died just two years later, greatly loved by all those whose lives he had touched. Two years after his burial it was discovered that his body had not decayed in the ground.

In 875 Vikings took hold of Lindisfarne and the monks left the island with Cuthbert's body. They wandered for seven years before settling at Chester-le-Street. Cuthbert's remains were moved again following further Danish invasions, this time to Ripon. Finally Lindisfarne's most famous saint came to rest in Durham in 995, where the cathedral that bears his name was built to enshrine him. Despite a number of disturbances, some of his relics remain there.

THE LINDISFARNE GOSPELS

Soon after Cuthbert's death, work on the Lindisfarne Gospels was started by a monk named Eadfrith, in his honour. They are a beautiful and decoratively illuminated version of the four Gospels in Latin, and were once covered by an ornate metal case made by a hermit monk named Billfrith. This was stolen during the first Viking raids of the late 8th century, but the pages survived, and were removed from Lindisfarne to a safer home and eventually found their way to Durham. In the 10th century a monk named Aldfrith (or Aldred) added a 'gloss' to the text of the Lindisfarne Gospels. This gloss is an Old English translation inserted in the lines between the Latin, and is now the oldest surviving Anglo-Saxon version of the Gospels. Since then the Lindisfarne Gospels have survived the ravages of the centuries and are now housed in the British Museum in London.

LINDISFARNE TODAY

A Tudor castle is now the dominant structure on Lindisfarne, while the priory is just a group of ruined, yet atmospheric stone structures – a memory of a time when Celtic Christianity flourished throughout northern England. Today the wind-blown island of Lindisfarne welcomes pilgrims from the Northumberland mainland across a narrow causeway that is submerged twice a day by the tides. Despite warnings, many people are caught out by the fast-moving waters, and enforced days and nights on the island are not a rarity. Perhaps in this way they receive a more vivid impression of the monastic life of St Aidan, St Cuthbert and their brothers.

Below *This aerial view shows the ruins of Lindisfarne Priory in the foreground. In the distance, on top of a small rock crag, is Lindisfarne's Tudor castle.*

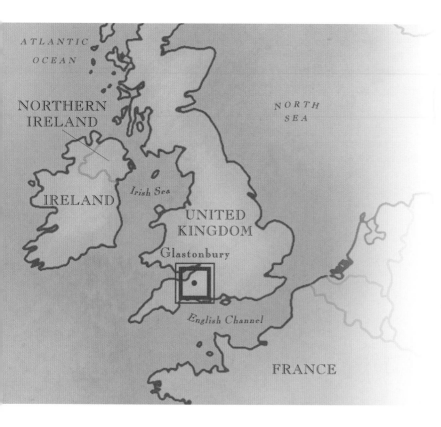

On the map: ATLANTIC OCEAN · NORTHERN IRELAND · NORTH SEA · IRELAND · Irish Sea · UNITED KINGDOM · Glastonbury · English Channel · FRANCE

Glastonbury, Somerset

Glastonbury's role in the history and mythology of the British Isles is unique. As well as being an important centre of pagan worship, the site has been linked with Christianity since the 1st century CE when stories emerged about the young Jesus visiting the area. Its place in the historical development of the Christian Church in Britain is crucial, and the combination of these influences with the potent legends of King Arthur and the Island of Avalon make Glastonbury an enduring place of contemplation and exploration.

Staring at the ruined remains of Glastonbury Abbey in Somerset today, it may be hard to believe there were times during its history when the Christian abbey complex was the richest and most important religious community in England – more important even than London's Westminster Abbey. And yet Glastonbury Abbey's story is a long and winding series of progresses and setbacks covering all of Christianity's two thousand years.

HISTORY AND DEVELOPMENT OF THE ABBEY
Indeed, Glastonbury's religious significance dates back to the earliest Christian times and the stories of Joseph of Arimathea's arrival in England after Jesus' death, bringing with him the Holy Grail – the cup with which Jesus established the ritual of the Communion at the Last Supper. It was also believed that Joseph had used the vessel to catch the blood from Jesus' wounds as he was dying on the cross. Why Joseph had brought the precious object to Glastonbury, or even England, is unclear, but may be traced to an even earlier legend.

It is a story held dear by some that Joseph of Arimathea – a merchant in metals and the uncle of Mary, Jesus' mother – had already taken the young Jesus to England on one of his trading trips involving tin and lead mining, which were then prevalent commodities in the West Country. For the young Jesus, however, this journey may have been one of inspiration and initiation, and some versions of the legend even report that he and Joseph built a small church. While it may seem improbable, the story is enshrined in the words of William Blake's famous hymn 'Jerusalem' in which the visionary author asks: 'And did those feet, in ancient times, walk upon England's pastures green?'

Joseph of Arimathea's return to Glastonbury in 63 CE, 30 years after Jesus' death, led to a meeting with the local leader Arviragus and the granting of 'twelve hides of land'. It was on this land that the first simple monastery was built, forming the initial centre of Christian evangelism in England: the notion that Glastonbury was the New Jerusalem had taken root in English myth, and for some (including William Blake) this idea never completely died.

The establishment of the first church and its surrounding community by Joseph of Arimathea was enough to carry the site through its early centuries – a time that saw the departure of the Romans and the arrival of the Saxons. It was not until the early 8th century that the Saxon King Ine of Wessex captured Somerset and took hold of Glastonbury. As a converted Christian, Ine decided to build the first stone church, the foundations of which still form the west end of the abbey nave. His commitment to the Christian community at Glastonbury substantially increased the church's wealth. The abbey took further steps forward in the 10th century under Dunstan, the Abbot of Glastonbury, with the lengthening of Ine's church and the building of new cloisters. In 960 Dunstan also became Archbishop of Canterbury – effectively head of the Christian Church in England. In 968, confirming Glastonbury's importance in the country's ritual life, King Edmund was buried at the abbey.

However, with the arrival of the Normans in 1066, Glastonbury came under threat. Its wealth and strength could not defend it from

'The notion that Glastonbury was the New Jerusalem had taken root in English myth.'

Left *The terracing on Glastonbury Tor is believed to form a maze, or labyrinth, which can be walked as part of a spiritual initiation into the energies of Avalon.*

the invasion and it was taken over by the first Norman abbot, Turstin. While his rule was ruthless towards the existing Christian community, he was responsible for great building works. From 1077 onwards the old church was demolished and an entirely new, Romanesque structure erected in its place. But Turstin was dismissed after his soldiers killed monks at the high altar, and his building works were destroyed in 1100 to make way for another church initiated by the new abbot, Herlewin, and completed in 1118. With the arrival of Abbot Henry of Blois in 1125, further key buildings were added: the cloisters, bell tower, chapter house, refectory, infirmary, outer gate, brewery and stables. Most of these survived a fire in 1184 that consumed the abbey and much of the old church, along with its religious treasures.

The struggle for control of the abbey's wealth and position in the Church continued until 1539, when King Henry VIII's Dissolution of the Monasteries witnessed the abbey's ransacking for the benefit of the King's treasury, and the merciless hanging of Abbot Whiting from the tower on top of Glastonbury Tor. The abbey would never again be a Christian community.

While the abbey has remained the key location in Glastonbury's Christian heritage, there are other features of the town and its surrounding landscape that still hold spiritual significance for many people whose sense of worship extends beyond the orthodox. Of these the Tor, Wearyall Hill and Chalice Well are the most important, and together they continue to provide a realm of spiritual experience that makes Glastonbury one of the most important living sacred sites in the British Isles.

GLASTONBURY TOR

Glastonbury's most famous topographical landmark is Glastonbury Tor. A 150 m (500 ft) -high hill, on which is perched an 18 m (60 ft) church tower dedicated to St Michael, the tor's shape seems to be an intriguing blend of the natural and the man-made. The highest point for many miles around, the hill dominates the landscape and its strange shape, with its apparent terracing, has been the subject of much study. Many experts now believe that this massive mound was worked on by early humans over a long period at a similar time to the erection of Stonehenge. One possible purpose of the earth-workings was to create a massive, walkable labyrinth on the whole hill; more precisely, some experts argue, the entire tor has been turned into a ritualized version of a 'Cretan maze', with the aim of providing seekers with a powerful experience of union with the energies present at the place. Even more dramatic versions of the theory suggest that the hill is a gate into other worlds and that some people have actually disappeared on the tor.

Also at the heart of myths about the tor is the idea that the hill is actually the Island of Avalon at the centre of the Arthurian legends, where once the sea lapped across the marshes where the Somerset Levels now extend for many miles. At one time the tor was called Ynys-witrin, the Island of Glass: surrounded by waters, it would have looked very much like an island. In Celtic legend it was the demi-god Avalloc, or Avallach, who ruled the Underworld and the name of Avalon is believed to derive from his persona. Another name for the Lord of the Underworld was Gwyn ap Nudd, and the tor was believed to be his home and a place where the fairy folk dwelt.

CHALICE WELL AND WEARYALL HILL

Another important legend in Joseph of Arimathea's story tells of the burial of the Holy Grail at a place believed to be an entrance to the Underworld, close to the foot of Glastonbury Tor. As soon as it was buried, a spring appeared and has continued to flow ever since. This place is now a retreat and sanctuary called Chalice Well, to which many

thousands of pilgrims still come annually in search of inspiration, peace and healing from the ever-flowing waters.

Joseph's return with the Holy Grail was accompanied by a further miraculous event. After his boat landed in the marshes near Glastonbury, Joseph is believed to have planted his staff – grown from the crown of thorns that Jesus wore on the cross – into the ground on Wearyall Hill. The staff took root immediately and by the next morning had put forth flowers. Even more unusually, the tree blossomed not once but twice a year, with its second flowering at Christmas time. This original tree grew unharmed until it was cut down by Oliver Cromwell's army during the English Civil War. Even so, a number of thorn trees in the area are believed to have grown from cuttings of the original hawthorn that Joseph brought from Jerusalem.

THE ISLE OF AVALON?

It was during rebuilding work at the abbey in 1191 that the tombs of King Arthur and Queen Guinevere were discovered in the cemetery, together with a lead cross with the Latin inscription *Hic iacet sepultus inclitus rex arturius in insula avalonia*: 'Here lies buried the renowned King Arthur in the Isle of Avalon'. Although some experts doubt the veracity of the find – seeing it as a possible strategy to increase the abbey's importance – for many people this discovery confirmed the link between King Arthur and Glastonbury as the Island of Avalon.

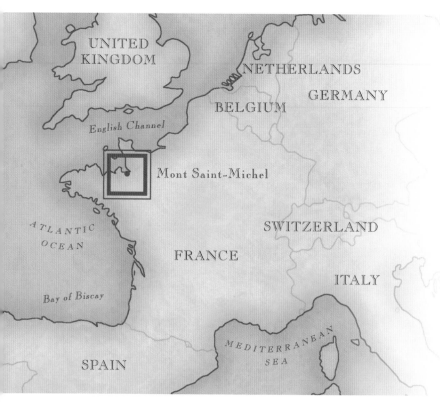

Mont Saint-Michel, France

Mont Saint-Michel is sometimes called the 'Wonder of the Western World' – a title it earned in medieval times when the sight of its striking outline greeting pilgrims and visitors was as precious as a glimpse of Jerusalem. It is one of a number of granite or granulite outcrops that have survived the sea's erosion, which washed away surrounding land. The mount now stands in a huge bay where the River Cousenon meets the sea, and where Brittany and Normandy once argued over the small island's ownership.

Once a tidal island, cut off from the world twice a day by a sea that can sometimes rise 14 m (46 ft) in one tide, Mont Saint-Michel has undergone modernization that has brought a permanent causeway for visitors and pilgrims. Those who still attempt to cross the sands from the coast can expect the twin dangers of quicksand and incoming waters, whose speed was described by author Victor Hugo as that of a horse's gallop. Although there are plans to build a bridge to update the permanent causeway, there are adventurous souls who still lose their lives here each year.

HISTORY OF THE MOUNT
Once called Mont Tombe, the mount was renamed and rededicated in the 8th century CE when Bishop Aubert of Avranches received a vision of the Archangel Michael, in which he was told to build a church on the mount. Aubert at first tried to ignore the request, but further apparitions persuaded him. In one version of the story the Archangel Michael used his finger to burn a hole in Aubert's head as a more effective means of convincing the disobedient priest.

Aubert's first church on the mount was consecrated on 16 October 709 and is one of the great symbols of early medieval worship of St Michael in the Western world. To the people of Aubert's time, the significance of St Michael's role – as the weigher of souls following death, as the protector from demons of those who had earned their place in heaven, and as guardian of the gates – would not have been lost. His association with mountain summits added a further link to this sea-bound peak.

In 966 a community of Benedictine monks arrived at the request of the Duke of Normandy and established Mont Saint-Michel as a place of isolation and contemplation. In the 11th century the building of the first Romanesque abbey began. The Italian architect William de Volpiano took the bold step of siting the transept crossing on the very summit of the mount. To compensate for this dramatic placing, it was necessary to build numerous supporting structures to bear the abbey's weight – most of which became crypts and chapels. At the same time the first dedicated monastery buildings were installed against the north wall of the abbey, and these were further extended in the following century with the flourishing of the monastic community.

RISE, FALL AND RECOVERY
At its spiritual height, Mont Saint-Michel was considered one of the most important pilgrimage destinations in Europe, along with Santiago de Compostela (see pages 42–43) and Rome (see pages 16–17). In addition, further linked communities were established, such as the English one at St Michael's Mount in Cornwall.

The Gothic parts of the structure that form today's striking silhouette were initiated in the 13th century after the King of France,

'The abbey is sometimes referred to as the Merveille – or "marvel".'

Philip Augustus, captured Normandy and offered Abbot Jourdain funds to improve the abbey. The *Merveille* – or 'marvel', as the abbey is sometimes known – was given two three-storey additions and crowned by a cloister and refectory. These remarkable structures are still breathtaking, both from within and without, and mark the high point in Mont Saint-Michel's architectural development.

Religious practice dwindled during the Reformation and gradually the community diminished. By the time of the French Revolution the abbey was closed and the mount requisitioned as an Alcatraz-like prison for clerics and celebrity members of the bourgeoisie. During the 19th century a campaign, led by the author Victor Hugo and other luminaries, resulted in the closing of the prison and the restoration of Mont Saint-Michel's status as a French national treasure. In 1874 it was declared a historic monument and has been protected ever since. The abbey is now topped by a gold-leaf-covered sculpture of its inspirer: the Archangel Michael.

Left The striking outline of Mont Saint-Michel has been enhanced over centuries by increasingly 'aspiring' structures that seem to reach up to receive the blessings of God and St Michael.

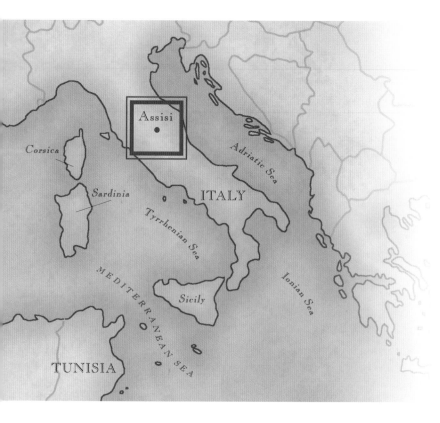

Assisi, Italy

The north Italian town of Assisi is bound up in popular imagination with St Francis, the wandering monk whose love of nature and life of poverty inspired a religious movement that threatened to overshadow the Roman Catholic church. Some 145 km (90 miles) north of Rome, set in the rolling hills of Umbria, Assisi was felt to be a place of special religious significance long before the birth of St Francis.

The Etruscans worshipped at a holy spring at 'Assisium' as far back as the 8th or 9th century BCE, and were followed in their reverence for the place by the Romans, who built a temple to the goddess Minerva in the 1st century BCE. In early Christian times the Minervan sanctuary was destroyed to make way for the first of a series of churches. Around this time, however, the holy spring seems to have stopped flowing.

THE CONVERSION OF FRANCIS

When Francesco (Francis) di Bernadone was born in Assisi in 1182 CE (some say 1181) the town was involved in conflicts with nearby Perugia, which were to play a part in his personal journey. Known as a bookish, yet headstrong youth, Francis dreamed of being a great soldier for Assisi, but a series of mystical experiences led him to abandon this idea and seek out a different life.

Following a pilgrimage to Rome, where he begged on behalf of the poor, he had an experience in the Church of St Damiano near Assisi that was to change his life for ever. According to accounts of his life, Francis was praying before an icon of Christ crucified when the image of Jesus started to speak, telling him that he should repair the church that lay in ruins. At first he took the request literally, selling his horse along with some of

Right The Umbrian hills where Francis once walked still attract those who are inspired by the saint's life. The basilica complex sits majestically at the north-west corner of the hill town of Assisi.

his father's cloth and giving money to the priest of the local church for its rebuilding. His father was furious, but Francis decided to cut himself off from any patrimony that he might receive and became a beggar travelling around the Assisi area helping to rebuild a number of churches.

While listening to a sermon from Matthew's Gospel in 1209, Francis was inspired to follow a life of apostolic poverty and spiritual repentance. He was soon joined by others and, with ten 'brothers', travelled to Rome to ask Pope Innocent III whether he could establish his own order. The Pope at first refused, but a dream the following night showed a poor man rebuilding Christ's church, and Francis was recalled and the decision reversed. The Franciscan order soon flourished under Francis' inspirational example and more and more of his peers, including the sons of noblemen, began to join him. A young woman named Clare (later to be known as Clare of Assisi) was also inspired by Francis and began her own religious order, known as the 'Poor Clares'.

FRANCIS' LOVE OF NATURE

Francis, who was never ordained as a priest, wandered the hills around Assisi, glorying in nature's creation. At the same time he became famous both for his love of animals and for his exhortations to them to worship God. A famous story tells of his sermon to a flock of birds, encouraging them to express their love of the Creator. His love of nature and his simple approach to life represented a challenge to the Church and the papacy, which had become associated with high living and hypocrisy.

In 1224, during a Lenten fast, Francis was visited by a six-winged angel on a cross and given the five wounds of Christ to his hands, feet and torso. He never spoke publicly of the event during his life, even though he suffered great pain as a result, right up to his death in 1226. This strange, painful blessing was the first example of stigmata in the history of the Christian Church.

After his death, the Basilica of St Francis was built in Assisi between 1228 and 1253, a remarkably rapid building achievement that

Above The nave of the Upper Church at St Francis' Basilica contains scenes from the life of St Francis, created by Giotto and his circle.

many have taken to demonstrate the local people's love and devotion for their saint. Francis' uncorrupted body was installed in the basilica; and the church, along with the adjacent friary, soon became a significant pilgrimage site. Many great artists, including Giotto di Bondone, were asked to paint scenes from Francis' life and from the events of the Gospels. A number of sublime works have survived the ravages of time and are still marvelled at for their spontaneous portrayals of Francis' experiences. Pilgrims continue to come for worship and retreat in this beautiful area, often commenting on the peaceful atmosphere of the Umbrian hills, where Francis once walked.

Holy Trinity, St Sergius Lavra, Russia

In the Russian Orthodox tradition a lavra *was originally a collection of monastic cells, although it later came to be the name for the most revered churches in Orthodoxy. The Troitse-Sergiyeva Lavra – or Holy Trinity, St Sergius Lavra – was one of the earliest monastic communities in Russia and is still considered the spiritual centre of the Russian Orthodox Church.*

The monastery is 88 km (55 miles) north-east of Moscow in the town of Sergiev Posad, also formerly known as Zagorsk. It was founded in 1345 by Sergius of Radonezh, an early monk and spiritual teacher who constructed a wooden church to honour the Holy Trinity on Makovets Hill. Contemporary accounts of Sergius' life and the lives of his adherents provide a detailed picture of early monastic life.

ST SERGIUS' HERITAGE

In 1355 Sergius defined a 'charter' for monasteries and monastic life, which defined the physical and practical requirements of such communities and included the need for a kitchen, bakery, refectory and a number of other buildings. This model was replicated throughout Russia, with as many as 400 cloisters being built to house monastic communities, including the well-known Kirilov, Simonov and Solovetsky monasteries.

St Sergius was not simply a hermetic monk, but was willing to become involved in the defence of his wider community. When the Tartars threatened his country in 1380, Sergius gave a special blessing for the Russian military leader Dmitri Donskoi and sent two of his monks to join the forces at the Battle of Kulikovo. One died in the battle and it was a sign of worse things to come: a group of Tartars attacked the monastery in 1408 and it was severely damaged by fire.

Following his death, Sergius was canonized and made the patron saint of Russia in 1422. In the same year construction of the church of the Holy Trinity began, the work being undertaken by a group of Serbian monks who had sheltered in the monastery following the Battle of Kosovo. The church was completed the next year and became home to St Sergius' relics, which can still be seen today. Andrei Rublev and Daniil Chyorny, the great medieval icon painters, were commissioned to decorate the new building with frescoes. Rublev's stunning icon image of the Trinity is still the focal point of worship for the many thousands who travel to the site each year.

THE HOLY TRINITY BECOMES A *LAVRA*

Between 1540 and 1550 the small monastery and its architectural ensemble was expanded to become a structure more like a castle. High rock walls with 12 towers were built around the perimeter of the monastery buildings, and when the Polish siege of 1608–10 took hold, the monks were able to withstand the onslaught. In 1744 the monastery gained the status of a *lavra* within the Russian and Ukrainian Orthodox Churches: it was only the second monastery

'In 1744 the monastery gained the status of a lavra *within the Russian and Ukrainian Orthodox Churches: it was only the second monastery to attain this honour.'*

to attain this honour, the first being the Kievo-Pecherskava Lavra in Kiev in the 16th century. This status provided the community with a stability and wealth that it was able to build on over the centuries. As well as becoming a highly respected religious school, the complex became the first-choice location when Moscow's elite wished to have important events celebrated, and many princes and princesses were baptised there. It also amassed a large collection of relics, artworks and scared texts, which, at the start of the 20th century, made it the wealthiest monastery in Russia.

SURVIVING THE COMMUNIST ERA

With the October Revolution of 1917, however, everything changed. The famous priest and mathematician Pavel Florensky, who had studied at the monastery and was the most articulate spiritual voice of his generation, attempted to protect the sacred artefacts, but was unable to fully resist the new communist regime. Many of the monastery's treasures were stolen, dispersed and never seen again. Florensky is thought to have been executed in 1937 for refusing to disclose the whereabouts of St Sergius' relics.

Some parts of the *lavra* became museums, which secured their future to some extent, but there were times when all the structures of the monastery were threatened with demolition. Some people believe that their fate was saved by the strange religious conversion to Orthodoxy that Stalin underwent during the Second World War. On 16 April 1946 the *lavra's* Cathedral of the Assumption, built by Ivan the Terrible in the 16th century, held its first divine service since the communists closed the monastery. Whether this may be considered a miracle of St Sergius, the father of 'Holy Russia', remains an open question.

Right *Part of the St Sergius Lavra, the 16th-century Cathedral of the Assumption has emerged from Communism's shadow to become an important place of worship again.*

Mount Athos, Greece

The Greek myth of the Gigantomachia, or 'war of the giants', tells how Athos was one of the giants (or Gigantes) who challenged the gods to battle. In the conflict Athos aimed a huge rock at Poseidon, which missed its target and fell into the Aegean Sea, creating Mount Athos. Another version of the story credits Poseidon with burying Athos under the rock that forms the peninsula. Whatever its origins, the result is that Mount Athos is both the name of the mountain and that of the peninsula on which the mountain stands.

The Mount Athos peninsula is the eastern part of the much larger Chalkidiki peninsula in Greece, which projects in a south-easterly direction into the Aegean Sea and is around 60 km (37 miles) long and 6–12 km (3¾–7½ miles) wide. The eponymous mountain is located towards the furthest, south-eastern tip of the peninsula and its heavily forested slopes rise steeply to the 2,033 m (6,670 ft) summit.

A MONASTIC STATE

The status of Mount Athos within Greece – indeed, within Europe – is unique. The 400 sq km (155 sq mile) peninsula which is known as the 'Autonomous Monastic State of the Holy Mountain', forms a separate 'theocratic' state within the overall sovereignty of the Republic of Greece. Spiritually, the entire peninsula is under the jurisdiction of the 'Ecumenical Patriarchate of Constantinople' – the leadership of the Christian Orthodox Church.

There are 20 monasteries on Mount Athos and each has a place in the 'Athonite hierarchy' – the order of importance. Of these, 17 monasteries are Greek, while three belong to the Orthodox tradition of other countries. In descending importance they are: Megísti Lávra, Vatopédi, Iviron (Georgian), Chilandariou (Serbian), Dionysiou, Koutloumousiou, Pantokratoros, Xiropotamou, Zografou (Bulgarian), Dochiariou, Karakalou, Filotheou, Simonos Petra, Agiou Pavlou, Stavronikita, Ksenofondos, Osiou Grigoriou, Esfigmenou, Agiou Panteleimonos and Konstamonitou.

Each monastery has an abbot, or *igoumenos*, who is elected by his own brotherhood and who leads the monastery, as its spiritual lord and father, until he dies. On the peninsula there are other buildings, such as hermitages, retreats, cells and cloisters, but all are linked to one of the monasteries that oversee their care and repair.

OUR LADY'S GARDEN

One of the more controversial aspects of the Mount Athos peninsula is its attitude to women, who are completely banned from setting foot on any part of the land. This rule was instituted in the belief that it helped the male monks avoid any problems of sexual temptation. The rule, though, is believed to extend to all female animals. There may be an exemption for chickens, however, since their egg yolks are used in the composition of the tempera paint employed by the monks in their painting of icons.

There is a more traditional explanation for the exclusion of women from Mount Athos. It is said that after Jesus Christ's crucifixion, his mother Mary and John the Evangelist were travelling from Joppa to Cyprus, when they were forced off course by poor weather and came to land at Athos. Overwhelmed by the beauty of the place, Mary is said to have prayed to her Son, asking Him to preserve this place as her own garden. A voice spoke, telling Mary that this would be her inheritance: a paradise and a haven for those seeking salvation. From then on Mount Athos was consecrated as Our Lady's Garden, and since the time when monks first formed their communities here, all women were excluded. This was to be Mary's garden alone, and it continues to be so, despite attempts by the European Parliament to change the situation.

Left *The Simonos Petra monastery is the 13th most important in the hierarchy of 20 on Mount Athos. It was founded in the 14th century by St Simon of the Eastern Orthodox Church.*

THE PILGRIM'S PRAYER

Although monks were on Athos from the 4th or 5th century CE, of the 20 monasteries still in existence today the earliest date back to the 9th and 10th centuries. Despite a history of conflicts and some invasions, the peninsula now enjoys a period of relative stability. The two thousand or so monks who live on Mount Athos today all adhere to the relatively strict religious practices of the Eastern Orthodox Church. The great majority of their day is taken up with prayer and work in the service of their community. Fasting and strict obedience to the Spiritual Fathers of the monasteries is an essential aspect of monastic life, and for many the additional benefits of absolute solitude lead them to become hermits. At the heart of the spiritual practice, however, is prayer and in particular the Jesus Prayer, also known as the Pilgrim's Prayer. Although it appears in slightly different versions, it is often expressed in the words: 'Lord have mercy on us, Christ have mercy on us'. Constant repetition of this prayer is said to lead to 'prayer of the heart' – a state in which the practitioner's heart is in constant contact with the Divine.

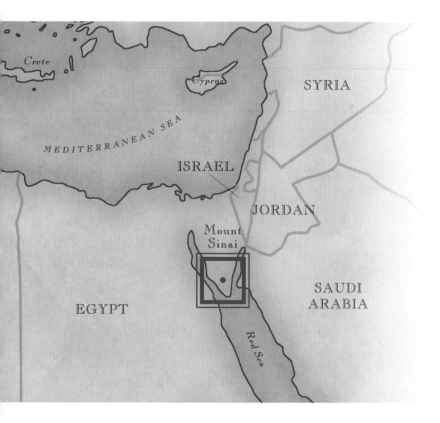

St Catherine's Monastery, Mount Sinai

In keeping with the traditions of the Orthodox Church, St Catherine's Monastery on Mount Sinai is a centre for the archiving of many religious relics and sacred texts. The library is second only to the Vatican in its extensive collection of codices and manuscripts. The monastery also holds some remarkable early icons. The most famous of these is the 7th-century Pantokrator of Sinai – *regarded by some as the world's most moving portrayal of Jesus.*

Before he became leader of the Israelites, Moses fled Egypt and went to live with Jethro close to Mount Sinai, where he would later receive the Ten Commandments. It was there, while he was shepherding Jethro's flocks of sheep, that Moses discovered the burning bush – a green leafy plant that was on fire without being consumed by the flames.

MOSES' MISSION

Moses heard God's voice, speaking from the bush, saying (according to Exodus): 'I am your father's God, the God of Abraham, the God of Isaac and the God of Jacob.' He commanded Moses to remove his sandals, as he was standing on Holy Land. Moses was then told that God had heard the Israelites' pleas for an end to their suffering and that Moses should go to the Pharaoh and demand their freedom from enslavement, so that he could lead them to a Promised Land 'flowing with milk and honey'.

At first Moses was unsure how to respond, not knowing how he would convince the Pharaoh, but God showed him three signs: his staff turned into a serpent; his hand became leprous, but was miraculously cured;

and he was told that he would be able to turn water into blood. All three of these signs he would be able to demonstrate before Pharaoh. God also told Moses that He would be with him. With this inspiration, and with the knowledge of God's presence and support, Moses was able to embark on the mission to free his people.

FROM SHRINE TO MONASTERY

The building of a shrine at the place of such religious importance for the Jewish and Christian peoples was a natural step – particularly as it seemed that the bush, although no longer burning, was very much alive. The significance of Mount Sinai in Moses' and the Israelites' lives added to the spiritual power of the place. A Spanish pilgrim from around the 4th century CE named Egeria, who travelled extensively in the Holy Land, reported how a church had been built beside the Burning Bush, which at that time was still growing verdantly. This first church, the Chapel of the Burning Bush, was built by Helena, mother of the Emperor Constantine I, establishing its connection to the eastern branch of Christianity.

The monastery at Mount Sinai was founded in 527 by the Emperor Justinian and his wife Theodora, around the Chapel of the Burning Bush, and the main buildings were completed between 548 and 565. Although it is usually called St Catherine's Monastery, its more accurate name is the Monastery of the Transfiguration. Its connection with the female saint came from the legend that the holy relics of St Catherine of Alexandria had been carried to Mount Sinai by angels. Catherine herself had been executed for her religious faith: the first attempt by placing her on a wheel, the second, fatal attempt by beheading. Monks did not find her remains on Mount Sinai until around 800, but her significance as an Egyptian in what was still a Muslim country gave the Christian monastery increased status and security.

The position of the monastery in Islamic lands was considerably strengthened by a Charter of Privileges, written by Muhammad in 623 after the monastery offered the Prophet asylum from his political enemies. Of the many tolerances outlined in the letter, one states that the Christians in the monastery should be left to worship without

interruption. The letter also implicitly acknowledges the common heritage of Jews, Christians and Muslims as 'people of the book'. Later, in the 10th or 11th century, possibly as part of an attempt to placate the local Islamic rulers, a Fatimid mosque was built within the walls of the monastery. Although many believe it has never been used by practising Muslims, partly because of its incorrect orientation relative to Mecca, the mosque remains (depending on the observer's perspective) a small symbol of interfaith dialogue or a demonstration of religious pragmatism.

In the time since monks have lived and survived within the high and protective walls of the monastery, they have been adherents of the Eastern Orthodox branch of Christianity. The abbot is also Archbishop of the whole 'Church of Sinai', which comprises St Catherine's monastery, the nearby monastery of Raithu and a number of other dependencies. The Archbishop is appointed by the Orthodox Patriarch of Jerusalem.

Above *The ancient monastery of St Catherine is nestled at the foot of Jebel Musa, or Mount Sinai, where Moses found the burning bush and later received the Ten Commandments.*

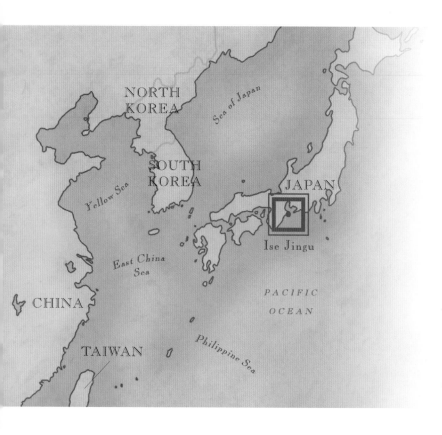

Ise Jingu Shrine, Japan

The Ise Jingu Shrine holds a special place in the spiritual life of Japan and of the Japanese people. It was the first great Shinto shrine, founded more than two thousand years ago by Yamatohime-no-mikoto, daughter of the Emperor Suinin, after a 20-year search for a permanent place of worship for the goddess Amaterasu Omikami. In Shinto history, Yamatohime's journey came to an end in the Mie Prefecture, when she heard the goddess' voice telling her that she wished to be venerated in Ise, close to the beauty of both mountains and sea.

The Ise Jingu Shrine (sometimes simply called the Jingu) is actually a shrine complex made up of more than a hundred separate shrines. The complex is divided into two distinct parts by a pilgrimage road some 4.8 km (3 miles) long. The inner shrine, or Naiku, is in the town of Uji and it is this part of the shrine that is dedicated to Amaterasu Omikami. The outer shrine, or Geku, is dedicated to a different Shinto deity named Toyouke no Omikami and is located in the town of Yamada.

THE RITUAL OF TRANSFERRING THE SHRINE

Although historians place the origins of the older Naiku as far back as the year 4 CE, evidence of the shrine's construction in its current form was first recorded in 690. This is also the first recognized date of a remarkable ritual process known as Shinkinen Sengu, or 'transferring the shrine', which takes place on a regular timescale. Every 20 years since this time (except for the period of warring states during the 15th and 16th centuries) the main part of the central shrine, the Kotaijingu, has been replaced by another

identical building on an adjacent plot. During the climactic ritual of Shinkinen Sengu, before the redundant shrine is taken down, sacred objects (including vestments and tools) are transferred from the old shrine to the new. The most important of these objects is the sacred eight-sided mirror, or *yatakagami*, of the sun goddess Amaterasu Omikami. Twenty years later the shrine is returned to the previous plot, as it perpetually alternates between east and west.

The process of building the new shrine reveals much about Shinto reverence for the natural world. By an interesting paradox, the new building requires the cutting and fashioning of a huge amount of fresh wood. Although the shrines are surrounded by the 5,500 ha (13,585 acres) of the sacred Kumano forest, timber was only ever cut from the special 'shrine forest' or *misomayama*. Since 1391, however, no timber for the new shrines has come from these forests, having been sourced elsewhere. But for the next Sengu ceremony in 2013, 20 per cent of the timber for the building will once again come from the 'shrine forests' – for the first time in more than seven hundred years.

'Shinto is an animistic religion, which focuses on the everyday, the present and the quality of people's connections with each other.'

USING AND REVERING THE NATURAL WORLD

The process of selecting the timber for the shrine is a long and painstaking one, and requires the advance identification of trees likely to provide the highest quality and greatest size of cedarwood, as required by the exacting designs of the shrine. The great doors to the shrine, for instance, require planks of cedar that are 1.2 m (4 ft) wide and completely without blemishes or imperfections. Some trees have been identified for use as far as two hundred years ahead. The cutting of trees is performed by three specially trained craftsmen, who work with axes to perform the ritual felling. At the end of the process the top of the tree is placed in the stump, as a symbol of reverence for the tree's gift to the people.

The Naiku is not the only part of the shrine complex that is renewed every 20 years. A number of other buildings are literally 're-placed', including the Uji bridge, which links the shrine to the opposite bank of the Isuzu River and provides access for pilgrims. Although many thousands of rituals are performed at the Ise Jingu every year, entrance to the Kotaijingu within the Naiku is restricted. Followers are permitted only to approach the four rows of tall wooden fences that protect the inner sanctum from being overlooked.

Shinto is an animistic religion, which focuses on the everyday, the present and the quality of people's connections with each other and with the natural world. The Ise Jingu shrines are the highest and most important expression of Shinto in Japanese culture, and reverence for the mysteries of their cycles and for the natural beauty of the place is still very strong.

Below This bridge in the inner Naiku shrine, passes over the waters of the Isuzu-Gawa river. The peaceful atmosphere reflects Shinto dedication to maintaining good relations with the natural world.

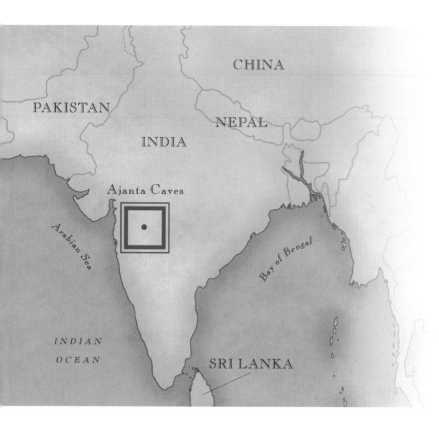

The Ajanta Caves, India

The Ajanta Caves are arranged around a horseshoe-shaped ravine close to the village of Ajintha, in the Aurangabad district of India's Maharashtra State. The 29 caves, cut into the basalt rock of the steep escarpment, have all been given identifying numbers by the ASI (Archaeological Survey of India). As well as revealing much about the development of Buddhist practice and monastic living in early India, the caves also display some of the most beautiful religious paintings and sculptures to have survived for two thousand years.

From careful study and excavation since the rediscovery of the caves in 1819, it has been possible to reconstruct a timeline for the original creation of the caves and the execution of the art contained within them.

PHASES OF CREATION

There are two main types of building here: *viharas*, which are halls of residence for monks, and *chaitya-grihas*, which are rooms for worship containing stupa monuments. It is now generally thought that the building work occurred in two main phases, which relate to the way in which Buddhism evolved in India.

The first group of caves, usually said to include caves 9, 10, 12 and 13 (as well as one known as 15A, which was only rediscovered in 1956), date from around the 2nd century BCE to the 1st or 2nd century CE. They are said to be part of the Hinayana or Sthaviravada phase of Buddhism. During this phase the Buddha was more normally enshrined in the form of a stupa (shrine) or mound, rather than in his bodily form. The Hinayana, or Lesser Vehicle, form of Buddhism was generally superseded by the less strict Mahayana, or Greater Vehicle, form, in which the Buddha was freely personified and worshipped in a number of ritualized poses, each expressing a different aspect of the Buddhahood.

The second phase of cave development at Ajanta has been a subject of differing opinions, but there seems to be some growing consensus around the idea that at least the majority of the caves of the Mahayana phase were created in the second half of the 5th century CE. The 25 caves are numbered 1–8, 11 and 14–29.

Building in both Hinayana and Mahayana phases involved the creation of *viharas* for the accommodation of monks and *chaitya-grihas* for worship. Externally the *viharas* vary tremendously, some being very simple, while others have ornate carved façades supported by columns. Internally, it is believed that shrines and other objects of worship were included in the *viharas*. In the later *chaitya-grihas* the Buddha is often portrayed in the *dharmachakrapravartana mudra* – the pose of the master dispensing teaching, or *dharma*.

Left *This detail from the* Mahajanaka Jataka *mural painting in Cave 1 shows King Mahajanaka on the right.*

CAVES 1 AND 2

Caves 1 and 2 are renowned for their artwork. Internally, Cave 1 is supported by 12 pillars, and at the rear is a shrine housing a seated image of the Buddha in the teaching pose. Each of the surrounding walls measures almost 12 m (40 ft) long and 6 m (20 ft) high. They carry ornate fresco-type images of scenes from the life of Gautama Buddha and from his former existences as a Bodhisattva – someone who willingly chooses to continue the cycle of death and rebirth, delaying full enlightenment for the sake of all other sentient beings. The paintings of Cave 2 also depict the Buddha's lifetimes and would have required of the monks that they learn and understand the lessons of the successive teachings from the episodes of his life.

ARTISTIC TECHNIQUES

For many years after their full rediscovery in the mid-19th century, the paintings in the Ajanta Caves were referred to as 'frescoes', identifying their technique with those of a number of Italian Renaissance painters who worked natural pigments into fresh, wet plaster. After much research, however, it has now been discovered that the technique employed at Ajanta is unique – not just within southern Asian traditions, but within world art. However, it is unfortunate that since the modern excavation of the caves many of the wall paintings have suffered significant decay and loss of colour and detail. As solid as the Ajanta Caves look, the fleeting beauty of their artwork may yet prove the impermanence of things.

Dogon Shrines, Mali

The Dogon people of Mali in West Africa have attracted attention from anthropologists all over the world for their unique animistic rituals and their extravagant cultural practices. Numbering between 300,000 and 400,000, their lives have changed considerably over the last century as their ancient rites have come under increasing scrutiny and suffered from the distorting effects of tourism. Nevertheless, the core of their spiritual world view remains intact.

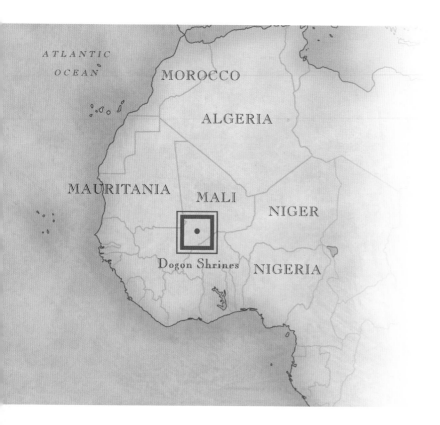

The land that forms the Dogon's world is a harsh environment dominated by a geological feature known as the Bandiagara escarpment. This sandstone cliff, sometimes as tall as 500 m (1,640 ft) and running for around 145 km (90 miles), divides the sandy plains of the south-east from the Bandiagara highlands in the north-west. Thirteen of the Dogon villages are focused around an area known as the Sanga, which lies east of the town of Bandiagara on the top side of the escarpment and includes the villages of Ogol-du-Haut and Ogol-du-Bas, which have been carefully studied by anthropologists.

DOGON CULTS

From studies of their lives, it has emerged that the Dogon people have three main cults: the Binu, the Awa and the Lebe. The Binu cult is sourced in the creation myth that talks about Nommo, the first human being. Nommo, who was created by the sky god Amma, proceeded to subdivide himself into four pairs of twins, all referred to as Nommo. When one of these twins rebelled against the will of the sky god, it became necessary to re-establish the cosmic order. Another Nommo

had to be sacrificed and his body parts were scattered to different parts of the world. Where the parts came to rest, shrines were built, which subsequently became places where ancestor worship of Nommo, spirit communication and agricultural sacrifice took place. These Binu shrines have remained an essential part of Dogon belief and religious practice and are overseen by a Binu priest.

The Awa cult is also concerned with the restoration of order to the spiritual realm following the death of the first Nommo. Its rituals are reserved for funerals and the anniversaries of deaths, and involve members dancing with the Dogon's carved wooden masks. The ceremonies are intended to guide souls of the dead to a peaceful resting place in the world of the ancestors, while maintaining their beneficent influence over their family line through a continued presence at the family altar.

The Lebe cult relates the Dogon people to the earth, the landscape and the source of their physical life, the earth god Lebe. The earth god is mediated through a chief priest, the Hogon, who oversees most of their

agricultural ceremonies. At night he is visited by Lebe, who appears in the form of a serpent and licks him clean, purifying his soul and preparing him for his role as mediator between two worlds.

AN EXTRA-TERRESTRIAL BELIEF SYSTEM

The Dogon have attracted particular interest – among both experts and lay people because of their extraordinary cosmology. While they were being studied by French anthropologist Marcel Griaule in the 1940s, it emerged that the Dogon's creation myth of the Nommo was founded on the belief that their ancestors had originally come from a star system many light years away. They told Griaule that the star known to Western astronomers had a twin 'white star', as well as a third star with a planet, from which the Nommo had originated. At this time the star known as Sirius B had only been speculated about (it would not be photographed until the 1970s) and was certainly not visible to the naked eye. The Dogons also said that the 'white star', Sirius B, was very heavy and made from a substance heavier than iron; it turned out to be a super-heavy 'white dwarf' star. The third star has not been detected.

The Dogon also seemed to be aware of the rings of Saturn and the moons of Jupiter, which again cannot be seen under normal conditions. The idea that the Dogon's ancestors lived on another planet many light years away understandably created a huge amount of controversy. There were many sceptics who thought that perhaps the Dogon's beliefs had been 'contaminated' by other cultures, or even by the anthropologists who were studying them. At the other end of the spectrum a number of cults grew up in Western culture around their extra-terrestrial belief system. Between the two were those for whom the world of the Dogon was possibly more complex than they could have imagined.

To some extent the controversy has obscured the beauty of a culture that seems to have kept its relationship to the Earth and the spirit world intact.

Below The priests of each Binu shrine maintain the sanctuary where the Dogon come to make contact with the spirits of mythic ancestors. The ostrich eggs placed atop the spires symbolize purity and fertility.

CHAPTER 5

SACRED STONES: STONE CIRCLES AND MEGALITHS

As we reach further back in time, we discover how little we know about the lives of our ancestors. All that we have to base our understandings on is the evidence they left behind: the artefacts of their lives, the objects they held sacred, the materials of their ritual lives. So why all the stone formations? It is possible the answer is simple: that stones are simply fragments, small chips off the old block of our own parent, Mother Earth. Our ancestors found pieces of their parent beneath their feet and raised them up towards the other world, the world of suns and moons and stars and spiritual parents of a different kind. As above, so below. The stones, they may have thought, have the power to link the world above to the world below, to mediate between the two and help bring heaven to Earth, and vice versa.

The variety of stone circles and other configurations to be found across northern Europe shows an extraordinary development in the ideas and capabilities of early humans. To uncover, fashion, move and erect the stones that make up some of these sites required extraordinary feats of strength, technology and faith. Early people must have believed in the power of the stones, in their ability to enhance their ritual behaviour. Without that belief, they would not have made such extreme efforts to create what are, in effect, the earliest temples.

Stonehenge, Wiltshire

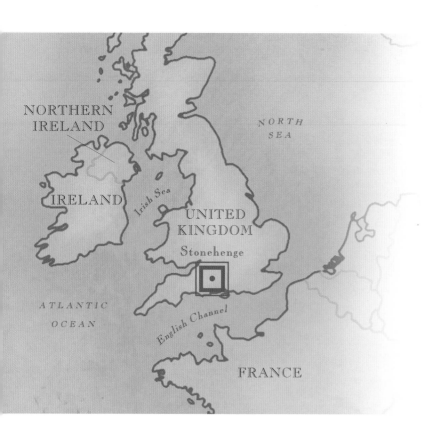

The Salisbury Plain area of England contains the most important megalithic monuments in the British Isles. The landscape here – for a long time part of the Kingdom of Wessex – is home to Stonehenge, Avebury (see pages 128–129), Woodhenge, the Cursus, the Amesbury Archer, a variety of barrows, earth workings and other sites of significance to early humans. Very little is known, however, of the people who lived and died in the times of these works and who devoted so much energy to building what might be considered the 'cathedrals' of their time.

Science has played an important role in the understanding of Stonehenge. Using modern techniques of excavation and radiocarbon dating, archaeologists have now established that the site was developed in a number of distinct phases.

PHASES OF CONSTRUCTION

Phase one, from 2950 to 2900 BCE, saw the creation of a large ring of 56 wooden posts, with a diameter of 97 m (320 ft). Just outside this were a ditch and a bank. Even at this early time, the ring appears to have had two main entrances: one directly to the south and another in the north-east.

The second phase of building occurred between 2900 and 2400 BCE and saw further timber posts put up in the central part of the circular enclosure. The original timber posts in the outer ring appear to have been removed during phase two, and some 25 of the post-holes filled with the results of human cremation, indicating a ritual function for the site and a commitment to the honouring of ancestors.

Construction of the third phase, which began around 2400 BCE and continued to

1900 BCE, focused on the introduction of stone into the Stonehenge complex. Modern archaeologists now break down this phase into a further six substages relating to the introduction of new elements. The first of these (3i) saw the digging of holes for up to 80 standing stones, laid out in two concentric crescents around the centre of the site; 43 of these 'bluestones', weighing around 4 tons each, are known to have originated in the Preseli Hills in Pembrokeshire, Wales, some 400 km (250 miles) away. How these enormous stones could have made such a journey 4,500 years ago remains an unsolved mystery. This third stage of Stonehenge's development also saw the arrival of the Heelstone.

Left During phase 3ii five giant trilithons were erected in the centre of the Stonehenge complex. Arranged in a horseshoe shape, they are open to receive the sun at the midsummer sunrise.

SOPHISTICATED TECHNIQUES

The next substage (3ii) saw the creation of a new ring of central stones to replace the 80 blue stones: 30 giant sarsen stones erected in a circle. What marked out this phase of building was the high level of craftsmanship employed in the preparation and working of the standing stones and their lintels. Techniques borrowed from woodworking, such as 'mortise-and-tenon' and 'tongue-and-groove' joints, meant that the structure was given permanence and stability as well as a high level of refinement. Even so, it is unclear whether the full circle, which would have required 74 stones, was ever completed.

Another ambitious development in this key phase was the building of the horseshoe crescent of five vast trilithons – arches made of two standing stones and a lintel – inside the perimeter of the new sarsen ring. Now just three trilithons stand as originally intended and, of the other two (including the largest arch), just one standing stone is upright, while its partner and lintel lie nearby. One of these giant sarsens bears the carving of a dagger and 14 axeheads, which have been dated to the Bronze Age.

Above Stonehenge was certainly built as a way of marking solar events. On midsummer's morning the sun rises over the Heelstone when viewed from the centre of the giant stone circle.

During the substage that followed (3iii) some of the bluestones that had previously been removed were again erected within the sarsen circle and may have been worked on at this time. The next substage (3iv) involved two further uses of the bluestones: the first as an oval inside the trilithon horseshoe, and the second as a circle between the trilithons and the outer sarsen ring.

The final stages of construction (3v and 3vi), believed to have been completed in around 1600 BCE, involved the removal of a portion of the bluestone circle to enable a clear sight to the north-eastern alignment, and the digging of holes for a further two concentric rings of stones, both outside the main sarsen circle. It appears these circles were never completed and that the holes were subsequently filled in.

Stonehenge: a look at its meaning

When the first modern, Christian-era historians started to write about Stonehenge in the Middle Ages, they were ill equipped to come to enlightened conclusions about the meaning and function of the monument. Of the medieval chroniclers, Henry of Huntingdon and Geoffrey of Monmouth were some of the first to record its presence, the latter giving King Arthur a more than slightly fanciful role in the monument's creation.

DRUID LINKS DISPROVEN

Writing in the 17th century CE, the influential English architect Inigo Jones asserted that Stonehenge was a Roman creation and a temple to their god Caelus. Others believed that the Danes were its originators. Even in Victorian times serious scholars were attributing the monument to the Saxons or even to more recent civilizations.

Only with the advances in radiocarbon dating has it become possible to assert the facts of Stonehenge's historical timing. This has sifted out some of the explanations of its origins, but has done little to tell us more about its originators and their beliefs. The influence of the Greeks, the Mycenaeans and the Egyptians – all of whom postdated Stonehenge – has been ruled out. Its age has also, for some experts at least, excluded the possibility that the builders were Druids. Since the Druids were an expression of Celtic culture, the argument runs, which only really emerged in England and Wales in around 300 BCE, the construction dates of 3100–1600 BCE would be too early for their participation. Nevertheless, various orders of Druids have firmly claimed Stonehenge as part of their culture, and some have been granted special rights to use the henge for their midsummer solstice rituals.

NATURAL ALIGNMENTS

Whatever their identity, the people who built and used Stonehenge had clear ideas and were strongly motivated. So how much of its function can be read from the placing of the monument in its particular landscape? The north-east alignment of the Heelstone clearly points to a culture that valued the sun, but there are directional alignments in the structure that may also relate to the moon. Some people have suggested that the site can be regarded as an observatory with the power to predict eclipses and incorporate the Earth's 'wobble' or precession. Others believe that there are important ley-lines passing through the site and that the centre of Stonehenge forms a significant acupuncture point on the surface of the Earth – a place where worshipful ritual has a particularly beneficial effect on the ailing planet's energy systems.

More conventional interpretations lean towards the idea that the site, together with its role as a cemetery, was important in funeral rituals – which themselves may have involved other sites in the Salisbury Plain complex. Whatever the truth, Stonehenge will probably continue to intrigue the minds of modern humans for at least as long as it nurtured the spirit of our early ancestors.

① THE ALTAR STONE

What became known as the Altar Stone – a 6 ton, 4 m (13 ft) high monolith of green micaceous sandstone – is believed to have been sourced in Wales, either from South Pembrokeshire or from the Brecon Beacons, during phase 3i of construction.

② THE NORTH-EASTERN ENTRANCE AND THE HEELSTONE

The entrance to the site in the north-east was aligned with the direction of sunrise at the midsummer solstice (21 June in the northern hemisphere). The Heelstone, a large upright unworked stone, which was placed well outside the main structure at 80 m (260 ft) from the centre of the henge in the widened north-eastern channel, took the role of sighting stone for the rising of the midsummer sun.

③ CIRCULAR BANK AND DITCH

These earthworks were constructed during phase one (2950–2900 BCE), just outside the well-defined circle of wooden posts. The excavated ditch contained both flint tools and the bones of oxen and deer, which had been kept by their owners for many years prior to burial.

④ THE SARSENS

A total of 30 giant sarsen stones were brought from the Marlborough Downs 40 km (25 miles) north of the site and erected in a 33 m (108 ft) diameter circle – each stone standing around 4 m (13 ft) high, 2 m (7 ft) wide and weighing about 25 tons. Along the tops was raised a ring of 30 curved lintels, which seem to have been intended to form a perfect circle. Seventeen of the 30 are still standing.

⑤ THE STATION STONES

There are four Station Stones, each dating back to around 2600 BCE. Two of these stones stood on top of mounds, known as 'barrows', even though they do not actually appear to contain any burial materials. Only two of these are still visible today.

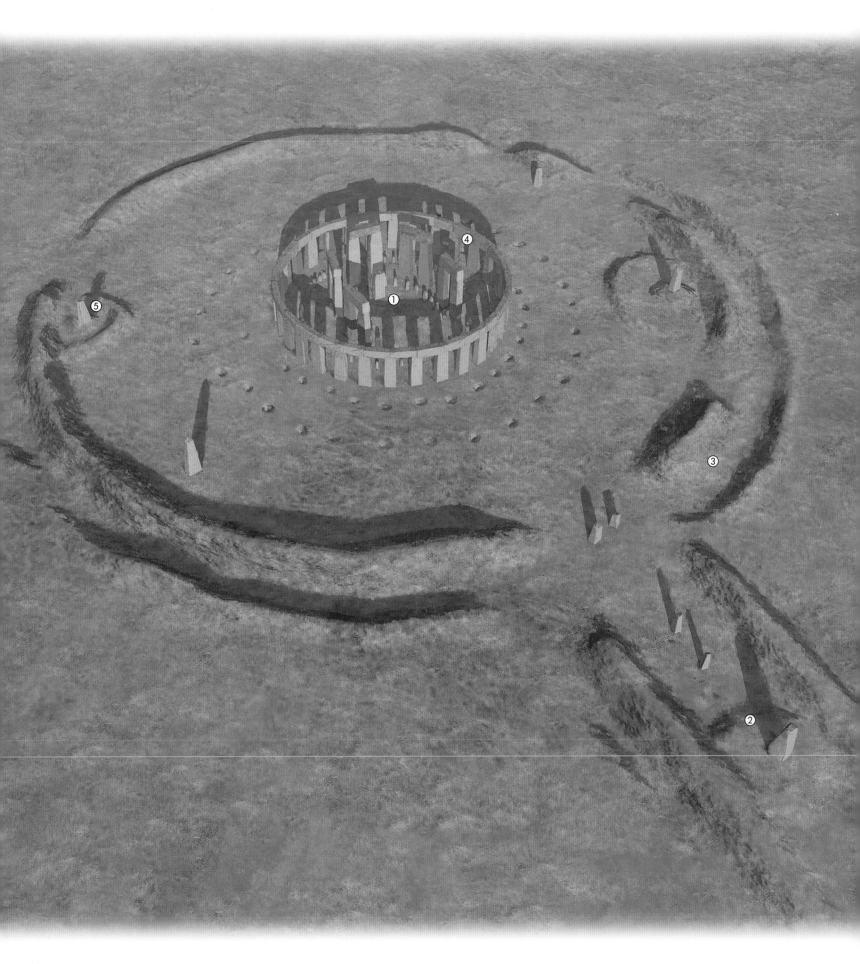

Avebury, Wiltshire

Avebury, in the English county of Wiltshire, is the site of the largest and most highly developed of all the stone circle and henge complexes in the British Isles. Although less immediately photogenic and impressive than Stonehenge – its relatively near neighbour, just 32 km (20 miles) away – Avebury's size and complexity, together with its links to other nearby sites, make it part of the most impressive creation of megalithic times.

The main feature at Avebury is the henge, a massive circular ditch and bank with a diameter of 421 m (1,380 ft), enclosing an area of 11.5 ha (28½ acres). Within this, the Outer Ring is about 335 m (1,100 ft) in diameter. Of an original 98 stones, each weighing around 40 tons, only 27 now survive and in many cases are not positioned exactly as they once were. The stones are sarsens, very similar to those used at Stonehenge and, most experts agree, probably from the same source on the Marlborough Downs. Construction dates for Avebury, taken from radiocarbon dating, suggest a similar period to Stonehenge, between 3000 and 1700 BCE.

OTHER KEY STRUCTURES

Within the main circle there is clear evidence of two smaller circles, each with a diameter of 103 m (338 ft). The circle in the north-north-west of the site was formed of 29 or 30 stones, some 3.5–4 m (11½–13 ft) high. Inside was a smaller concentric circle made up of 12 equally high stones. At its centre was a cove or horseshoe made up of even larger stones, which faced north-east. The smaller circle in the south-south-east quadrant was probably made up of 30 large sarsens with one enormous 5.5 m (18 ft) high central stone known as the Obelisk.

From the great circle, two long 'avenues' of standing stones would have led away: the Kennet Avenue to the south-south-east and the Beckhampton to the west-south-west. Silbury Hill, the remarkable mound about 1.6 km (1 mile) away to the south, stands as another important landmark in the Avebury landscape

NEGLECT AND REDISCOVERY

Unfortunately the stones that once formed the Outer Ring have not been well cared for over the centuries. The presence within the circle of half the modern village of Avebury is a clear indication of the neglect that the site has suffered. It is believed that the stone structures at Avebury were substantially intact until the 14th century CE, when Christians started to dig up and bury the large stones, to dismantle the pagan meaning of the place. During this excavation a barber-surgeon was crushed beneath one of the giant pillars in the south of the ring when it fell on him; his body was never recovered and he became an integral part of Avebury's history.

John Aubrey, the 17th-century antiquarian who rediscovered both Avebury and Stonehenge, wrote that 'Avebury does as much exceed in greatness the so renowned Stonehenge as a Cathedral doeth a parish Church'. William Stukeley – the 18th-century historian, and a supporter of the Druid connection for Avebury and other megalithic sites – became intimately involved in its protection and in the raising of its importance in the public psyche. Such was his regard for Avebury's significance that he described it as 'the most august work at this day upon the globe of the earth'.

PART OF AN ENERGY GRID?

Interest in Avebury's significance has risen again, and many theories have been put forward for its ritual and everyday functions. Its sheer size would have enabled many huge gatherings (and even living and trading arrangements) to take place within its boundaries. In their recent book *The Sun and the Serpent*, Hamish Miller and Paul Broadhurst proposed a function for the

Avebury 'temple' that had never before been explored. They believed that, using dowsing, they had detected a powerful pair of energy lines that stretched from St Michael's Mount in Cornwall across southern England to the coast of East Anglia. What characterized these dual 'Serpent' lines was their passing through an unusually high number of chapels, churches and other sites that were named, or associated with, St Michael. Apart from St Michael's Mount and Glastonbury Tor (where the church was dedicated to St Michael), one of the other key sites that they believe forms part of this double line is Avebury. The behaviour of the lines at the Avebury complex seemed particularly remarkable, entering and exiting via the curved, constructed 'avenues', and led the authors to dub Avebury a 'Serpent Temple'.

Miller and Broadhurst's ideas bring together two important notions: that the Avebury site was a place of power where ritual activity contributed new energies to a grid of energy meridians flowing through the land; and that, in some way unknown to us, a tradition existed of people (including perhaps the builders of Avebury) who knew of the 'straight line' relationship between a myriad of important sites across the whole of England.

Below *The circular Avebury henge takes in the village of Avebury and many of its important buildings and roads. For those who view the site as the most important outdoor temple in Britain, these modern 'advances' are a savage attack on their spiritual heritage.*

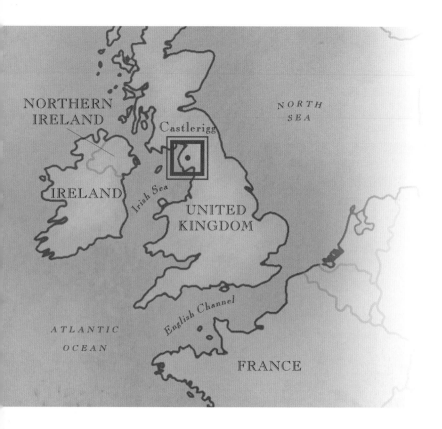

Castlerigg, Cumbria

Castlerigg stone circle, which is also known as the Carles, stands on a natural plateau surrounded by some of the most dominating and beautiful hills of the Lake District: Skiddaw, Blencathra and Helvellyn form part of the stunning 360-degree amphitheatre to Castlerigg's staging. The spectacular location adds to the drama of the circle's presence in the Cumbrian landscape, and this is only emphasized by the transient weather conditions that pervade this part of Britain.

Castlerigg does not form a perfect circle: its north-east side is flattened slightly where it appears to have lost some of its original stones. There are now 38 stones of variable shapes and sizes forming the circle, and all of them are rough, unhewn boulders. Some stand more than 1.5 m (5 ft) high, while other, smaller stones have fallen over. From the arrangement of the remaining stones it is estimated that the circle would originally have been formed of 41 stones. At the north side two larger stones seem to form an opening, perhaps a formal entrance, and in the south-west there is an outlying stone, a feature that Castlerigg shares with other Cumbrian stone circles.

One unique aspect of the Castlerigg circle is a small rectangular enclosure of ten stones, known as a cove, just inside the eastern point of the circle. Much speculation has gone into the cove's function. While its exact purpose is still far from clear, some experts believe that it was a burial site, even though an archaeological excavation in 1882 unearthed only charcoal. While many stone circles in the United Kingdom have been found to contain human burials, Castlerigg has not revealed such evidence.

DATING AND LOCATION
Castlerigg is believed to be one of the earliest stone circles in Britain, dating back to around 3200 BCE. Features that indicate its early status – according to the circle scholar Aubrey Burl – include its larger diameter, its greater number of stones (more than 20), the height of the stones (greater than 1 m/3¼ ft), an entrance marked by larger stones, an outlier or significant stone at some distance from the ring, a flattened – not perfectly round – circle and the presence of a bank around the stone circle.

Very little is known of early humans' lives around these times, but there are a series of circles along the west coast of England and Scotland that were developed after Castlerigg's creation by Neolithic and early Bronze Age peoples. Some scholars believe that for much of this time the inhabitants of Cumbria would live close to the coast, as boats were their most efficient means of transport and enabled them to move quite heavy loads and come to shore at many different points. The land, which was often undulating, rough and thickly wooded, offered a harder journey between sites and settlements.

'While its exact purpose is still far from clear, some experts believe that it was a burial site, even though an archaeological excavation in 1882 unearthed only charcoal.'

SPECULATION ABOUT ITS PURPOSE

The function of the Castlerigg site – whether for ritual, spiritual or more pragmatic purposes – is difficult to assess. What we do know is that the efforts required to establish such stone circles were always very great and would have required significant motivation and commitment. The fact that later circles elsewhere contained burials indicates that death rituals would have taken place in them, and that the presence of the stones offered a permanent reminder of the deceased's lives and, perhaps, their continuance in another world. The excavation of a stone axe head in 1875 was a further confirmation that the Lake District was a major source of Neolithic axes. Indeed the Langdale Pikes, another Lake District site, are often described as a stone-axe factory, and there is a close link between the earliest of Britain's stone circles and the axe industry.

In more modern times stone circles have been associated with certain anomalous experiences. In 1919 a Mr Singleton, together with a friend, claimed to have seen small moving balls of light – what would today be called 'ball lightning' – travelling slowly around the stones of Castlerigg. These kinds of phenomena have led some people to speculate that the stone circles were sited at particular places on the land where certain

Above The Castlerigg megalithic circle is surrounded by some of the Lake District's most beautiful mountains. The site, in the Lake District National Park, forms part of this constantly changing and spectacular landscape.

invisible energies were already active (see pages 126–127 and 128–129). Whether, as some suspect, Neolithic man and woman was more sensitive to these energies is a question that has yet to be fully answered.

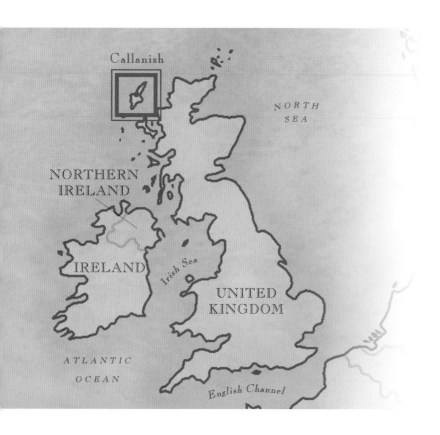

Callanish, Isle of Lewis

Callanish is one of the most sophisticated and multi-faceted standing-stone complexes in the British Isles. It is located on the Isle of Lewis, the most northerly of the main islands in the Outer Hebrides off the north-west coast of Scotland. Situated 25 km (15 miles) from the island's main town of Stornaway, the main Callanish complex lies just 200 m (650 ft) from the shores of the bay known as Loch Roag.

While many standing-stone configurations may have a circle, an outlier, a burial chamber, an inner ring of stones or a central stone, Callanish is remarkable in possessing all of these features. Its overall layout can be loosely likened to a Celtic cross, laid out almost on the points of the compass. It has a central circle with four radiating arms or avenues, the northern avenue (some 80m/262 ft in length) being considerably longer than the rest and directed some 15 degrees east of north. Within the main circle, which is formed of 13 tall, jutting, thin and angular Lewissian gneiss stones, there is a smaller circle (half the larger circle's 13m/42 ft diameter) perfectly occupying the eastern part.

DIFFERING BUILDERS AND BELIEFS

The smaller circle, which is itself composed of 17 variously sized stones, contains a further four large stones marking the chambered burial site. The largest stone in this circle is 4.75 m (15½ ft) high and weighs in at a relatively light 5 tons. It is also very close to the true centre of the large main circle. The presence of the small chambered tomb,

which was first found to have human remains during an excavation in 1857, has led some to think that this part of the Callanish complex was added to the original circle some time after its creation. Perhaps it was even put there by those who wished in some way to possess the power of the earlier site. There is also some evidence that those who came after the first builders may have deliberately attempted to destroy parts of the stone circle, possibly as part of a mission to assert a differing belief system.

The main circle and avenue complex at Callanish are often called Callanish I, since there are also a further 19 sites with significant stones at Callanish, as well as remnants of a timber circle close to Loch Roag. This extensive site of standing stones is much more complex than the first excavators of the modern period could possibly have imagined.

EXPLANATIONS

First recorded by John Morisone, a Lewissian, in 1680 as 'great stones standing up in ranks', the Callanish stones' possible function was speculated upon: '(they) ... were sett up in

place for devotione'. Callanish was described in 1695 by Martin Martin as 'ye Heathen temple'. First excavated in the 19th century, Callanish has been of great interest to archaeologists and other interested parties ever since. The site has attracted a raft of theories to explain its sophisticated and apparently careful construction and orientation by the Neolithic people of Lewis. It has been viewed as a deliberately despoiled astronomical observatory, a calendrical computer, a fusion of burial and ceremonial architecture and, during the 1970s, as a lunar and stellar site capable of highly refined astronomical observations.

Right Overlooking the waters of Loch Roag, Callanish is a large and complex arrangement of gneiss stones. In the eastern part of the complex is a small chambered tomb, which revealed human remains when it was excavated in 1857.

LEGENDS

As well as being subjected to scientific analysis, the stones on Callanish have also been the subject of numerous legends. Local lore recalls that the giants who lived on Lewis refused conversion to Christianity by St Kieran and were summarily petrified into the stones we now see.

Another story relates that a 'shining one' – a special being – once walked along the great stone avenue on midsummer's morning and that this event is heralded by the singing of a cuckoo, although normally the bird's eerie call would be associated with the arrival of spring and also the Beltane festival.

A further extraordinary tale, which benefits from a certain improbability in its telling, concerns the arrival of a priest-king. Adorned with the feathers of a mallard, the man came to Lewis with a fleet of ships and a good many black slaves and proceeded to erect the stones. The story also tells how many of the black people died during the mission, but spares us details of the causes.

Stone circles are often, it seems, the meeting place of ornate story and scientific speculation. The enigma of Callanish's stones is still a long way from being solved.

Men an Tol, Cornwall

Men an Tol stands on the southern slope of a wild, gorse-covered piece of moorland 4.8 km (3 miles) north-west of Madron, near Penzance in Cornwall. Its central and strangest feature is a partially buried stone disc around 1.5 m (5 ft) in diameter and penetrated in its centre by an empty circle with a diameter of around 45 cm (18 in). Known as the Crick Stone or Devil's Eye, the stone has often been attributed with magical powers for those who pass through its void.

On either side of the holed stone (Men an Tol means 'stone of the hole') are partially buried cuboid stones, standing about 1.2 m (4 ft) above ground. Both appear to lean away from the central circle, and one of them is additionally supported by a smaller superficial stone.

Holed stones of this type are rare in the catalogue of British stone megaliths and circles. Other stones with holes do exist: the Long Stone in Gloucestershire and Davidstow Well (also in Cornwall) are examples. Another used to stand outside the circle ring at Avebury (see pages 128–129), and the Stone of Odin used to stand between the Ring of Brodgar and the Stones of Stennes on Orkney island. Nevertheless, it is only at Men an Tol that the stone may have formed part of a significant stone circle.

THEORIES AND SPECULATION

A number of theories have grown up around the significance of this unique site and about the missing elements that may have formed its particular configuration. For instance, there have been suggestions that the holed stone formed an entrance to some form of passage grave or other burial chamber. But now, following work by local archaeologists, there appear to be strong indications that there was a 16 m (52 ft) diameter stone circle formed by 19 or 20 upright stones, including the Crick Stone. They found evidence for the existence of 11 of the stones that could have formed this arrangement, taking in those that are visible and others that are buried beneath the turf of the moor.

As with many stone circles and other such forms, there has been speculation about the stones' relationship to a number of astronomical phenomena. In Men an Tol's case, the three visible stones appear to line up with the north-east sunrises at Beltane (1 May) and Lughnasa (1 August) and with the sunsets at Imbolc (1 or 2 February) and Samhain (1 November), if viewed from the south-west.

Other speculation has included the idea that there are connections with various stars for the Men an Tol configuration. As with many stellar-alignment ideas, however, it is far from clear whether megalithic peoples ever valued these as highly as the more obvious solar orientations.

HEALING ATTRIBUTES

The legends and folkloric tales relating the power of the holed stone are many, and generally talk of healing and fertility. For example, a woman wishing to get pregnant would come to Men an Tol and pass herself through the stone a ritual number of times. Whether the stone stimulated parthenogenesis (so-called 'virgin births') or simply increased the potential to conceive is not recorded. This birthing idea may also contain echoes of religious rituals of birth, death and rebirth, in which a novitiate was passed through the hole from one world to another – from the womb to the tomb, as it were – in initiatory experiences.

'In general it was thought that nine passes were required for full healing to take place.'

The healing folklore of the stone is recorded in some detail, with its powers being particularly related to the twin medieval perils of scrofula and rickets, both of which are now known to be related to poor diet and adverse living conditions. In earlier times, great faith was put in the power of the megalith, and young children with either condition would be passed naked through the stone three times, before being ritually dragged in anti-clockwise circles through the gorsy grass in an effort to rid them of their scrofulous or rickety symptoms. Adults would also use the hole for their own conditions, but in general it was thought that nine passes were required for full healing to take place.

It remains a curious enigma that a gap, an absence, a simple void of matter could – like some modern physicist's wormhole in space – become a site of such imagined power.

Above *The obvious fertility symbolism at Men an Tol has been enshrined in a number of rituals involving people passing through the hole to simulate both intercourse and birth.*

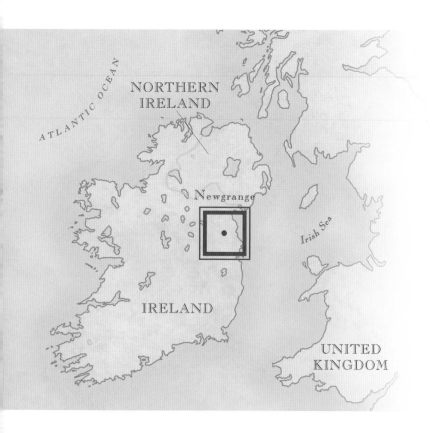

Newgrange, Ireland

Newgrange is acknowledged to be the oldest and most important ancient site in Ireland. Situated close to modern Donore in County Meath, Newgrange is an example of a sophisticated Neolithic passage tomb and is part of the Brú na Bóinne complex, which contains three large tombs and 37 smaller tombs. What makes this site unique is the quality of its construction, the artistry of the workmanship and its extraordinarily good state of repair after what is believed to be around five thousand years since its creation.

In modern times Newgrange was only rediscovered in 1699 when some road builders searching for construction materials discovered what they thought was a cave. Despite the importance of their unlikely find, Newgrange was not fully excavated until 1962, when its complex structure and artistic design were fully revealed and gave a clearer sense of its ritual purpose.

MOUND AND BURIAL CHAMBER

The main outer structure is a large kidney-shaped stone and turf mound more than 50 m (164 ft) across, with a retaining perimeter of 97 large kerbstones topped by a tall façade wall of granite and white quartz extending on either side of the entrance. While the majority of the stone for the mound was found locally, the sparkling white quartz and granite of the imposing wall were probably sourced from further away, perhaps from the bays of Wicklow and Dundalk.

Around the mound, which covers an area of more than 0.4 ha (1 acre), there once stood a ring of giant standing stones. Although only 12 of these still remain, it is believed that as many as 37 once contained

Left An unusual-looking dome in the Irish landscape, Newgrange is instantly recognizable from its façade of granite and white quartz. It was once surrounded by a ring of 37 large standing stones.

the Newgrange passage grave. The circle is believed to have been erected around one thousand years after the mound's original construction during the Bronze Age.

Inside the mound an 18 m (59 ft) long passage reaches towards the centre, where it opens onto a cruciform chamber. The burial chamber is an extraordinary structural achievement. An early example of a corbelled (or trussed) roof, it rises steeply to a height of nearly 4 m (13 ft). Apart from standing intact for more than five thousand years, the structure has also kept the burial chamber free from water. It is estimated that work on the Newgrange project would have consumed six thousand man-years of labour.

SOLSTICE EVENT

The most important feature of the passage and the cruciform chamber is its directional alignment. Between 19 and 23 December, either side of the winter solstice, sunrise illuminates the burial chamber with searing shafts of sunlight, which enter the passage via a 'roofbox' over the entrance to the Newgrange tomb. The sun beams its way to the back wall of the chamber, illuminating the interior and revealing the carved stonework, which is richly decorated with ornate spirals (both single and triple), lozenge shapes and other natural forms. The event lasts just 17 minutes before the Earth's turning again obscures the sun from the entrance. Nowhere else among the megalithic structures of the British Isles is the relative movement of Sun and Earth so precisely recorded as it is here at Newgrange.

What seems clear from archaeological evidence is Newgrange's function as some kind of tomb or centre for death rituals. During excavation the remains of five bodies were found; and recesses in the cruciform chamber contained large stone basins, which it is believed would have held the cremated remains of those recently deceased. It is only possible to wonder at the precise nature of ritual events that may have occurred in the inner chamber at those rare moments when the sun relieved the darkness.

Radiocarbon dating has placed the date of Newgrange's original construction at 3,300

and 2,900 BCE, making it one of the oldest surviving megalithic structures in Europe. To put its age in context, Stonehenge's giant trilithons were erected some thousand years later, and the Celts – who are sometimes erroneously credited with Newgrange's spiral designs – did not arrive in Ireland for another 2,500 years. It is hard to imagine that the industrious early people who created Newgrange and left artwork to honour their ancestors had any notion of the way their work would reach into the future.

Above *During the winter solstice the sunrise illuminates the burial chamber at the end of Newgrange's passageway, revealing ornately decorated and carved stonework.*

Carnac, France

The stones of Carnac are at least five thousand years old and represent one of the most concentrated collections of standing stones and other megalithic sites still visible on the planet. More than three thousand stones are collected together as alignments, tumuli, dolmens and other configurations in a relatively small area close to the northern French village of Carnac in Brittany.

The remarkable feat of the early builders who erected the Carnac stones is immediately evident in the long rows of standing stones that traverse the French countryside. Although they may once have been linked in a united formation, the stones now appear in three distinct groups – perhaps due to the removal of some stones over the years – and are known by the names Menec, Kermario and Kerlescan.

MENEC, KERMARIO AND KERLESCAN

Closest to the village of Carnac and the most westerly of the three groups, the Menec alignments are made up of 11 rows of stones or 'menhirs', some 100 m (328 ft) wide and 1,160 m (3,805 ft) in length. The rows are more spread out in the west, where the tallest stones can be as high as 4 m (13 ft). In the central portion many of the stones are less than 1 m (3⅓ ft) high, but in the east the stones become taller again. At either end of the site there appear to be the remains of stone circles.

The Kermario, or 'house of the dead', alignment starts some 300 m (985 ft) east of the Menec alignment and possesses the same gently fanning structure, with the wider section again at its west end. It is made up of 1,029 stones in ten ranks and stretches for around 1,300 m (4,265 ft), with some partial interruptions. Again it terminates at its east end with a stone circle.

The Kerlescan alignment is rather different from the others. Situated north-east of Kermario, the Kerlescan is a group of 555 stones in 13 columns and ranging in height from 4 m (13 ft) to a little under 1 m (3⅓ ft). At the west end is another stone circle formed from 39 megaliths.

The facts of Carnac sound simple, yet little in this prosaic description can prepare the visitor for the actual sight of so many stones laid out across the landscape like an army of giant marching soldiers. Their very presence is enough to provoke myriad questions about their age, their origins, the people who placed them there and what they represented.

REARRANGEMENT AND RE-EXAMINATION

Serious interest in the Carnac stones in the modern era did not occur until the 18th and early 19th centuries, when vague theories about Druidic and star-map connections started to emerge. But it was not until the arrival of Scottish antiquarian James Miln in the 1860s that important excavations started to take place. At that time Miln recorded that only some 700 of the three thousand stones were standing; the rest, it seemed, had given in to the force of gravity. The great majority were not reinstated until the 1930s, and then again in the 1980s when road-building programmes brought in machinery to rearrange and reposition some of the stones to fit in with the public works. Since then there have been attempts to create a more historically accurate reconstruction of the site, in the context of a serious study of the stones' original function.

Apart from the common explanation of solar alignment with the winter-solstice sunset for the arrangement of the standing stones, Carnac has thrown up one possible explanation for the use of megaliths that has not appeared elsewhere. French scientist Pierre Méreaux spent 30 years researching at Carnac and came to the conclusion that the stone dolmens that are scattered throughout

the area, and which comprise upright stones with connecting flat lintels, are actually primitive earthquake-detectors. He cites their carefully balanced 'tables' as sensitive seismic instruments, able to react to movements in the earth below. He connects this theory to the well-known fact that Brittany is the most seismically active part of France.

Recently it has become more difficult for worshippers to get close to the stones. As at sites like Stonehenge, there have been moves to protect the stones from erosion, damage and theft. At Carnac this has resulted in demonstrations from those who wish to have free access, who in many cases believe themselves to have some connection with the work of their Neolithic ancestors.

Above *This view reveals the incredible achievement of the early builders of the stone temples at Carnac. Around a thousand stones form the Menec alignments close to the village of Carnac.*

'The tallest stones can be as high as 4 m (13 ft).'

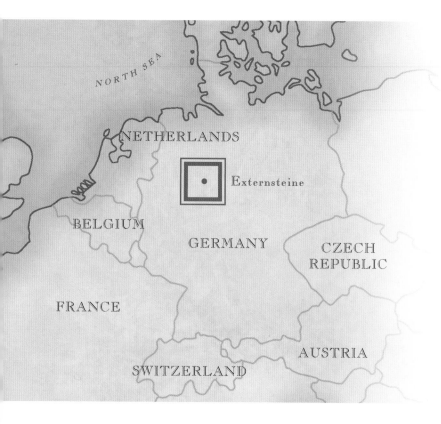

Externsteine, Germany

Pagan tradition in Germany is most clearly evident at the strange and jutting rocky outcrop known as Externsteine, or 'the stones of the Egge' (where the Egge are the Eggegebirge Hills). Located close to Detmold in the Teutoburger region of north-western Germany, the Externsteine formation appears like a prehistoric stone backbone out of the wooded hills that surround it. Its position in the heartland of Teutonic Germany has given the site an attraction for different peoples throughout its long history – some with more spiritual aims than others.

According to some scholars, the sacred rocks of Externsteine lie at the geomantic centre of Germany's ancient heart. They certainly seem to have been a place of gathering and pilgrimage since prehistoric, Celtic and early Saxon times. Evidence has been uncovered that reveals the early presence of nomadic reindeer hunters at this sandstone monument.

A SITE OF PAGAN AND CHRISTIAN RITUAL

Teutonic hero myths are embedded in this area, along with the heavy defeat of the German people at the hands of Arminius' Roman legions. After this turning point it appears that Roman soldiers may have established a shrine to the Persian cult of Mithras here, although some experts believe that other deities – such as Wotan, the Norse god, or Weleda, the Bructerian prophetess – were worshipped here.

One of the central man-made features of the stones is an ancient observatory. Possibly the only one of its kind, its carefully built structure may date back as far as Neolithic times. Perched high on the central peak of

Externsteine's five pinnacles, nearly 40 m (131 ft) above the ground, a roofless pagan temple contains an early astronomical instrument. Carved from the natural limestone of the edifice and positioned above a small dome-topped altar, it has a 50 cm (20 in) circular opening, which acts as a lens, focusing the light of the midsummer sunrise and the most northerly rising of the moon, and transmitting them to other points within the temple, where it is believed that sacred objects once received the direct or reflected rays of the sun.

It is known that pagan rituals happened here until 772 CE when Charlemagne (Charles the Great), ruler of the Holy Roman Empire, carried out the decisive act of cutting down the Tree of Irminsul, the great symbol of nature in the pagan world. After this time the site was occupied by Christian monks, and a programme of Christianization was initiated. As well as the development of monks' cells, a number of beautifully carved reliefs were carried out on the natural stone of the pillars.

The most remarkable of these was created in the 12th century and depicts Christ's

descent from the cross. Romanesque in style, the carving is heavily influenced by Byzantine art and is the only known example of Byzantine sculpture in Germany. Its symbolism expresses precisely the struggle for the spiritual heart of Externsteine. As Nicodemus lowers the body of Jesus from the cross, he steps on the sacred tree – the Irminsul – which bends under his weight. At the same time the sun and moon (both pagan symbols of power and fertility) are shown weeping. A snake, symbolizing earth energies and natural wisdom, is trodden down by the

feet of Jesus' disciples. The message seems clear: Christ's crucifixion put an end to the power of pagan spirituality. Next to the ornate carving is a group of caves, once inhabited by monks and carrying an inscription revealing its consecration as a chapel in 1115.

DARKER ASSOCIATIONS

In more modern times the place has attracted interest from different groups wishing to adopt the real or symbolic power that Externsteine offers. As the heartland of the Teutonic race, the stones' value was quickly grasped by Nazi Heinrich Himmler, who in 1933 initiated the 'Externsteine Foundation' with the intention of creating a sacred grove of trees for the worship of Teutonic ancestors. A branch of the SS, the Ahnenerbe division also studied the stones in search of folkloric history that would serve the Nazis' purposes.

Now the site plays host to various groups of neo-nationalists, neo-pagans and others who use the site as a place of nature worship. The presence of Externsteine in the psychological landscape of the German people is deeply ingrained, and its role in the country's ongoing struggle with its own soul seems likely to continue for many years to come.

Far left *Five pinnacles form the limestone crag of Externsteine: the tallest, central peak houses an ancient, open-air temple with an observatory that records the midsummer solstice.*

Below *This ornate carving shows Jesus being taken down from the cross by Nicodemus. Beneath his feet (no longer present) the Tree of Irminsul is bent towards the ground.*

CHAPTER 6

SACRED LAND AND WATER

Planet Earth offers an extraordinarily rich diversity of natural features, all formed by the expression of huge forces that are referred to scientifically as physical or geological. For most spiritual traditions, however, the origins of the Earth and the rest of the universe are the result of a beneficent creator. These teachings tell of the creator or his team of workers, who formed the world with its land, seas, rivers, plains and mountains. The two approaches – scientific and religious – are not necessarily incompatible; scientific processes do not necessarily exclude a creator.

If all the features of our world were created by divine forces, then they are worthy of respect or worship, as a reminder of the forces that created us and our ancestors. We – along with the ants, the frogs, the birds, the mammals and the fish – are all part of the same landscape that we call 'the environment'. By honouring the features of our world and the resources that support our life, many religions tell us that we are reconnecting to the source of our creation and thereby fulfilling a significant part of our human destiny. Some places are simply respected for their natural, pre-existing form; other sites become sacred or significant through human intervention, through the markings people have made to celebrate their special connection with the landscape. Whatever the perspective, the ways in which these sites are appreciated cannot help but challenge our own view of the world.

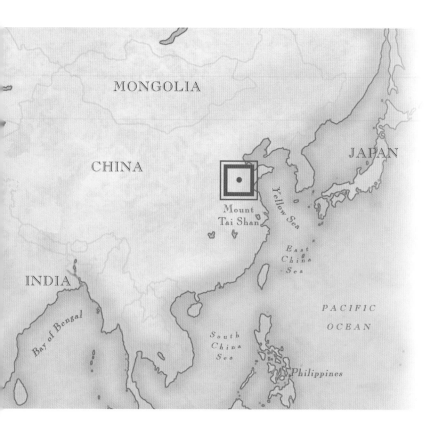

Mount Tai Shan, China

Mount Tai Shan, with its tallest Jade Emperor peak rising 1,545 m (5,065 ft) above sea level, is the most famous and important of China's five sacred mountains. Located in the centre of Shangdon Province in the eastern part of China, the mountain has been a focus of pilgrimage for the last three thousand years. During this time worship at the site evolved into an official imperial ritual and Mount Tai Shan became one of the principal places where rulers would pay homage to Heaven (on the summit) and Earth (at the foot of the mountain).

In 219 BCE Qin Shi Huang, the first emperor of China, held a ceremony on the summit of the mountain to proclaim the unity of his empire – an event recorded in one of the 1,018 inscriptions that now adorn the cliffsides.

The natural beauty of the site has also attracted artists, poets and philosophers and has been a source of inspiration in Chinese literature for hundreds, if not thousands, of years. Confucius himself, whose home town of Qufu was only some 70 km (44 miles) away, visited the site many times in the 6th and 5th centuries BCE and, as well as writing about the mountain, left his own calligraphic carvings on the rocks.

On the mountain complex there are a total of 22 temples, 97 ruins and 819 stone tablets. A flight of some 7,000 steps leads the pilgrim up the more favoured East Peak of Mount Tai Shan and the long journey to the summit will take most people a whole day to complete. Along this so-called 'stairway to heaven' there are 11 gates, 14 archways and four pavilions and every step of the way provides a different view of the surrounding landscape for the pilgrim to experience and respond to spiritually.

Right The Temple of the Jade Emperor at the summit of Mount Tai Shan. According to Chinese mythology the Jade Emperor is the ruler of Heaven and among the most important gods of the Chinese Taoist pantheon.

SACRED TEMPLES

Of all the temples on the mountain, perhaps the one dedicated to the god of Mount Tai himself – the Dai Miao – is the most impressive. It is certainly the largest and most complete ancient building in the Tai Shan complex and covers an area of 96,000 sq m (1 million sq ft). First built during the Qin Dynasty around 210 BCE, it was transformed into an imperial palace during the Han Dynasty (206 BCE–220 CE), making it one of only three such palaces in China.

Of the other temples on the mountain, the most important have been the Temple to the Heavenly Queen Mother, built before the period of the Three Kingdoms (220–280 CE), and the Azure Cloud Temple, whose religious influence once extended over more than half of China.

NATURAL BEAUTY

As well as the constructions of human hand, natural wonders are ever present at Tai Shan. The mountain is home to some of the oldest trees in China. These include the Han Dynasty cypresses, which were planted around 2,100 years ago by the emperor Wu Di; the Tang Chinese Scholartree, which is 1,300 years old; and the 'Welcoming Guest Pine', which is 500 years old. There are also the famous five 'Dafu' pines, which were replanted 250 years ago, to replace five original pines that once sheltered the emperor Qin Shi Huang during a precarious and rainy descent of the mountain.

Mount Tai Shan is supposed to offer the pilgrim the possibility of four distinct wonders: the view of the morning sunrise from the east side of the mountain; the foggy clouds that envelop the peak, which are said to instil the desire to fly like a celestial being into the sea of mist; the beauty of the snow-covered mountain in winter; and what is described as the 'Buddha light' or rainbow aureole that sometimes enfolds the very peak of the mountain and those who stand upon it. Each visitor, though, may find their own unique wonder in the myriad impressions that Tai Shan provides.

Confucius once said that when you witness the sunrise from Mount Tai Shan, you see

both the past and the future of China. More recently, modern scholars have put forward the idea that Mount Tai Shan represents a microcosm of the highest level of Chinese culture, of its creative artistry and expression. In an attempt to blend harmoniously human construction with the beauty of nature, the mountain expresses a cultural archetype, or ideal, which, in a time of great change and technological advance in China, has found a renewed attraction.

Above The climb to the summit of Mount Tai Shan starts from the Tai Shan Arch. The climber first passes the Ten Thousand Immortals Tower, then Arhat Cliff and the Palace of the Goddess Dou Mu. The entire ascent may take up to seven hours.

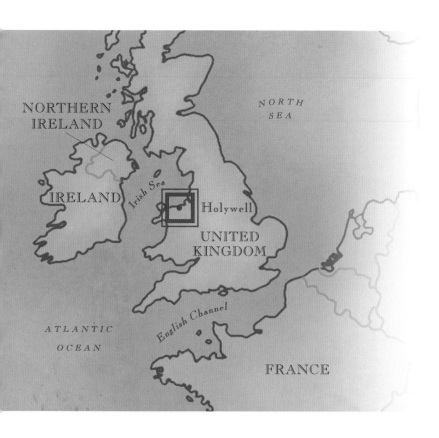

St Winefride's Well, Holywell

St Winefride's Well (also spelt St Winifrid's) can be found in the town with the eponymous name of Holywell, in Flintshire, north Wales. In modern times it has been described as the 'Lourdes of Wales', but while its claimed healing powers may be similar to those of the French shrine, its origins are considerably more ancient. St Winefride's Well is believed to be the oldest continuously attended Christian pilgrimage site in Great Britain, dating back to the 7th century CE, and is considered one of the 'Seven Wonders of Wales'.

The sacred spring that gives the site its name, and which has been attributed with many miracles over nearly 1,350 years, first issued water in 660 CE following the miraculous healing of St Winefride. The story of Winefride, whose original Welsh name was Gwenfrewy, the daughter of Welsh nobleman Tyfid ap Eiludd, is a strange and somewhat sordid one.

WINEFRIDE'S STORY

Her suitor Caradog became enraged when she told him that she had pledged herself to God and intended to become a nun. Depending on which version of the story you read, the action describes Caradog's attempt to rape Winefride, but when she tried to escape from him, he drew his sword and decapitated her with a single blow. The legend then relates how her head rolled down a hill and finally came to rest: on this very spot a spring began to flow spontaneously. Winefride's maternal uncle (later to be canonized as St Beuno) quickly arrived on the scene, picked up her head and, in a miraculous medical procedure, rejoined her head to her body and 'resurrected' her. Some say that Beuno then put a curse on Caradog, causing him to melt into the ground; a more reliable version appears to give the spurned suitor a different ending. Following these extraordinary events, Caradog is thought to have been the victim of a revenge killing by St Winefride's brother Oswain, an event detailed in historical records.

Winefride's original wish to become a nun was fulfilled and she entered Gwytherin Abbey in Denbighshire, where she eventually took over the role of abbess from her maternal aunt St Tenoi. Stories of her life also relate that she made a personally important pilgrimage to Rome. Following her death she was buried in the abbey, and pilgrims started to come and visit the holy well where Winefride's miraculous reheading had taken place – and hence the town received its new name.

Right *The well at Holywell was built on the spot where Winefride's head is said to have come to rest following her beheading by Caradog. Pilgrims believe the waters have healing powers.*

'It has been
described as the
"Lourdes of Wales".'

WOOLSTON WELL

There is also a well named after St Winefride
in the hamlet of Woolston near Oswestry in
Shropshire. In 1138 CE a group of monks –
some say relic-stealing monks – were on their
way to Shrewsbury Abbey when they were
forced to break their journey and stay the
night in Woolston. When they arose in the
morning they disovered that a new spring
had sprung up from the ground. The water is
believed by some to possess healing powers,
being particularly good for bruises and
broken bones. The well is now covered by a
half-timbered cottage, from beneath which
the water flows into a series of stone troughs
and eventually a stream. The monks
continued on their journey to the abbey at
Shrewsbury, where the remains of their
shrine containing some of Winefride's relics
can still be found.

In 1415, following his victory in the Battle
of Agincourt, King Henry V made a 72 km
(45 mile) thanksgiving pilgrimage from
Shewsbury Abbey, taking in Woolston and
finally arriving at Winefride's spiritual home
in Holywell. All these sites continued to
be important pilgrimage destinations
throughout the late Middle Ages, but with
the arrival of Henry VIII's ecclesiastical
reformation, the Shrewsbury Abbey shrine
was all but destroyed in 1540, along with
many of the country's other religious
buildings and communities.

Holywell, however, escaped the worst of
the king's zeal and the town has continued to
attract pilgrims up to the present day. It is the
only place of pilgrimage in the United
Kingdom to have functioned continuously
throughout the Reformation. The shrine
now offers worshippers the opportunity to
bathe in the sacred waters, and many enter
the pool a number of times in one day during
their sojourn, in search of Winefride's
healing blessings.

Above *Shrewsbury
Abbey hosts a shrine
to Winefride where
pilgrims pay their
respects and ask for
blessings from the saint.*

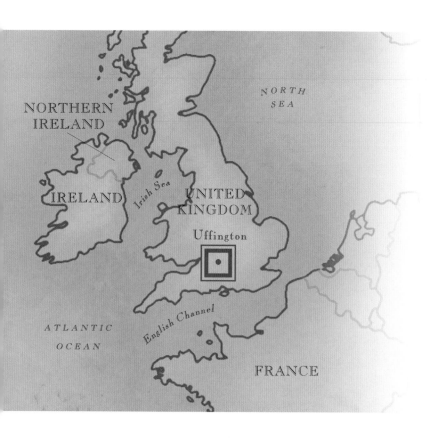

The White Horse, Uffington

The White Horse of Uffington is an unmistakable design cut into the English chalk bedrock of the Ridgeway in Oxfordshire. Both elegant and stylized, the image is some 113 m (370 ft) from nose to tail. Until 1995 it was believed to have dated from the Iron Age, but new archaeological techniques have revealed that the figure was probably created between 1200 and 800 BCE, dating it to the Bronze Age.

For the experts this was an interesting discovery, since similar semi-abstracted horse images have also been found on coins from this era. However, the real purpose of the Uffington White Horse has been harder to understand and its original function has been the subject of much speculation.

AN OBJECT OF WORSHIP?
It is believed by some scholars that the hill figure actually represents a horse goddess, who would have been connected with the local tribe known as the Belgae. The horse was the main form taken by Epona, a goddess worshipped by the Celts in Gaul and also known as Rhiannon in Britain. This connection is generally considered to be later than the Bronze Age dating, although it is possible that the horse was adopted by people who came after that period. There is some evidence that the sun god Belinos, who was worshipped around this time, was connected to horses: he was often portrayed riding horses or being carried in a chariot.

As well as representing an object of worship, the chalk horse could have had a more prosaic explanation as the badge or emblem of a particular tribe who owned the land and wished to let others know that was the case, by making their particular mark or stamp. Generally, though, the amount of work involved in the creation of such a large figure indicates a significance beyond the simply material – an importance that is normally associated with religious or spiritual activity. Given the horse's position on the peak of a hill, there have been suggestions

SCOURING THE WHITE HORSE

As well as being the oldest major hill figure in the English landscape, the Uffington White Horse is also one of the best preserved and maintained. It is very likely that the process of keeping the horse figure clean and visible in its dramatic location was an important activity for people close to the horse since it was first established. What is perhaps more surprising is that even in more modern times a festival continued to be held around what is known as the 'Scouring of the White Horse'. Involving games, music, wrestling, cheese rolling and other events, the three-day festival was held every seven years at the cost of the local lord, to encourage the participation of the local people in the clearing and recutting of the horse's chalk form. Most of the events took place at Uffington Castle, the partially enclosed earthen banks that once formed an ancient hill fort. It seems that the festival stopped around a hundred years ago, but the horse was kept clean by local enthusiasts until English Heritage took over the task.

that it was an attempt to communicate with the gods themselves, to show the tribe's respect for the horse god or goddess and to invoke a blessing on their people.

There are thought to have been many hundreds of such chalk figures in the British landscape over the past three thousand years. Many of them have, interestingly, portrayed horses, demonstrating the creature's enormous importance to humans until the recent arrival of the car. Other figures have featured different creatures and human images, but, of the total number, just 57 now survive in the southern part of England. The rest have been grown over by vegetation and have simply returned to the earth.

Inscribed on an escarpment high on White Horse Hill, the figure is one of only four known horse figures that look to the right. The Uffington White Horse's position on top of White Horse Hill also means that it can be seen as far as 32 km (20 miles) away on a particularly clear day. It can be also be viewed from the top of nearby Dragon Hill, which was once believed to be the site of St George's slaying of the beast that had entrapped a maiden. This led some to think that the chalk figure was an image of St George's own horse, or even perhaps of the famous dragon. Whatever the truth of the myth, the first sight of the chalk horse on the Ridgeway hills can be as thrilling today as it once was to its Bronze Age makers.

Left *Almost certainly the oldest surviving landscape figure in Britain, the Uffington White Horse has been dated at over 3,000 years old. Its situation on Oxfordshire's Ridgeway makes it visible from many miles away.*

Mount Kailash, Tibet

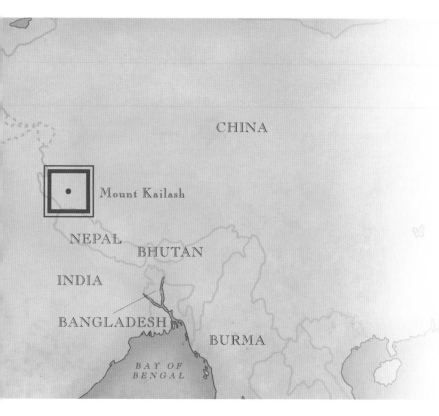

CHINA

Mount Kailash

NEPAL

BHUTAN

INDIA

BANGLADESH

BURMA

BAY OF
BENGAL

Mount Kailash is a crystal-shaped peak high in the Gangdisê mountains in western Tibet. Close to the mountain is the source of four of the great rivers in Asia: the Brahmaputra, the Karnali, the Sutlej (a tributary of the Ganges) and the Indus. Kailash, which means 'crystal' in Sanskrit, is an important sacred place in four of the world's great religions: Buddhism, Hinduism, Jainism and the ancient Tibetan religion of Bön Po.

Close to the base of the mountain are two lakes: Rakshastal and Manasarowar. The latter plays an important part in the ritual pilgrimage that draws many people to this remote, yet symbolically central part of the world. The 8,848 m (29,000 ft) Mount Everest may hold a special place for its sheer height, but the 6,638 m (21,775 ft) peak of Mount Kailash can be described as the most spiritually important natural form in all Asia.

DIFFERING MYTHOLOGIES

In Hindu mythology, Shiva is believed to live on the peak of Mount Kailash. In some Hindu schools of thought, the mountain represents heaven or paradise, the place where departed souls reside in their sojourns between lives. In the Hindu Puranas, Kailash is the central pillar of the world, its four crystalline faces – quartz, ruby, gold and lapis lazuli – looking out to the four directions of the compass. In some versions of Shiva's story, Mount Kailash is the ultimate manifestation of the god's lingam, or phallus, while the adjacent Lake Manasarowar represents the yoni, or vagina, of his consort Parvati.

Tibetan Buddhists have a legend of Milarepa, their founder, arriving in Tibet to challenge Naro-Bonchung, the master of the native animist Bön Po religion. Both were powerful spiritual magicians and, when they battled against each other, neither was able to overcome the other. Another solution arose: the first of the two to reach the summit of Mount Kailash would lead their triumphant religion in Tibet. Naro-Bonchung was soon being carried through the air on a magic drum, while Milarepa – to the distress of his devotees – was simply sitting in meditation. And yet, just as Naro-Bonchung had nearly reached Kailash's peak, Milarepa began to fly and, travelling on the sun's rays, was quickly beamed to the top ahead of his adversary. From then on Buddhism would be the religion of Tibet and has been challenged only by the Chinese invasion of 1950, which led to the flight of the Dalai Lama in 1959 and to the deaths of many Buddhist monks, nuns and laiety who wished to continue their religious practice.

For the people of the ancient Tibetan religion of Bön Po, Mount Kailash is viewed as the nine-layered or nine-storeyed mountain that is represented by the symbol of the swastika. Jains, who call Kailash Mount Ashtapada, maintain that their original founder Rishabhadeva achieved his enlightenment on the sacred mountain.

PILGRIMAGE TO THE HOLY MOUNTAIN

For many years after the Chinese invasion of Tibet in 1950, pilgrimage to Mount Kailash was made impossible for members of all religions, some of whom would view this journey as the spiritual culmination of their lives. But since 1980 the road from Tibet's capital, Lhasa, across the Tibetan plateau to Mount Kailash has been opened up again to pilgrims. Those who do decide to embark on this spiritual journey can expect a physically harsh experience involving weeks of difficult and sometimes dangerous travel before they have even arrived at the remote mountain and its surroundings.

Each religion has a different spiritual requirement for the formal pilgrimage. For example, although most follow a similar 52 km (32 mile) route, which circles the mountain and Lake Manasarowar. Hindus

Left *Tibetan prayer flags line the 52 km (32 mile) pilgrimage route around Mount Kailash and Lake Manasarowar. For many pilgrims the journey to Kailash is the fulfilment of a lifetime's ambition.*

and Buddhists work around the mountain in a clockwise direction, while Jains and followers of Bön Po travel anti-clockwise. Some pilgrims attempt to cover the whole route within a single day – an arduous demand under normal circumstances, but with the added hardships of high altitude it can be fatal. Others cover the route (albeit taking considerably longer) by a seemingly endless series of full-length prostrations along the rough ground.

All pilgrims seem to be wary of a long-held taboo that seems even to have carried through to Westerners who might have been tempted to climb the mountain. Out of respect for the importance of the sanctity of the place, no one should ever set foot on the actual mountain. It is believed that anyone who breaks this taboo will suffer severe consequences – even death. Although it is perhaps symbolic, the legend serves to reinforce the sense of reverence in which the mountain is held by so many people of such diverse faiths.

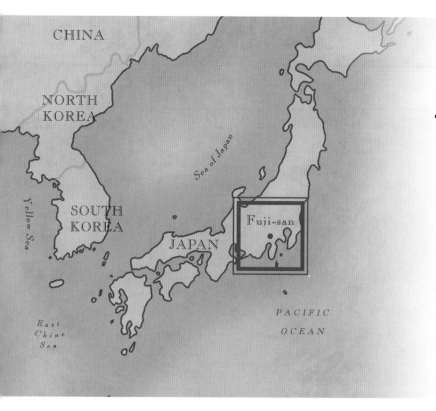

CHINA

NORTH KOREA

SOUTH KOREA

JAPAN

Sea of Japan

Yellow Sea

East China Sea

Fuji-san

PACIFIC OCEAN

Mount Fuji, Japan

Mountain worship in Japan goes back at least two thousand years, and mountains were recognized as sacred places and the homes of spirits well before Shinto was formalized as a religion in the 5th and 6th centuries CE. Shinto upholds the idea that spirits called kami *dwell in natural places such as rivers, woodlands, lakes and mountains and that, through prayer and ritual, they can offer a positive influence over the affairs of humans. Mount Fuji, or Fuji-san, is the greatest – both literally and spiritually – of all Japanese mountains.*

The arrival of Buddhism in Japan in the 6th century CE only increased Fuji's spiritual importance, since the new religion also contained elements of mountain worship, with some Buddhists viewing mountain climbing as a metaphor for the search for spiritual enlightenment. Buddhist adherents soon adopted Shinto's sacred mountains as pilgrimage destinations, and the first ascent of Mount Fuji is believed to have been achieved by an anonymous Buddhist monk in 663 CE.

VOLCANO OF FIRE

Geologically Mount Fuji has undergone a number of transformations before arriving at its current size and shape. As an active volcano, the mountain has a history of eruptions dating back many thousands of years, and its current incarnation – believed to have been formed ten thousand years ago – is built upon three previous stages of development. The 3,776 m (12,385 ft) high Mount Fuji is currently considered to be 'active with a low risk of eruption'. Its last major eruption occurred in 1708 when a new crater formed halfway down the mountain.

Scientific experts continue to study the volcano in order to better predict its future behaviour, and emergency plans for residents of the neighbouring areas are continually under review. Its situation, just 100 km (62 miles) from Tokyo, lends its geological condition additional importance.

With its volcanic identity, Mount Fuji has often been connected with fire spirits or fire gods – indeed, its name is believed to be an old native Ainu word meaning deity of fire. For those living nearby, the need to placate the *kami* of such a powerful and potentially dangerous place was obvious, and the first shrine built at the mountain in around 800 CE was dedicated to the fire god. Over time, though, another Shinto deity – Konohana Sakuya Hime or 'the Goddess of the Flowering Trees' – found her dwelling place at Fuji-san and became the most important *kami*. She is worshipped in shrines at Fuji's base and at its summit, and each year she is honoured in a fire ritual to mark the end of the climbing season in August.

MOUNTAIN-CLIMBING WORSHIP

In the ninth century a new religious sect called Shugendo emerged, which was focused entirely on the spiritual practice of mountain climbing. It taught that devotees could develop spiritual powers by climbing important mountains and communing with their deities on the summits. Shugendo followers established the first major climbing route to the peak of Fuji-san in the 14th century. Four centuries later a new religious movement called the Fuji-ko was formed, to continue the mountain-climbing worship of Mount Fuji. Made up of many societies, the Fuji-ko is still active today, and many of its members are among the 200,000 people who

'The first ascent of Mount Fuji is believed to have been achieved by an anonymous Buddhist monk in 663 CE.'

come to climb Mount Fuji annually, to pray at the shrines, worship at the summit or walk around the volcano's crater.

The official Fuji climbing season starts on 1 July each year and runs until the end of August. As well as the devoted pilgrims, there are many tourists from Japan and other countries who choose one of a number of well-defined routes that take them to the mountain's summit and back again to safety within the day.

Around two thousand religious organizations have their bases close to the foot of Mount Fuji, including one of Japan's largest Buddhist sects. Fuji's role in the spiritual life of the nation is assured: its image as a symmetrical mountain peak forever topped with snow appears throughout Japanese iconography and has inspired many famous artworks, including Hokusai's *36 Views of Mount Fuji.*

Nevertheless the mountain's popularity has a modern price: despite numerous attempts to secure Fuji's place as a World Heritage site, progress has been hampered by increasing amounts of pollution from human activity. While the mountain may be sacred to some, it has yet to achieve the same status for others.

Above *The view of Mount Fuji across Lake Kawaguchi is just one of the images of the mountain captured by the Japanese artist Hokusai in his* 36 Views of Mount Fuji.

COLOMBIA
ECUADOR
PERU
BRAZIL
PACIFIC OCEAN
Nazca Desert
BOLIVIA
CHILE

Nazca Lines, Peru

Flying over the Nazca Desert in the coastal plains of Peru, one could be forgiven for believing that the ancient people of this remote place once believed they could communicate with the gods. Why else would they create hundreds of images of animals, humans, flowers and geometric shapes that can be viewed properly only from the air? Perhaps, though, their motivations are not as simple as we might imagine.

Since the first commercial flights between Lima and Arequipa in the 1930s led to the aerial revelation of these designs, theories have flourished as to the secular purpose or religious function of these beautifully designed and carefully constructed figures.

UNIQUE DESERT CONDITIONS

Given that they are believed to have been created between 200 and 600 CE, it is a minor miracle that the hundreds of figures on the Nazca Desert surface are still visible at all. That we are able to witness their splendour is a product of the strange, almost unique conditions that prevail in this barren and unusual landscape. The Nazca plateau, which stretches from Nazca to Palpa, is 518 sq km (200 sq miles) of dry, windless desert, which manages to keep a constant temperature of around 25°C (77°F).

The lines that compose the figures were originally created by removing superficial stones covered in dark iron oxide in order to reveal the lighter soil beneath; they vary in depth from a few centimetres to almost 1 m (3⅓ ft). One of the chief reasons why the lines and figures have not been covered over again

in the intervening hundreds of years since their creation is the general lack of wind and eroding rain: it usually rains here for around only half an hour every few years. Another reason for the stability of the surface is the high gypsum content in the soil, which tends to 'glue' the small superficial stones to their pale clay substrate.

Perhaps the most striking aspect of the images, spread – apparently at random – across the whole Nazca plateau, is the sheer size of some of the individual designs. For instance, the figure of 'Alcatraz', the snake-necked heron, is 275 m (900 ft) long. The lizard, now bisected by the Pan-American Highway, is 188 m (615 ft) long. The monkey, which lies next to a complex geometric form, is around 122 m (400 ft) long and 90 m (300 ft) across. Many other designs are well over 30 m (100 ft) in length and are impossible to make out from the ground.

SPECULATION AND MYSTERY

Another interesting feature of the Nazca images (or geoglyphs, as they are sometimes called) is that they are generally made up of one continuous 'drawn' line. In the case of

the monkey, for example, the length of this unbroken line is several kilometres long. This has led some people to speculate that the figures represent some form of labyrinth or trackway that the peoples of the Nazca Desert required themselves to walk, for the sake of their religious or nature rituals. It is certainly likely, from their choice of subject and their dedication to the task, that the figures' creator greatly revered these animal and plant forms. To walk their outlines was, perhaps, a way to ingest and reconnect to their shamanic power.

This explanation is by no means the only one to have been put forward over the last half-century since their revelation to the world. To some people they are an astronomical zodiac that provides a map of the heavens, or a calendar for predicting solstices and equinoxes. To others they are evidence of an alien landing site and an attempt to communicate with extra-terrestrial intelligences. For yet other people, the lines are indicators of underground water supplies, a map of precious resources to be handed down from generation to generation. There are many more major

Right *Inscribed into the desert floor, geometric figures like this giant trapezoid, demonstrate the extreme accuracy in the Nazcans' drawing ability. Viewed from the air, such shapes have led to speculation about their role as alien landing strips.*

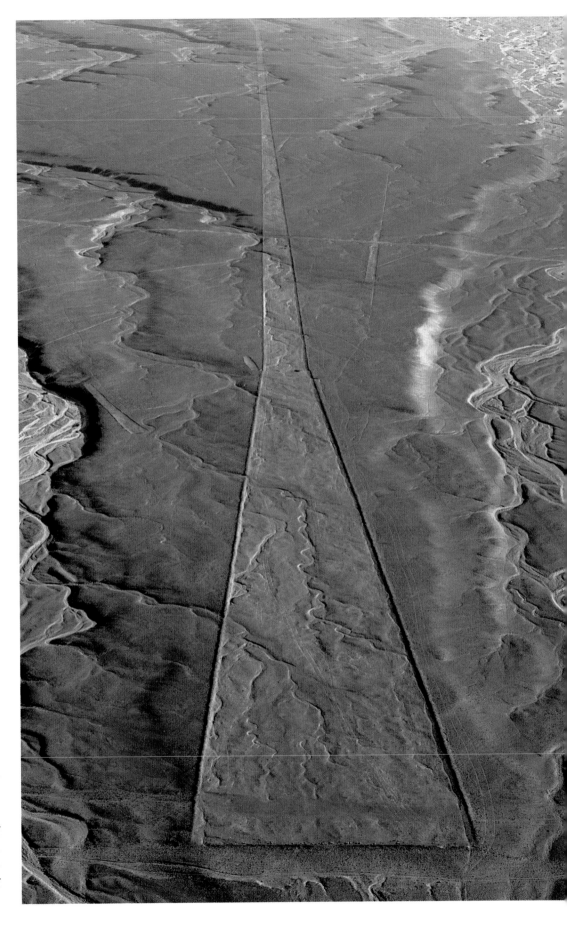

theories, and each year seems to bring new ideas, as well as refinements to the existing collection of speculations about the enigmatic Nazca 'Lines'.

Whatever the correct answer, it is clear to the naked, aerial eye that the draughtsmanship involved in the creation of the figures is remarkable, for it is both artistic in its graphic simplification of the images and has, in many cases, also been executed with a specific biological accuracy.

THE DESIGNS

The images from the Nazca Desert can be divided into groups and, potentially, historical periods. It is clear that some images predate others, since some lines have been drawn over other figures, but in these cases the time difference is almost impossible to calculate. There is, however, a distinctly different approach to the drawing of the animal, human, flower and spiral designs to that taken with the large geometric shapes of triangles, rectangles and trapezoids that fill the plain. In some cases it appears that the geometric shapes have been drawn on top of the more 'life-like' images.

The recent discovery of the nearby settlement of Cahuachi, complete with artefacts and mummified bodies, is helping to shed more light on the Nazcan culture and the beliefs that guided the builders of the lines. Cahuachi was built nearly two thousand years ago and was mysteriously abandoned around five hundred years later, deliberately submerged under thousands of tonnes of pampa sand. Paintings on pottery and ancient forms of weaving have all helped archaeologists to recognize the sources of the Nazca designs. Further work at the site may help us to understand even more about these remarkable people.

PROTECTING THE LINES

Like many sacred sites, the Nazca Lines are under constant pressure from the twin threats of weather and human interference. In 1998 floods and landslides caused by the El Niño weather pattern eroded several of the Nazca figures. Destructive human activity has taken many forms on the Nazca plain. In some cases 'tomb raiders' looking for pre-Incan artefacts have caused damage through unauthorized excavation. Gold and copper mining has become more prevalent in the area: one mine was built very close to one of the 2,000-year-old, 3.2 km (2 mile) long trapezoids.

In more extreme examples of human carelessness, advertisers have mimicked the figures by carving their own modern commercial versions. And in some cases the Nazca Lines are becoming confused with truck routes from utility companies, which are running new power cables across the plain to keep up with the demand for electricity. Without further protection from local authorities, it is hard to see how the Nazca figures will be able to survive the ravages of the 21st century. In the meantime the figures – both eloquent and enigmatic – continue to haunt the imagination.

THE HERON (ALCATRAZ)

The largest figure on the Nazca plain, the heron or large bird, has attracted attention not just for its size, but also for questions about its exact species and the origins of the

model for the drawing. One researcher, Maria Reiche, has even named it the 'solstice bird' after her belief that the line across its wingspan relates to the sun's position at one of the annual solstices.

THE MONKEY

The monkey may not be one of the largest figures, but it is one of the most interesting and remarkable. The drawing of the figure is exceptional and includes a large spiral that forms the monkey's tail. Many people believe it to be an image of a spider monkey, although the direction of the spiralling tail is incorrect. The monkey is accompanied by a set of lines – a large quadrangle intersected by a zigzag line.

THE SPIDER

Until recently it was thought that the spider's long rear leg was a misdrawing or aberration by Nazcan designers. But then a researcher pointed out that there is a species of rare spider, called *Ricinulei* and occurring only in the Amazon rainforest, that actually possesses one rear leg longer than its others because it forms part of the animal's reproductive system. This theory raises a further question:

how the Nazcans knew of an intensely rare species occurring many hundreds of kilometres away on the other side of the Andes. It has also been suggested by a number of researchers that the spider is actually a representation of the great star system of Orion. This naturally leads on to the theory that many of the figures may also be representations of star systems perceived by the Nazcans.

THE HUMMINGBIRD

The hummingbird plays an important role in the local Peruvian ecology, helping to fertilize plants that rely on its busy darting flights between flowers. Even the staple crop of maize is a beneficiary of the hummingbird's activities – although whether the Nazcans were aware of this remains unknown. What is clear is their reverence for this, the smallest of all bird species.

THE WHALES

There are two whale figures on the Nazca plateau, one of which appears to be a killer whale. The Nazcans' knowledge of the creature is not so improbable given their proximity to the coast, but the confident drawing and beauty of the image seem to imply a close affinity with the animal.

THE ASTRONAUT, OR OWL MAN

When this figure was first rediscovered in 1982 by Eduardo Herran, many extra-terrestrial researchers were excited by its appearance and dubbed it 'The Astronaut' for its 'goggle-like' eyes. Maria Reiche, a German researcher who lived at Nazca until her death in 1998, resisted this theory, insisting that it was an 'owl man', a familiar depiction combining aspects of bird and human that often appeared on Nazcan pottery. The figure's arms are seen to be pointing in different directions – above and below – perhaps indicating the link between heaven and earth. The figure is one of the examples of anthropomorphic figures that appear on the Nazca plain. Others are known as 'The Man with the Hat' and 'The Executioner' and, as a group, these appear to be the most primitive designs.

THE PAIR OF HANDS

The pair of hands is one of the strangest of all the glyphs, as it appears to be a creation of the Nazcan imagination. Like a figure from a nightmare or from some hallucinatory experience, the oversized hands, small body and deformed head seem to bear little relation to reality.

TRAPEZOIDS

The enormous trapezoid figures – some as long as 3,000 m (9,850 ft) – are very accurately inscribed into the desert floor. Whether they represent astronomical directions (pointing to specific stars or star systems) is unclear. While some people have speculated on their role as landing strips for alien intelligences, their true function is still a matter for speculation.

Far left This is the smaller of two hummingbird images. The hummingbird played an important part in Peruvian ecology, fertilizing the indigenous peoples' staple crop of maize.

Below The spider's extended rear leg (top left) has led to the idea that the image shows a rare species named Ricinulei, *which lives in the Amazon jungle hundreds of kilometres away.*

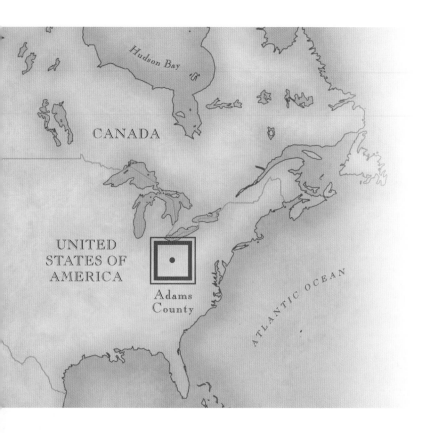

Serpent Mound, Ohio

Located in Adams County, Ohio, the great Serpent Mound is the largest and most distinctive serpent-effigy mound in the world. The curving serpent lies on part of a plateau that was created by what is described geologically as a crypto-explosive event. A number of theories have emerged to explain the massive forces behind the raising of this 6.4 km (4 mile) diameter plateau, including a meteoric impact or volcanic activity. Whatever the real cause, it serves only to add to the enigma of the serpent's placement on its cliff edge.

Mystery surrounds the origins of the Serpent Mound, a figure that measures 405 m (1,330 ft) from its coiled tail along its zigzagging back to a head that appears to be devouring a shape variously described as an egg, a frog or the sun.

DISCOVERY OF THE SERPENT
In the modern era the mound was first discovered in 1846 by two surveyors named Ephraim G. Squier and Edwin H. Davis, who published a book about the ancient native monuments of the Mississippi Valley. In 1885 the publication eventually attracted a Harvard University archaeologist named Frederick Ward Putnam to the site, where he found it threatened by farming activity. Quickly raising funds, he managed to secure the Serpent Mound and 24 ha (60 acres) of land around, before embarking on the first serious excavation of the site in 1886. As well as the Serpent Mound itself, Putnam's land also encompassed three conical mounds, an ancient village site and a burial place.

In three years Putnam excavated the contents of the Serpent Mound and two of the conical mounds, coming to the conclusion that they were created by the native Adena people who lived in parts of the Mississippi Valley from around 800 BCE to 100 CE. Putnam went on to be known as the 'Father of American archaeology', but discussion and debate about the dating of the Serpent Mound and the people who created it have continued well after the completion of his work.

Recent radiocarbon-dating analysis of three pieces of charcoal discovered in the mound seems to give a more confusing picture. Two of the artefacts gave a date of around 1070 CE – much later than the Adena people, and during the period of a Mississippian culture known as the Fort Ancient People. The third piece of charcoal provided a divergent piece of evidence: it was more than 2,900 years old, placing it as part of the very early Adena culture or even earlier. While the timing of these datings provides interesting evidence, it does not conclusively place the building of the serpent. There are experts who attribute the mound to other groups of Native Americans, specifically to the Hopewell culture and a pre-Adena culture of the Ohio Valley known as the Allegheny or Allegewi people.

THE ENIGMA OF ITS CREATION
The purpose of the Serpent Mound for those who originally built it is difficult to assess. Since human remains have never been found, this appears to rule out burial purposes. Snake cults, and in particular rattlesnake cults, have played parts in American, Mexican and, to some extent, European ancient peoples' cultures. Cherokee peoples tell of a legendary snake called Uktena with supernatural powers, and some historians have questioned whether the Serpent Mound was actually a shrine to a totemic animal god: a place where the snake's power was revered and worshipped.

'There appear to be solar alignments with different parts of the snake.'

The very real fact that snakes had the power to take human life would always have given them a power beyond the ordinary.

A growing movement has speculated about the astronomical significance of the Serpent Mound. There appear to be solar alignments with different parts of the snake: the head and oval shape in front of it are in line with the sunset at the midsummer solstice; the coils align with the midwinter sunrise, and the autumn and spring equinox sunrises in September and March, as well as the summer solstice. Others have suggested lunar alignments related to the coils of the snake's tail.

The recent dating of charcoal artefacts to 1070 CE gave some additional frisson to those who adhere to the theorized connection with star alignments. It was 1066 when Halley's Comet passed, and in 1054 the light from the exploding supernova that became the Crab Nebula was visible in the skies, both day and night, for two weeks. Is it possible that the early Native American peoples associated remarkable events in the skies with the animals that seemed to rule their lives on the ground? Whatever the answer, their artistry and commitment will continue to fascinate those who are still able to witness the results of their work.

Below Set on the edge of a plateau, Serpent Mound may have been positioned so as to point at various astronomical events such as the midsummer solstice and the autumn and spring equinoxes.

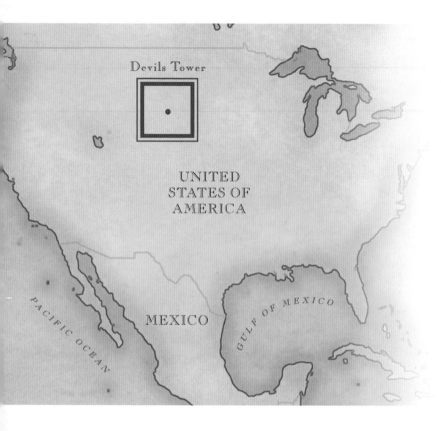

Devils Tower

UNITED STATES OF AMERICA

PACIFIC OCEAN

MEXICO

GULF OF MEXICO

Devils Tower, Wyoming

For many people the remarkable geological phenomenon known as Devils Tower, in Wyoming, first came to their attention through Steven Spielberg's blockbuster film Close Encounters of the Third Kind, *in which the tower plays a key role in the main character's meeting with alien life. The movie is not the only story to feature the huge basalt tower, and a number of Native American legends tell of the rock's history as a sacred object in the natural landscape.*

The strange appearance of Devils Tower, and its seemingly unique volcanic origins many millions of years ago, only add to the aura of mystery that surrounds it.

THE SEVEN SISTERS AND THE BEAR
One story, which is common to the Arapaho, Crow, Cheyenne, Kiowa and Sioux Native American tribes, tells of seven sisters who were playing in the woods one day when they were startled by a giant bear. They ran from the huge animal and took refuge on a small rock, where they began to pray to the Great Spirit to save them from the aggressive bear.

The Great Spirit was touched by their plight and the innocence of their faith, and the rock suddenly grew up high into the sky, carrying the girls out of harm's way. The giant bear was still determined to catch the young girls, however, and started to climb the rock. And yet, even with his sharp claws, he could not make it to the top and began to slide down, digging deep grooves into the rock tower, breaking his claws as he went and finally crashing to the earth below. The Great Spirit then took the girls into the sky, where they live today as the seven stars of the Pleiades cluster. The great rock, with its distinctive grooved profile, remains today as the Devils Tower. It is known to a number of northern plains tribes as Bear Lodge or Mateo Tepee and is regarded by them as an important sacred site where vision quests have regularly taken place.

Geologically, the tower is the remains of a volcanic 'extrusion' that pushed its way up through the Earth's crust at least 40 million years ago. At that time it was still many metres below the surface, but constant erosion by wind and water eventually revealed the tower of solidified volcanic magma, formed of predominantly five-sided rock columns. It now rises around 265 m (870 ft) clear of its surrounding base and some 380 m (1,250 ft) above the nearby Belle Fourche River.

THE BLACK HILLS

The Black Hills area around Devils Tower is known for its large underground caves – some of the largest in the world, including Jewel Cave and Wind Cave. One Native American legend tells of a group of three people discovering a tunnel under or close to Devils Tower. Inside the tunnel they found human bones, before the space opened onto a small lake; on the shores of the lake were huge quantities of gold. Unable to recover the huge weight of the treasure they had found, they decided to hide the tunnel's entrance and return later. And yet, according to the Native American who told this story on his deathbed, they never returned to the cave. Of all the seekers who come to this place, perhaps some look for treasures of the Earth, while others look for rewards of the Spirit.

A SOURCE OF BEAUTY, RITUAL AND REWARD

The tower of volcanic rock was first discovered by non-native people during the US Geological Survey of 1875 and was given the name Devils Tower as an adaptation of the native name, which meant 'Bad God's Tower'. In 1906 President Theodore Roosevelt declared Devils Tower a National Monument and established the United States' first National Park around it. The beautiful rolling hills of the 545 ha (1,347 acre) park are covered with deciduous woodlands, pine forests and prairie grasslands. The National Park is also something of a sanctuary for deer, prairie dogs and other wildlife and welcomes hundreds of thousands of visitors each year.

Since the first ascent by wooden ladders in 1893, the Devils Tower has become a major venue for climbers and more than 20,000 ascents have been made. For the Native American peoples this has become a source of some sorrow, and the most recent accommodation to local sensitivities and the conflict between the two groups has seen a climbing ban of Devils Tower during the sacred month of June to enable prayer offerings, vision quests and other rituals to continue undisturbed.

Above Devils Tower rises out of the surrounding landscape in such dramatic fashion that Native Americans were understandably intrigued by the presence of the volcanic feature and attributed power and legendary status to it.

Sedona, Arizona

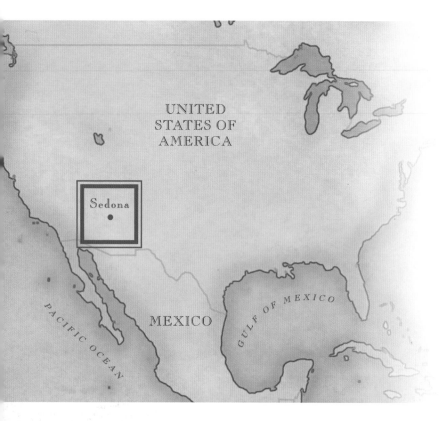

Sedona has justly been described as one of the most beautiful natural landscapes in the United States, if not the world. Located in northern Arizona on the vast, high Colorado plateau, the famous red rocks of Sedona are the result of millions of years of geological action. Many people today are attracted to this unique landscape recognizing that it represents a myriad of sacred places, a tapestry of earth energies that offers a thinning of the veil between the seen and the unseen worlds.

Sedona's story is nearly as old as the planet itself. Its red canyon walls reveal nine layers of stone from a succession of geological periods that traverse hundreds of millions of years. There are six sandstone layers, two of limestone and a top layer of igneous basalt from volcanic eruptions more than 14 million years ago, which covered the entire Verde Valley in many metres of lava. The under-layers are believed to have been deposited by the mud of inland seas or wind-blown sands.

THE VERDE VALLEY

The features that can be seen today – the hugely tall rock outcrops that appear to surge from the underlying plateau – are believed to be what was left after the eroding forces of high-speed winds had done their work. The Verde Valley in which Sedona sits is named after the green colour of the natural copper that can be found in the ground, the mining of which has been a regular commercial activity in the area for many years. It contrasts well with the dominant and intense red of the rocks, which is the result of iron-oxide staining over very long periods of time.

Human activity in the Verde Valley is believed to have started around 4000 BCE when hunter-gatherer peoples first arrived. The Hohokam native peoples are known to have been farming the dry red soil in the area from around 300 BCE. By 700 CE they had developed farming techniques that involved the creation of irrigation channels, but they mysteriously abandoned the area some time later – perhaps because of a local volcanic event that is known to have occurred in 1066. At around the same time the 'Sinagua' Native Americans, so called because of their ability to farm the waterless soils, settled here. They built cliff dwellings and pueblos that are similar to (although less sophisticated than) those of the Anasazi of Chaco Canyon (see pages 66–67).

The Sinagua were travelling, trading peoples and were known to have connections with other peoples towards the Pacific coast and further south in what is now Mexico. They traded copper, which they mined close to Sedona, and other craft artefacts such as pottery and jewellery. They are known to us now from the remains of their pueblos, which are common around Sedona. The best-known sites are Palatki, Honanki and Wupatki, all of which had many rooms in two-storey structures. These contain decorative and functional artwork: petroglyphs showing tribal loyalties, mysterious creatures and images that seem to represent observations of the skies. It is believed that the Sinagua people carried out religious rituals connected to the timing of celestial events. At the beginning of the 15th century CE the Sinagua left the Sedona area, for reasons that have never been fully explained.

THE NAMING OF SEDONA

Around the same time as the Sinagua's departure, the Yavapai and Apache native peoples started to settle in Oak Creek Canyon, a beautiful river valley close to Sedona, which is still an important part of the wider Sedona area today. The arrival of 'modern' Europeans came in 1583 when Spanish explorers found the remote area in search of gold and silver. After the American Civil War, and with the establishing of the state of Arizona, the Verde Valley – Sedona and Oak Creek Canyon in particular – began to be settled more quickly. Sedona gained its current name only in 1902 when it was named after the postmaster's wife, Sedona Schnebly, in honour of her hospitality and dedication to the promotion of the locale.

Now, a hundred years later, the area around Sedona has become a magnet for New Age seekers who believe that the area is a major centre of 'energy vortices', places where earth energies can be experienced directly. Whether as a result of particular geological features or through the activities of previous human cultures, this phenomenon has continued to grow, and Sedona now attracts many millions of people in search of inspiration and upliftment from the place of the red rocks.

Below The distinctive red rocks of Sedona, such as these in the Red Rock/Secret Mountain Wilderness area, are the result of millions of years of erosion following both volcanic activity and mud/sand deposits.

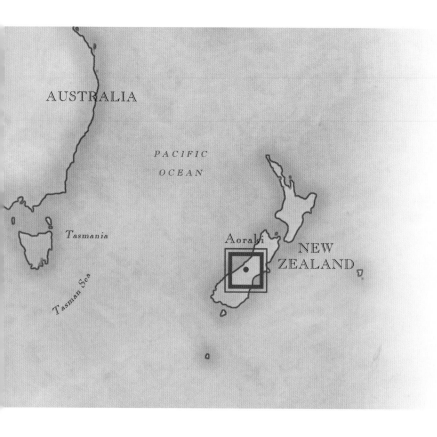

Aoraki/ Mount Cook, New Zealand

Mount Cook on the South Island of New Zealand is also known by its Maori name Aoraki (Cloud Piercer). In 1998, by agreement between the Ngai Tahu Maori peoples and the British Crown, the mountain was renamed Aoraki/Mount Cook. Of all the indigenous sites in New Zealand that have been renamed, this is the only one where the Maori term takes precedence, a milestone in the Maori struggle for recognition of their heritage.

Before the arrival in New Zealand of the British explorer Captain James Cook, Aoraki (or Aorangi as it is also known) was unchallenged as the most important representation of the living presence of Ancestors in the entire Maori landscape.

CLOUD PIERCER

Rising to 3,754 m (12,313 ft) above sea level, the triple-peaked Aoraki is New Zealand's highest mountain and forms part of the chain of Southern Alps that runs almost all the way down the South Island. Aoraki is also surrounded by four major glaciers: the Tasman, the Hooker, the Murchison and the Mueller. Concentrated in the Mount Cook National Park, which covers an area of some 700 sq km (270 sq miles), are 22 of New Zealand's 27 tallest mountains – all of which have an Ancestor significance to the Ngai Tahu people. Indeed, for the indigenous peoples the idea of climbing these mountains is a sacrilegious one, evoking the idea of treading on the Ancestor's very face.

This clash has become more overt as New Zealand has taken on its role as adventure sports capital of the world. While the Western world views nature's riches as opportunities for 'extreme' activities, native peoples can often only stand by and watch as their sacred lands are treated like the playground of the infantile rich. Aoraki has been a target for Western climbers since the first ascent of the summit in 1894 by three New Zealanders, Tom Fyfe, James Clarke and George Graham. Shortly after their success, a Swiss mountain guide named Matthias Zurbriggen was the first man to climb Aoraki solo. Since then the mountain has become an increasingly attractive destination for climbers, and guided ascents can be undertaken by people of all abilities.

THE MAORI CREATION MYTH

To understand the full significance of Aoraki to the Maori people, it is necessary to appreciate quite a different worldview – one in which nature and natural objects are living embodiments of characters within the creation myth. These go back to a time before the existence of the islands that we call New Zealand.

To the Ngai Tahu people, Aoraki was originally the first child of Raki, the heavens or Sky Father, and Poharua Te Po, the 'breath of life found in the womb of darkness'. Later Raki wedded Papa-tui-nuku (the Earth Mother) and soon afterwards some of Raki's sky children came to meet their father's new wife. Aoraki (Cloud in the Sky), Raki-ora (Long Raki), Raki-rua (Raki the Second) and Raraki-roa (Long Unbroken Line) descended from the skies in a canoe called 'Te Waka o Aoraki'. They found a huge continent called Hawaiiki, but when they looked for more land they were unable to find any. Together they said a *karakia*, or incantation, to lift their canoe back into the heavens and return them to their sky home. However, the prayer did not work properly and the canoe fell into the sea, transforming itself into earth and stone. It settled with its western part further out of the water than its eastern part and, seeking safety, Aoraki and his brothers clambered onto the high part of the upturned canoe, where they were petrified in turn.

This was how New Zealand's South Island, or Te Waka o Aoraki, was formed – with Aoraki as the tallest peak and his brothers as the three highest mountains close by: Rakiro

(Mount Dampier), Rakiru (Mount Teichelmann) and Rarakiroa (Mount Tasman). This was not the end of the creation process; it took the great works of another Ancestor, Tu Te Rakiwhanoa, to shape the land and make it ready for human life.

Today's Ngai Tahu still see their role as mediators between the natural and supernatural worlds. The strength and continuation of their tribal life depend on maintaining their rightful place in this relationship. What we see as 'simply nature' is, for them, the living embodiment of their forebears. Without the ancestors there would have been no life, and so their sense of interdependence with the past is irrefutable and immutable. Nevertheless they struggle to communicate their vision to the thousands of climbers who come to Aoraki/Mount Cook for the challenge of a lifetime.

Above *Glacial runoff from Aoraki/Mount Cook flows through the Hooker Valley on New Zealand's South Island. The Hooker glacier is just one of four glaciers that surround Aoraki/ Mount Cook's triple peak.*

'*The triple-peaked Aoraki is New Zealand's highest mountain.*'

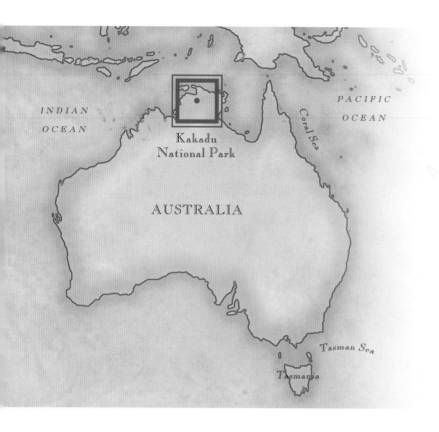

Rock paintings, Australia

Aboriginal paintings on rocks and caves can be found in various areas of Australia. They are the work of many different cultures in a number of time periods and were created, it seems, for a myriad of purposes. With some scientific experts believing that a portion of these paintings date back as far as 30,000–40,000 years, it is remarkable that we can still see them today. While many of the images were almost certainly made for ritual or ceremonial purposes, they also represent a way of storing visual stories.

Some of the most impressive, and possibly the oldest, Aboriginal paintings are found in northern Australia, particularly within Kakadu National Park, some 200 km (125 miles) east of Darwin.

CREATION CHARACTERS

Kakadu is often referred to as a 'cultural landscape'. Here it is believed that the very features of the landscape were formed by the spiritual ancestors of Aboriginal people during the Dreamtime (see pages 168–169), the time of Creation. The Ancestors, or 'first people', came from inside the Earth and started their journeying, creating the rocks, hills, rivers, plants, animals and the 'Bininj', or 'Mungguy', as the Aboriginal people are called. The 'first people' educated the Bininj in the ways of the world, telling them how to hunt and feed themselves and how to look after the land. They also brought with them laws of kinship, ceremony and language, and it is this world that the early rock paintings at Kakadu record and celebrate.

One of the most spectacular areas of Aboriginal rock art in the Kakadu National Park is at Nourlangie Rock. The rock's upper part is known as Burrunggui, and there are many key figures painted on the rocks here, including the figure of 'The Lightning Man' or Namarrgon. Namarrgon is an important Creation Ancestor who is still considered to be active today, creating the lightning storms that fill the skies every wet season. On his head and knees are the axes that he uses to split the clouds, while an arc over his head represents the lightning he makes.

Namarrgon's wife is represented in the same image, as are their offspring. These children are the 'Alyurr', a type of blue and orange grasshopper, and are considered very important to the local Aboriginal peoples because they were the Ancestors who provided them with language and other societal structures during the Dreamtime. They generally appear just before the start of the wet season: their role is to call to their father Namarrgon to bring the thunder and lightning storms.

Namondjok is another important character in the Creation stories, and a number of Aboriginal clans tell different stories about his role in their history. For some, Namondjok is a Creation Ancestor who now resides in the Milky Way and can be seen there at night, simply as a dark spot. For others, he has an even darker past that sends a warning to those who follow: his story tells that when he travelled through the Nourlangie Rock area he broke the sacred kinship laws with his clan sister (who, under Aboriginal definition, could have been a cousin rather than an actual sister; nevertheless, the taboo was broken). After the event, his sister plucked a feather from Namondjok's headdress and this is now a large boulder in the landscape.

In the same gallery is the single male figure of a spirit named Nabulwinjbulwinj (pronounced Nar-bul-win-bul-win). He is a dangerous figure, renowned for his terrible habit of killing women by striking them with a yam before eating them.

UNCOVERING A SACRED LANDSCAPE

Other Australian sites offer equally beguiling and sophisticated imagery. As well as images of human figures, there are complex images of animals such as turtles and wallabies and remarkable 'X-ray' images of fish, which appear to show accurate details of their internal organs. The Kimberly region in Western Australia is home to a wide variety of images, including very large 'Wandjina', spirit Ancestors who contributed to the laws and the landscape. Snake images also feature here in their traditional role of fertility spirits. And in the Northern Territory, at the Nganalam Art Site, there is an image of the Rainbow Serpent, another important character in Dreamtime mythology.

Discoveries of new rock artworks are regularly being made, and their care and protection can generally be assured. With each image, and the benefit of cooperative working between native Aboriginal peoples and 'settled Europeans', an increasing understanding of Australia's sacred landscape continues to evolve.

Below This rock painting at Nourlangie Rock depicts *Nabulwinjbulwinj, a dangerous spirit who kills women by striking them with a yam and then eats them.*

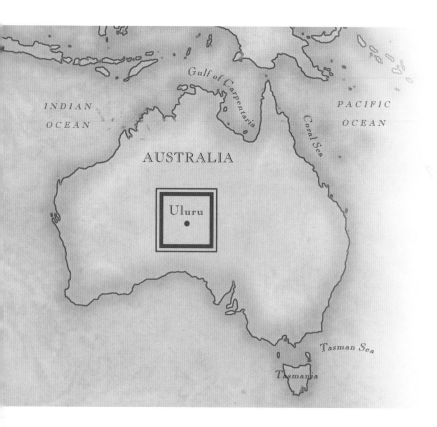

Uluru/Ayers Rock, Australia

Uluru is the Aboriginal name for a huge formation of red sandstone just west of Australia's geographical centre in the Northern Territory. Now referred to by its composite name of Uluru/Ayers Rock, the rock is 346 m (1,135 ft) high with a circumference of more than 9 km (5½ miles). Although it is sometimes called the world's largest monolith, the formation is in fact part of a larger rock system that continues beneath ground level.

Uluru is particularly well known for its stunning appearance during sunrises and sunsets, when the light striking the rock appears to make it glow in a constantly changing succession of red hues. The effect is the result of an iron oxide covering the rock, together with the relatively high level of reflective feldspar in the arkosic sandstone. But whatever the scientific explanation, little can prepare the spectator for the intensity of the vision that Uluru offers.

THE DREAMTIME

The Aboriginal people of Australia probably have the oldest tradition of landscape mythology on the planet, with evidence that their culture has existed in some form for more than 30,000 years. In Aboriginal mythology, during the period that marked the beginnings of the Earth, called Alcheringa or the Dreamtime (see also pages 166–167), Ancestor beings – totemic humans and animals – emerged from inside the Earth and began their wanderings over the land. Through their simple everyday actions such as giving birth, hunting, making music, forming relationships, eating and dying they

created features in the still-malleable landscape. Then, at the end of the Dreamtime, these features changed into stone and the bodies of the totemic Ancestors who had helped to form them became the features of the landscape: the hills, valleys, caves and rocks.

The tracks that the Ancestors had trodden during their wanderings in the Dreamtime became known as Songlines and were the routes that linked all the sacred places of power, such as Uluru and Kata Tjuta (see pages 170–171). In this way the interior of Australia was transformed into a sacred landscape, and the Aboriginal people saw it as their continuing spiritual duty to 'go walkabout' – to walk and sing as they followed the Songlines. In this way they would reinforce and connect with the energy and memory of the Dreamtime. Through rituals

carried out at sacred places they would (and still do) call on the *kurunba*, the spiritual power of the Ancestors available to them. Aboriginal peoples still believe that this power can be drawn on to strengthen their tribe and increase the health of the land that sustains them.

SACRED EARTH RITUALS

Uluru is held sacred by the Anangu, Pitjantjatjara and Yankunytjatjara Aboriginal peoples who live in this part of Australia, and has been an important ritual centre for many thousands of years. Of the many parts of the rock, different locations have historically been used for the practice of ceremonies and initiatory rites and have Aboriginal names that relate to their functions. The Anangu people, who still actively use the site for their rituals, ask visitors not to take photographs of

'The Aboriginal people of Australia probably have the oldest tradition of landscape mythology on the planet.'

certain parts of the rock for reasons related to their *tjukurpa*, or traditional beliefs. They have specific gender rites that are taboo for the opposite sex, and want to ensure there is no possibility that Anangu people of the 'wrong' sex can violate their taboos by accidentally witnessing a photograph of their forbidden ground in the 'outside world'.

The Anangu view themselves as the direct descendents of the Ancestors from the Dreamtime and are therefore responsible for the management and protection of Uluru and the lands around it. Recent developments in political land-ownership

issues have meant that the period of direct ownership by the Australian government has ended. In 1985 the title of the Uluru-Kata Tjuta National Park was given back to the Pitjantjatjara Aboriginal people, who then granted a 99-year lease to the Australian National Parks and Wildlife Service. The management board of the park now contains a majority of Anangu people. Given the hardships and human-rights abuses suffered by the Aboriginals since the arrival of European settlers, this is a remarkable turnaround and a triumph for the native culture of Australia's ancient continent.

Above Part of a larger rock system below ground, Uluru/Ayers Rock's remarkable presence in the landscape has provided a focus for sacred worship and ritual for Aboriginal peoples over thousands of years.

Kata Tjuta, Australia

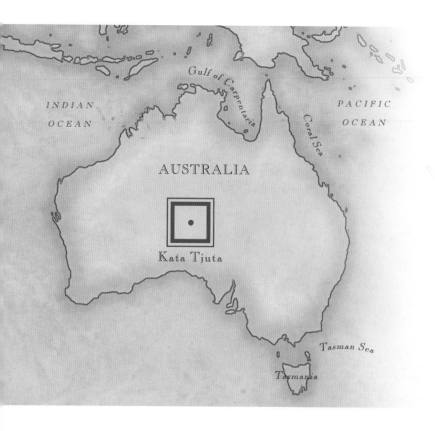

Kata Tjuta is a unique rock outcrop made up of 36 domed peaks, with the tallest – Mount Olga – rising 546 m (1,790 ft) out of the surrounding landscape. Also known informally as 'The Olgas', Kata Tjuta is situated about 450 km (280 miles) from Alice Springs and just 25 km (15 miles) from Uluru/Ayers Rock (see pages 168–169). Many believe that Uluru and Kata Tjuta are part of the same rock system, even though the composition of Kata Tjuta is rather different, being formed of a hard granite made up of quartz and feldspar.

Kata Tjuta, which means 'many-headed' in the language of the Pitjantjatjara people, covers an area of more than 20 sq km (7¾ sq miles) and is a very important landscape feature in the Aboriginal ancestral worship that traces its origins to the Dreamtime (see pages 166–169). With the intense tourist interest that focuses on Uluru/Ayers Rock, many people now find that the calm and tranquillity around the vast, impassive rocks of Kata Tjuta offer a more profound experience.

HISTORY OLD AND NEW

There are believed to have been Aboriginal settlements at Kata Tjuta dating from around 10,000 years ago, and some experts believe that the human presence here could date back twice as long. Aboriginal people do not date the Dreamtime in conventional ways, but Kata Tjuta has clearly been part of the Songline network that links sacred places since the beginning of their civilization and, together with Uluru, forms a most important ceremonial centre. Many legends are associated with Kata Tjuta, but perhaps the most powerful and enduring myths revolve around the

snake totem known as Wanambi, who is believed to live on the peak of Mount Olga.

This unbroken Aboriginal connection with Kata Tjuta was first threatened in July 1872 when the explorer-settler Ernest Giles initially approached the rocks from the north-east. As he made his way towards the distant, strangely shaped outcrop, his way was barred by a huge lake. Unable to reach his goal he decided to retreat, though not before he had named the feature Mount Olga in honour of the Queen of Württemberg (in what is now Germany). Giles returned the following year to explore Kata Tjuta further, but was eventually beaten to Uluru by William Gosse, who first saw the red rock on 19 July 1873 and decided to name it after the Chief Secretary of South Australia, Sir Henry Ayers. Giles then became the first European to climb the rock, accompanied by his Afghanisthan-born camel driver.

LEARNING TO RESPECT THE ABORIGINAL HERITAGE

Few white people ventured into the remote and austere landscape around Kata Tjuta and Uluru, but the area was declared an Aboriginal

Reserve in 1920. The first road access came in the 1940s and, together with rumours of gold and nascent ideas of tourism, began to threaten the area. In 1950 Ayers Rock and the nearby area were named a national park, and in 1958 this was combined with the Olgas to form the Ayers Rock National Park. The following year saw the first motel built close to Uluru, and an airstrip was created soon afterwards to bring increasing numbers of tourists. By the 1970s Uluru was the number-one Outback tourist destination, and Aboriginal concerns grew in tandem with visitor numbers. By 1983 the tourist facilities near Uluru were closed down and the site was now serviced by the resort of Yulara, some 20 km (12½ miles) away from the rock. Since the change of land ownership in 1995, Kata Tjuta's care and protection (like those of Uluru) are predominantly under the management of the Anangu Aboriginal peoples.

In 1993, under the dual naming policy of the Australian government, Mount Olga (or 'The Olgas') was renamed Kata Tjuta/Mount Olga in synchrony with the name change for Uluru/Ayers Rock. For the first time in more than a hundred years the Aboriginal peoples have been able to view the future of their ancestral heritage with greater confidence. At the same time they can hope that an understanding of their Dreamtime will benefit the white people in their struggle to form a healthy relationship with the world that supports them.

'The area was declared an Aboriginal Reserve in 1920.'

Index

Acknowledgements

PICTURE ACKNOWLEGEMENTS

AKG-images 99; /Bildarchiv Monheim 14; /Andrea Jemolo 43. **Alamy**/David Ball 98; /Danita Delimont 117; /Andy Hallam 135; /Christopher Hill Photographic/ scenicireland.com 136; /Geoff A. Howard 65; /JTB Photo Communications, Inc. 145; /John Lens 141; /David Muenker 67; /Sepp Puchinger/imagebroker 20; /Skyscan Photolibrary 101. **Art Directors & Trip**/Dinodia Photo Library 57, 58. **Bridgeman Art Library**/Jasna Gora Monastery, Czestochowa, Poland 87; /Stapleton Collection, UK 88. **Collections**/Michael Diggin 41. **Corbis**; /Peter Adams 153; /Alinari Archives 17; /Archivo Iconografico, S.A. 167; /Yann Arthus-Bertrand 22, 155, 156, 157, 169; /Christophe Boisvieux 33; /Jan Butchofsky-Houser 81; /Anthony Cassidy 95; /Elio Ciol 109; /Dean Conger 73; /Richard A. Cooke 159; /Ashley Cooper 131; /Tony Craddock/zefa 161; /Ric Ergenbright 142-143; /Gianni Dagli Orti 137; /Jose Fuste Raga 115 ; /Lowell Georgia 144; /Ali Haider/epa 51; /Tim Hawkins/Eye Ubiquitous 103; /Chris Hellier 113; /John Heseltine 72; /Angelo Hornak 39; /Andrea Jemolo 42; /Danny Lehman 83; /Charles & Josette Lenars 118; /Craig Lovell 6-7, 163, 165; /Krause, Johansen/Archivo Iconografico, SA 12; /Wolfgang Meier/zefa 140; /Kazuyoshi Nomachi 9, 52, 53; /Paulo Novias 70-71; /Altaf Qadri/epa 8; /Sergio Pitamitz 10-11; /Reuters 36-37; /Galen Rowell 151; /Skyscan 104, 149; /Kurt Stier 25; /Homer Sykes 146, 147; /Pierre Terdjman 89; /Luca I. Tettoni 29; /Richard Walker 107; /Patrick Ward 171; /Roger Wood 48, 49; /Adam Woolfitt 23, 125, 129, 133; /Alison Wright 93; /Jim Zuckerman 55. **Dinodia**/56, 69. **Getty Images**/; /Peter Adams 108; /Joe Cornish 139; /Patrick Ingrand 90-91; /John Lamb 15; /Alan Smith 79; /R. Strange/PhotoLink 124; /Stephen Studd 77; /Jeremy Woodhouse 122-123. **Martin Gray**/sacredsites.com 121. **PA Photos**/Beate Schleep/DPA 84. 85. **Photodisc**/H Wiessenhofer /PhotoLink 4. **Photolibrary Group**/JTB Photo 27, 59. **Steve Rich** 47. **Robert Harding World Imagery**/Gavin Hellier 7 bottom right. **SuperStock**/age footstock 78, 86, 111; /Koji Kitagawa 119; /SuperStock, Inc. 54. **The Art Archive**/Dagli Orti 13. **Three Blind Men**/Dominic Sansoni 63. **Topfoto**/Topham Picturepoint 80. **World Pictures** 21.

Executive Editor Sandra Rigby
Editor Charlotte Macey
Executive Art Editor Sally Bond
Designers Annika Skoog, Shane Whiting & Claire Dale (for Cobalt ID)
Illustrator KJA-artists.com
Production Controller Simone Nauerth
Picture Researcher Jennifer Veall